CERTIFIED
BEAUTIES

CERTIFIED BEAUTIES

MORE OF HOCKEY'S GREATEST UNTOLD STORIES

James Duthie

Collins

Certified Beauties
Copyright © 2025 by James Duthie
Foreword copyright © 2025 by Sidney Crosby
All rights reserved.

Published by Collins, an imprint of HarperCollins Publishers Ltd

FIRST EDITION

No part of this book may be used or reproduced in any manner whatsoever without written permission.

Without limiting the exclusive rights of any author, contributor, or the publisher of this publication, any unauthorized use of this publication to train generative artificial intelligence (AI) technologies is expressly prohibited. HarperCollins also exercise their rights under Article 4(3) of the Digital Single Market Directive 2019/790 and expressly reserve this publication from the text and data mining exception.

HarperCollins Publishers Ltd
Bay Adelaide Centre, East Tower
22 Adelaide Street West, 41st Floor
Toronto, Ontario, Canada
M5H 4E3

www.harpercollins.ca

HarperCollins Publishers
Macken House, 39/40 Mayor Street Upper
Dublin 1, D01 C9W8, Ireland

https://www.harpercollins.com

Background photographs © ArgitopIA/adobe.stock.com (pg. ii–iii), antusher/adobe.stock.com (pg. vi–vii), chandlervid85/adobe.stock.com (pg. viii)

All photographs are courtesy of the players unless credited otherwise.

Library and Archives Canada Cataloguing in Publication

Title: Certified beauties : more of hockey's greatest untold stories / James Duthie.
Names: Duthie, James, 1966- author
Identifiers: Canadiana (print) 20250243113 | Canadiana (ebook) 2025024313X | ISBN 9781443474702 (hardcover) | ISBN 9781443474719 (ebook)
Subjects: LCSH: Hockey players—Anecdotes. | LCSH: Hockey—Anecdotes. | LCSH: National Hockey League—Anecdotes. | LCGFT: Anecdotes.
Classification: LCC GV847 .D875 2025 | DDC 796.962—dc23

Printed and bound in the United States of America

26 27 28 29 30 LBC 7 6 5 4 3

*For two of the biggest beauties ever,
Mark Ward and Darryl Stoliker*

CONTENTS

Foreword by Sidney Crosby ix
Introduction xiii

The Snapping (Sticks) of Claude Giroux
BRADY TKACHUK'S PRANK BACKFIRES 1

The Beer-League Miracle
A MEN'S LEAGUE TEAM TAKES ON THE BEST PLAYERS IN THE WORLD 5

Bruce, There It Is!
THE NAKED TRUTHS ABOUT BRUCE BOUDREAU'S LIFE IN HOCKEY 11

Patient #1
ROBERTO LUONGO PLAYS TWO PERIODS, WITH A HOSPITAL VISIT IN BETWEEN 22

Lost Boy
MIKE JOHNSON'S FIRST NHL ROAD TRIP NIGHTMARE 29

Terry Ryan: The Movie
THE CINEMATIC LIFE OF A NEWFOUNDLAND LEGEND 37

Sharknado
THE PERFECT STORM THAT LED MACKLIN CELEBRINI TO NHL STARDOM 57

Touching Randy
BRAD MAY AND THE DUCKS ANNOY THEIR COACH AND WIN A CUP 65

The Masked Marvel
SARAH NURSE BECOMES A SUPERSTAR IN COVID CHAOS 70

O-Dog and the Peach Pit After Dark
JEFF O'NEILL STAYS OUT TOO LATE IN LA 76

The Prankster
TODD SIMPSON TORMENTS HIS TEAMMATES 81

The Elephant and the Mouse
BRENDAN MORRISON GETS A HARSH INTRODUCTION TO SALARY ARBITRATION 88

13 and 21
REMEMBERING JOHN AND MATTY GAUDREAU 93

Biron's Bizarre Buffalo Bookends
A GOALIE'S FIRST AND LAST GAMES FOR THE SABRES ARE EQUALLY UNFORGETTABLE 114

Walrus and Waffle Man
THE ARTISTIC COMEDY OF GEORGE PARROS 122

The Riga Redemption
A TEAM OF CANADIAN "MISFITS" TURN DISASTER INTO GOLD 126

Big Ko
DON KOHARSKI ON DOUGHNUTS AND THE FIGHT OF HIS LIFE 135

The Sleep-in Six
A GROUP OF OILERS PLAY GUILTY FOR GLEN SATHER 141

19 Teams, 14 Broken Noses, 2 Bunnies
THE PRO HOCKEY JOURNEY OF ZENON KONOPKA 146

Winning Is Infectious
BLAKE COLEMAN WINS TWO CUPS, AND ALMOST LOSES AN ARM 168

The Many Awkward Introductions of Emma Maltais
A BUDDING STAR LEAVES SOME STRANGE FIRST IMPRESSIONS 172

99 for a Night
SAM GAGNER'S UNLIKELY EIGHT 178

The Wounded Wizard of Waco
BRAD TRELIVING'S ADVENTURES BEFORE RUNNING THE LEAFS AND FLAMES 185

The Hangover
KEVIN BIEKSA GETS HIS BIG BREAK AT THE WORST POSSIBLE TIME 189

Burn the Boats
THE UNIVERSITY OF NEW BRUNSWICK REDS' HISTORIC 43-0 SEASON 194

Seven Short Stories by Keith Yandle
AND A COUPLE MORE FROM HIS SIDEKICK, KEVIN HAYES 208

The Hustler
DARCY HORDICHUK WHEELS, DEALS, AND WRESTLES ALLIGATORS 217

When a Killer Calls
KEVIN WEEKES GETS TOUGH LOVE FROM A LEGENDARY COACH 224

The Shiner
ROOKIE FRANK CORRADO CATCHES FRIENDLY FIRE IN A BRAWL BETWEEN TEAMMATES 229

One-Timers
STORIES THAT CAN BE READ DURING A SINGLE SHIFT 235

The Captain and the Swede
DARRYL SITTLER AND BORJE SALMING 245

Before He Was a Star
MARTY TURCO'S WILD RIDE TO DALLAS AND A STANLEY CUP 254

Free Megan
MEGAN KELLER'S BEST AND WORST CAREER MOMENTS HAPPEN IN ISOLATION 262

Jumpman
FUTURE CAPTAIN NICK FOLIGNO LEARNS THE ROPES AS A ROOKIE 266

Vinnie's Private Plane
VINCENT DAMPHOUSSE GETS TRADED IN THE SKY 271

Struddy's (Accidental and Intentional) Scraps
JASON STRUDWICK FIGHTS EVERYONE EXCEPT A HUNGARIAN RIOT SQUAD 275

Hockey Night in Kenya
THIS AFRICAN NATION WANTS TO TAKE ON THE WORLD 283

"The Biggest Bunch of Beauties Ever Assembled"
MATTHEW TKACHUK AND HIS FLORIDA PANTHERS 290

Revenge of the Cabbage Rolls
RAY WHITNEY TAKES THE *F* OUT OF OPENING SHIFT 295

Acknowledgements 301

FOREWORD

BY SIDNEY CROSBY

The bench during a hockey game can be a hectic place. Sometimes there is humour, sometimes tension . . . always chirps. Your coaches are barking out line combinations and adjustments. Guys are jumping on and off. It's controlled chaos.

One thing you always see on a bench when you watch a game is guys using smelling salts, to give them a jolt. Everyone has their own style. Some take a quick sniff. Others use it, then stick it under another guy's nose.

I haven't been one to use sniffers. Not sure why. I have always felt amped up enough without them. But they are always around on the bench. Usually after players use them, they give them to the trainer to throw out, or just stick them in the little water bottle holders.

So this one night during the playoffs I come back to the bench after my first shift, and I start to feel this burning sensation on my leg. I wear long underwear under my pants, and the pain is coming from between my underwear and the pants.

Right away, I think something is biting me. I stand up on the bench and start making a funny noise, moving around trying to shake out what I think is something biting me. My equipment manager, Dana Heinze, looks at me, puzzled, and says, "You . . . good?"

FOREWORD

No, Dana, I'm not good! This spider, or whatever it is, is attacking me. I'm freaking out. I'm jumping up and down, grabbing at my groin like my pants are on fire. Anyone who saw it must have figured I had finally lost it.

Sure enough, as I'm doing this crazy panic-dance, a sniffer falls out of my pants.

Not sure how it got in there. Someone must have left it on the bench, and it just slipped into my gear.

It scarred me. Ever since, I've kept a close eye out for those things. Trust me, you don't want one in your pants . . . your gloves . . . definitely not your jock.

I know Sid and the Burning Sniffer probably isn't worthy of a full chapter in *Certified Beauties*, but I figured it fits in the foreword. These are the kinds of ridiculous little moments we laugh about our entire careers, and likely will well after we're done.

In James's first *Beauties* book, you were introduced to my former teammate and roommate in Rimouski, Eric Neilson. The definition of a certified beauty. My first year in junior, a local Mazda dealership gives us a car to share, but I don't have my licence yet, so Eric's my driver.

One night he goes out after a game and I go to bed. When I come down for breakfast the next morning, Eric and our billets are laughing their heads off. Seems my face is totally covered in marker. I figure Eric's just pranked me. Wrote on me while I was sleeping. Standard junior hockey gag. Then he tells me the real story.

He'd crashed our car into a street sign while trying to impress some girls with his driving. He somehow managed to make a deal with the police officer who showed up. He would get me to autograph a bunch of hockey cards in exchange for staying out of trouble. So Eric shook me awake in the middle of the night—I have no recollection of this—and made me sign the cards for the officer. Since I was still half asleep, I went back to bed still holding the marker in my hand. And apparently, did some facial artwork the rest of the night.

I also share the story in *Beauties* of the time my Penguins roommate Colby Armstrong accidentally knees me in the groin during a hotel room wrestling match (we were waiting for our room-service chocolate cake at the Hyatt in Buffalo, a night-before-the-game tradition). I am in agony on the floor. And without painting too vivid a picture . . . there is some serious swelling.

We need to call the trainer to the room. He's not happy. He's worried I'm going to miss the game. All night long, Army is so nervous, constantly checking on me. "Sid, you okay? You have to play!" He thinks he's going to be sent down to the minors for giving me a nut shot in a wrestling match. So I gut it out and play. Just for Army.

Certified Beauties is full of countless stories like this. Stories of legendary characters, crazy pranks, incredible comebacks . . . unlikely heroes. No sport breeds better stories than hockey. We tell them constantly on team buses, long flights . . . over beers after a game. And now it's your turn to have a seat on the bench. No smelling salts necessary.

INTRODUCTION

This is only the second sequel I've been involved with.

The first was a movie called *Goon 2: Last of the Enforcers*, where I play a Canadian sportscaster named "James Duthie." So a nuanced, Daniel Day-Lewis–esque performance, where I completely immersed myself in the character for months to prepare. Nailing the accent was especially tough.

I loved the first *Goon* movie and told actor/writer/director/great guy Jay Baruchel this when I ran into him on the red carpet of the Canadian Screen Awards one year. Jay told me he was writing a sequel, and I made a crack about how he should put the TSN panel in it. One of those comments where five seconds after he walked away, I was saying to myself, "You're an idiot. Stop saying dumb things in front of people you admire."

So I think I'm being pranked six months later when Jay calls and says he really has written the panel into the movie. But the Hollywood execs get a hold of it, and the "panel" becomes just me and actor T.J. Miller, who plays Chad Bailey, an ex-hockey player turned TV analyst. Naturally, I take a stand and refuse to participate unless the rest of the TSN panel is put back in the film.

(That's not entirely accurate. I believe my actual response is "I'm in! Screw the panel!")

A few weeks later, we're shooting our scenes in the TSN studio. There are a few scripted lines central to the plot. We ad-lib the rest. Well, mostly T.J. ad-libs, and I laugh at everything he says, forcing them to shoot several scenes over. Amateur hour.

INTRODUCTION

Our show is called *Sportsdesk* in the movie, and T.J. keeps making up tag lines at the end of the scenes.

"Sportsdesk: It's sports. At a desk."

"Sportsdesk: We're all pink on the inside!"

"Sportsdesk: Fuck yeah!"

I figure one scene might make the final cut. But when I sit down in a Toronto theatre for the premiere 10 months later, I choke on my popcorn when we are the opening scene. And basically every single line we shot is in the movie. Only bummer is I never got to meet Liev Schreiber. I had really hoped to be cast as a Chechen gangster in *Ray Donovan*.

I'm pretty sure the only negative reviews *Last of the Enforcers* got went something like this: "The clown who played the *Sportsdesk* host was totally unbelievable in the role." Harsh, but fair.

The point is (sorry it took this long to get there), Jay did a second *Goon* because there was another story he wanted to tell. Hockey is a sport that breeds great stories, with its unpredictability, brutality and camaraderie. It's a game of character. And characters.

After the first *Beauties* came out, I started hearing from hockey people saying, "I wish I had known you were writing this. I have an unbelievable story for you . . ." They were too good to leave unwritten.

Don't try to make sense of the list of storytellers in here. There is no formula, no agenda, except hopefully entertaining you. Some tales come from people I've gotten to know during my time covering the game. Others from something I call Six Degrees of Kevin Bieksa. The former Vancouver Canuck turned TV analyst tells me his story during a day off at the 2024 Stanley Cup Final in Edmonton. When we finish, he says, "You have to talk to Darcy Hordichuk and Brendan Morrison." Later, Hordichuk says, "You can't write this book without a Todd Simpson story." On and on it goes.

INTRODUCTION

One small parental advisory warning. After the first book came out, I was caught off guard by the number of people who would message me, saying their young son or daughter loved the book and *Beauties* chapters had become their bedtime stories. I immediately start sweating, calculating how many f-bombs and inappropriate scenes there were. So Mom and Dad, maybe just have a quick read first, and redact anything you don't want little Ethan or Rachel sharing on the monkey bars tomorrow at recess. (Do schoolyards still have monkey bars? If not, that's a travesty.)

Many of the stories are told by one person. I always want you to feel like you are sitting at the bar next to them. Extra voices are added here and there. And there is one chapter that has a full chorus.

I was a month into writing when I turned on my phone after getting off a plane and learned that John and Matty Gaudreau had been killed. A tragedy still hard to fathom. I had interviewed John before but didn't really know him. I knew nothing about Matty, except that he played hockey too. In talking to family, friends and teammates for their chapter, I learned what you will: They were the very definition of the title of this book—true certified beauties.

—JD

THE SNAPPING (STICKS) OF CLAUDE GIROUX

Brady Tkachuk's Prank Backfires

Brady Tkachuk surveys the mess in front of him, and his brain screams two words: *CLAUDE GIROUX*.

His sticks have all been taped together. Clear tape—up and down the shafts, over the blades, around the knobs. It looks like one of those packages wrapped in cellophane that pop out of airport luggage carousels. It will take forever to separate them.

"Fucking Giroux," he says out loud.

It's February 18, 2023. A practice day for Tkachuk's Ottawa Senators. They have an afternoon game at home against the St. Louis Blues the next day.

"There aren't many guys who would pull something like that on me," Tkachuk says. "And I'm in one of those moods where the first guy I think of on my list is going to get pranked right back. And the guy at the top of my list is G."

The dressing room is mostly empty, so Tkachuk wastes no time planning and executing revenge. He goes to Giroux's stick stall and grabs three. He finds a saw and carefully cuts into each of them, at a specific spot on the shaft. When this is done right, there is no way the victim will notice. But as soon as he takes a shot or makes a hard pass, the stick will snap.

Tim Stutzle and Alex DeBrincat are the only players around to witness Tkachuk's carpentry. He swears them to secrecy. And gets a little giddy thinking of Giroux breaking stick after stick in the middle of a practice drill. He'll snap. The boys will get a kick out of it. And Tkachuk will have taught his good friend a lesson: Don't mess with my weapons.

But NHL players, especially captains, have a lot going on. And by the time the Senators hit the ice a couple of hours later, Tkachuk's mind has wandered elsewhere. He forgets the prank. Giroux must have grabbed a different stick because it doesn't shatter. Practice is routine, and Tkachuk's focus turns back to beating the Blues.

The Sunday afternoon start time means no morning skate. It's wake up and go play. Six and a half minutes in, the Blues take a too-many-men penalty. The Senators go on the power play. Tkachuk is on the first unit. After a minute or so, he changes and Giroux comes on.

"I'm excited as soon as I jump on the ice," Giroux says. "I just have this feeling I'm going to score on this shift, so I'm jacked up."

Giroux receives a pass in his own end and tries to make another as he hits the blue line. His stick snaps.

"It just breaks so easy," Giroux says. "I'm thinking, 'That's weird.'"

On the bench, Tkachuk doesn't even react. Sticks break all the time. The bell inside his head is silent. Giroux hustles back to the bench to grab another twig. Two seconds later, he knocks a puck out of the air, and his new stick breaks.

"Now the Blues have a two-on-one the other way, and Claude comes to the bench and he is snapping," Tkachuk says. "This is how clueless I am—I still don't think anything."

Giroux is confused. And furious. "All I can think of is that Brayden Schenn, who plays for St. Louis and is a good buddy, somehow messed with my sticks as a prank," Giroux says. "So I start barking at him, 'This is bullshit! You cut my sticks. What's wrong with you?!' And Schenner's just shaking his head, going, 'What are you talking about, G?'"

As Tkachuk sits on the bench, the bell finally goes off. "As soon as he screams at Schenn, it hits me. Oh my God! Those are the sticks I cut. He's using them in the game!"

Panicked, Brady grabs the Senators' equipment manager and tells him to get rid of the next Giroux stick on the rack, ASAP. "Break it now!" Tkachuk says. "Do not let him touch that stick!"

There is a TV time out the next whistle. Tkachuk turns his attention to silencing the witnesses. "I turn to Timmy and Brinks and say, 'You better both take this to your fucking graves and not rat me out.'"

But he can't handle the guilt. When Giroux sits down next to him on the bench, still fuming, Tkachuk comes clean.

"G, it was me," he says quietly. Giroux stares back at him, blankly.

"What are you talking about?"

"Your sticks. I cut them."

Brady tries a smile, but Giroux is not smiling back. No giggle. No "Good one, buddy!" with a slap on the back. Just one long death stare.

"I'm losing my shit," Giroux says. "I'm so mad. I can see DeBrincat and Timmy killing themselves laughing on the bench. I'm going, 'Why are you guys laughing?' I can tell Brady feels awful. He's so embarrassed. At one point, I think he's going to cry. I almost feel bad for him, thinking about it now. Well, not really."

"He just looks right through me," Tkachuk says. "And he doesn't talk to me the rest of the game."

When he gets back on the ice, Tkachuk gives new definition to the phrase "playing guilty." In the first 10 minutes of the second period, he scores a goal and adds two assists. The Senators score six straight and cruise to a 7–2 win. And Giroux, once he finally gets a fresh, uncut stick, adds two assists, including one on Tkachuk's goal.

"Finally, after the game, I look at G and this big smirk comes over his face," Tkachuk says. "He says, 'If they scored on that two-on-one and we lost the game, I would have fucking killed you.'"

There is still one part of this Senators edition of *Clue* that remains unsolved. Was Tkachuk's guess right that the initial crime was committed by Mr. Giroux in the dressing room with a roll of tape? Tkachuk eventually asks. "Nope, wasn't me," Giroux says. An eavesdropper starts laughing across the room.

"It was me," says Tim Stutzle. Yes, the real perpetrator is also one of the two guys who sat quietly and watched Tkachuk saw the sticks of the wrongly accused Giroux.

"You motherfucker," Tkachuk says with a bitter smile. He immediately starts quietly thinking of a way to get the young German back.

But only at practice this time. Most definitely, just practice.

THE BEER-LEAGUE MIRACLE

A Men's League Team Takes on the Best Players in the World

In the parking lot of a hockey arena in Newmarket, Ontario, members of a summer beer-league team are leaning on their cars, hanging out before their Wednesday night game. They do this every week, milking the warm August evenings before stepping inside the cold rink.

The team is called Dirty Mike and the Boys. They are still kids, most of them. Some junior and college players and an American Hockey Leaguer—21-year-old Amadeus Lombardi—a Detroit Red Wings prospect. So it's hardly your old-fart beer-belly team. Like most men's leagues, this one has several divisions. And the Dirty Mike boys are in the top one. It's quality hockey.

The boys have had a great summer season, going 11-1. Now it's quarter-final night. They are facing the AKI Icebergs, a more typical beer-league team. They're good, but most of the guys are in their mid- to late 20s and have stopped playing competitive hockey.

But the Icebergs do have one wild card on their roster. He's shown up for a handful of games over the last few years but hasn't made it out at all this summer. Seems his job had him working extended hours in June. He needed some vacation time. Plus, he just got married over the weekend. So the Dirty Mike boys figure there's little chance he shows tonight.

But just as they're about to go inside to get dressed for the game, an SUV pulls into the parking lot.

"Holy shit, that's his car," one of the players says.

The driver's door opens. Connor McDavid steps out.

"We'd been talking about it all week but figured there was no way he'd actually play," says Luke Strickland, a Dirty Mike and the Boys forward. "Then he gets out of the car, and we realize we're about to play against the best player in the world. And then the passenger door opens, and we're like, 'Oh boy.'"

Out the other side of the SUV comes Leon Draisaitl.

"It's this instant mix of excitement and dread," Luke says. "It's incredibly cool that you are about to share the ice with maybe the two best players on the planet. But we really want to win, and that seems . . . unlikely now."

Unlikely is about to become impossible. Tyler Hodges, the guy who is supposed to play goalie for the Dirty Mike squad, just texted. He can't make it. The goalie no-show is a classic beer-league buzzkill. But particularly when two of your opposing forwards combined for 517 points over the last two NHL seasons.

"We're so dead," one of the Dirty Mike players says. And the ones who don't say it, think it.

At another rink at nearby Saint Andrew's College, Ben Charette has just gotten off the ice after a two-hour skills skate. That makes four hours total for his day, after another long session at 6 a.m. Ben is getting ready for his freshman season playing goalie for Harvard University. He's still rehabbing from shoulder surgery. He's exhausted, sore and starving.

Ben takes off his gear and picks up his phone. There are a dozen missed calls from his hockey buddies. He calls one back. "Ben, we have no goalie, and we're going to have to forfeit! We need you! Oh yeah, and we're playing McDavid and Draisaitl!"

Ben checks the team group chat, and someone has already posted the video of the two Oilers stars arriving at the rink. "I'm thinking, 'Oh my God, I just skated for four hours today and now they want me to go get lit up by two NHL superstars,'" Ben says. "But at the same time, you don't get a chance like this . . . maybe . . . ever. So I get in my car and buzz over to the other rink."

They need to delay the game 15 minutes for Ben to get there, which will be a pretty cool part of the story he tells someday. *Ever tell you about the time 97 and 29 had their game put on hold . . . for me!*

"I throw my gear back on and get out on the ice, and Connor and Leon are just kind of standing there, waiting for me," Ben says. "I'm thinking, 'Is this real life?'"

Besides the Icebergs jersey, McDavid and Draisaitl are both wearing all their Oilers gear, which just adds to the intimidation.

Word travels fast in a town like Newmarket, and by puck drop, the arena is packed. There are three rinks in the Magna Centre complex, plus a skate park outside. Every kid around has run over to watch. There are only a few rows of seats, so most are pressed up against the glass, getting a close-up view of greatness.

Predictably, it doesn't start well for Dirty Mike and the Boys. On the first shift of the game, McDavid sauces a perfect pass through three guys to Draisaitl.

"He fires the hardest slapshot I've ever seen, right by me and off the bar," Ben says. "I can't believe the sound it makes. The puck almost hits the roof. I'm like, 'Oh my God, this is ridiculous.' A few seconds later, McDavid gets a breakaway, fakes far side, then pulls it back and goes backhand high glove and in. I'm thinking, 'What the hell just happened?' I've never seen a guy control a puck like that. It takes me a few minutes of the game for my mind to even comprehend how he is moving. It's so fast, it's like he's glitching."

Luke and the rest of the guys are having a similar experience trying to skate with the two superstars.

"Their skill is outrageous," Luke says. "All these fans behind the glass have their phones out, and I keep thinking, 'Don't get embarrassed and end up on TSN or BarDown.' And early on, they aren't really even trying. Especially Leon. He's just out for a skate, firing shots from everywhere. I take a few faceoffs against him. He has this custom stick that looks like a canoe paddle to me. He's so fast, he wins it clean before I even get my stick down. I win one, only because he misses it. So I'll always have that."

In no time, it's 4–1 for Connor, Leon and the Icebergs. But the pair can't play the entire game, and the rest of their team is made up mostly of McDavid's buddies from his days playing for the York–Simcoe Express. Really good beer-league players, but several flights down from their two teammates. So while Connor and Leon sit for a shift, Luke's line scores three straight goals to tie it.

This back and forth continues all game. McDavid and Draisaitl come on the ice and score. And when they sit, Dirty Mike and the Boys respond.

"They score about four goals each," Luke says. "And by the third period, when it's a really close game, their competitive juices start to flow and they seem to be playing pretty hard."

Though Ben is about to give up 11 goals, which is never great for your GAA, he's also making some spectacular saves. He stops McDavid on a breakaway, and again on the rebound. He slides across to make a couple of brilliant backdoor stops on Draisaitl.

When the final buzzer sounds, it's 11–11. Somehow Dirty Mike and the Boys have taken the best one-two combo in the universe to three-on-three overtime. Though that format likely doesn't bode well for the outcome.

Early in OT, McDavid and Draisaitl get a two-on-one. The crowd buzzes. Players on both benches stand. Ben gulps. This has to be game over. But as McDavid is making a move, the puck bobbles and ends up on the stick of Lombardi, the Red Wings prospect and Dirty Mike's best player. The third Iceberg player on the ice is not one of the best players in the world. He's just a guy. Lombardi blows by him and buries the game winner.

Dirty Mike and the Boys, 12. Connor and Leon, 11. Do you believe in miracles?

There are unwritten rules in beer league, especially one of this quality. It's a glorified scrimmage, so guys can stay in game shape for their real seasons. You aren't supposed to celebrate like you've won the Stanley Cup. Especially against two guys who just lost the actual Stanley Cup. So Lombardi doesn't even react to the goal. But on the bench, most of his teammates can't contain themselves.

"We try to play it cool, but it's wholesale off the bench," Luke says. "We're just so excited to have won this game. I didn't even think we were going to score a goal, let alone win 12–11. We can't believe it.

During handshakes, McDavid taps Ben on the chest and says, "Good job."

"Pretty freaking cool, not gonna lie," Ben says.

In the dressing room after, the boys joke about whether losing to a bunch of kids called Dirty Mike and the Boys is more devastating for the two Oilers than losing Game 7 of the Cup Final to the Florida Panthers. For the record, "They didn't look too upset," Luke laughs. "I think they were over it in about a minute."

Luke would soon return to his regular team at Nipissing University in North Bay. Ben would head off to Harvard. And McDavid and Draisaitl would go back to chasing a Stanley Cup. They would come close again the following spring, falling to the Panthers again in the finals. They've likely already forgotten their cameo in beer league. Their opponents never will.

"I'm twenty-one years old," Luke says. "I've idolized McDavid and Draisaitl most of my life. To play a real game against them . . . it's surreal."

POSTSCRIPT: *Alas, this isn't the last stacked team Dirty Mike and the Boys would face. After winning their semifinal, in the championship game they play a team featuring (then) Philadelphia Flyer Morgan Frost, budding Dallas star Wyatt Johnston and veteran NHL defenceman Sean Walker. Dirty Mike and the Boys lose 9–4 and have to watch Frost and friends hoist the prestigious league trophy . . . a beat-up old beer keg.*

BRUCE, THERE IT IS!

The Naked Truths About Bruce Boudreau's Life in Hockey

Like any great hockey story, this one starts with Bruce Boudreau running through a bar naked. (Suddenly the whole "Bruce, there it is!" chant has a completely different meaning.)

It's 1975, just in case you were imagining present-day Bruce in a bare-assed sprint.

In his defence, streaking is a thing in the '70s. And members of Bruce's junior team, the Toronto Marlboros, are keen participants. "We just won the Memorial Cup, and we have the world by the balls," Bruce says. "Everyone on our team had been streaking that season. That song "The Streak" is really popular, and we are a close team. So we go out, and it's just a thing that a few of the guys would run through the restaurant or bar naked. Just to get laughs."

Bruce, a 68-goal, 165-point junior superstar, had not partaken. Until a Monday night, just before the NHL Draft. "We go to Edelweiss, this bar at Ontario Place," Bruce says. "It's really late and there are only a handful of people left. So I decide, 'What the hell. Let's streak!'"

He convinces teammates Mike Kitchen and Mark Napier to join him. It's a simple route. They will take off their clothes in one bathroom, run across the circular stage where Edelweiss's one-man band has long since wrapped up his set, and end up in the other bathroom at the opposite end of the bar.

The boys make one questionable equipment choice. And it would prove costly. They put their underwear over their heads.

"And I trip over the stage and put my head through the drum," Bruce says. "I get up, shake the drum off my head and run into the bathroom. We are laughing our heads off. Just the dumbest thing ever."

Bar management isn't as amused. Before the trio leaves, two plainclothes police officers show up and charge them with indecent exposure. Bad timing, especially for Bruce, who is projected to be a first-rounder in the draft.

"We go home that night and make a vow we won't tell anyone," Bruce says. "And by eight the next morning it's on CHUM radio, and in big bold letters in the *Toronto Star*. My dad phones me and starts screaming."

Yes, the streaking story would be much funnier if it didn't end up hurting Bruce's draft status so much.

"I had gone to a meeting with the Oakland Seals people, and they told me they were drafting me third overall," Bruce says. "Then John McLellan, the assistant general manager of the Maple Leafs, tells me, 'We'd pick you seventh, but you won't be there.'"

Then the streaking story breaks.

The 1975 NHL Draft is conducted by phone. Bruce and his dad, Norm, are sitting in the basement of their bungalow in North York. The phone isn't ringing. "We're sitting there saying, 'What's going on?' The draft was supposed to start two hours ago!"

The Seals don't take Bruce third as they promised. They select Ralph Klassen, a centre from the Saskatoon Blades. Toronto passes too, taking Don Ashby, a centre from the Calgary Centennials. The phone in the Boudreau basement stays silent for what feels like an eternity. When it finally does ring, it's the secretary of

Bruce's agent, Alan Eagleson. Bruce is a Toronto Maple Leaf after all. But in the third round, 42nd overall. He never gets an explanation for what happened.

"I am just shattered," he says. "Forty-third, all because I dropped my laundry. But it's my own fault."

In 1975, there is an alternative to the NHL for a player turning pro: the World Hockey Association.

"There is no way I would have signed there if I went in the first round," Bruce says. "But because I get picked so far down, I decide to sign with the Minnesota Fighting Saints."

This move, it turns out, is like falling headfirst into a drum with your underwear on your head. Again.

Thirty games into Bruce's rookie season, the Saints fold. Most of the players rush to the bank to cash their last cheques. But Bruce doesn't bother. By the time he gets around to it a couple of days later, the money is all gone. The Saints also still owe him $10,000 of his $25,000 signing bonus.

Bruce is taken first in the Saints' dispersal draft by Indianapolis, but Eagleson refuses to let him sign there if he doesn't get the rest of his bonus. So Bill Watters, one of Eagleson's assistants, makes a suggestion. He's heard they are about to make a movie based around a minor-league team down in Pennsylvania. Why doesn't Bruce go spend the rest of the year there and have a little fun, and the Leafs will sign him after the season?

So just a few months after he was supposed to go third overall in the NHL Draft, Bruce heads to the North American Hockey League. "It's maybe the second dumbest thing I've ever done in my life, after the streaking," he says. "I could have signed with the Leafs right there, gone to their farm team in Oklahoma City and started my career properly."

Dumb move for his hockey career, yes. But for Bruce's future role as a world-class storyteller, it's the greatest decision ever.

Because the team he signs with is the Johnstown Jets. Better known by their fictional name, the Charlestown Chiefs. And the movie they are about to shoot is *Slap Shot*.

"When I go down there, I think it's just some small movie that will pass. Instead, it turns out to be the most iconic thing that's ever happened to me. Even today, every hockey team on every bus watches that movie."

There are entire books written about *Slap Shot*, so we'll condense the backstory. A guy named Ned Dowd had played for the Jets a few years earlier. His sister Nancy, a budding screenwriter, came to visit. What she witnessed, on and off the ice, inspired her to write *Slap Shot*. Academy Award–winning director George Roy Hill (*Butch Cassidy and the Sundance Kid*, *The Sting*) loves it and casts his go-to leading man, Paul Newman, to play Reggie Dunlop.

And landing in the middle of this big Hollywood production is Bruce Boudreau, soon to be forever listed in the credits as "Hockey Player #7."

"The whole thing is crazy," he says. "I have no idea how big it's going to be."

There is a scene where the Charlestown goalie is getting bombarded by the Hyannisport Presidents. Bruce is an extra, playing one of the Presidents. George Roy Hill tells the cast his camera is focused only on the net, but they are to keep playing the game.

"So I never leave the front of the net," Bruce says. "The play would go out around the blue line, but being the ham that I am, I never move. So I end up in a bunch of shots in the movie."

One day, Hill comes into the dressing room and tells the Jets players he needs to shoot a scene in an apartment that is supposed to be Reggie Dunlop's. He needs the messiest, sloppiest-looking place he can find. "Everybody in unison points at me," Bruce says. "So when Paul Newman is lying on the bed and can't get any sleep and the dog comes to lie with him, that's my apartment."

John Gofton is the oldest player on the Jets. He gets the role of Nick Brophy on the opposing Presidents—and a memorable scene with Newman before a faceoff.

"I'm drunk. I'm not bullshitting ya," Brophy says to Dunlop. "Got stinkin' shitfaced on the bus, Louise left me, and that son of a bitch over there keeps playing me when he knows I'm shitfaced. Anybody throws me against the boards, I'm gonna piss all over myself."

Of course, he does get hit hard into the boards, and . . . self-fulfilling prophecy.

"That shot where John gets hit, we all line up to take turns hitting him," Bruce says. "They end up doing thirteen takes, and every guy tries to hit him harder. We're jumping at him, just drilling him. Laughing our asses off. By the last take, he ends up with a concussion."

One night, Bruce and his roommate are invited to watch the dailies (the scenes shot that day) with Newman and Hill. "At one point, Paul Newman turns to us and says, 'I just finished making a movie called *The Life and Times of Judge Roy Bean* and I only did it for the money, but this movie is going to be great.'"

He's right. Bruce sees *Slap Shot* in Toronto when it premieres the next year. "The crowd goes nuts," he says. "The talk at the time is that it's far-fetched. And sure, it's exaggerated a bit. But those brawls, and the crazy off-ice scenes? That stuff really happened in the minors."

Case in point: The Jets (Bruce's non-fictional team) take a road trip to Cape Cod in a snowstorm. It takes 15 hours to get there. "We have sixteen bunks and seventeen players and I'm the only rookie, so guess who sleeps on the floor? As we go up and down hills, all the spilled beer is rolling back and forth all over me. I get soaked."

The next night they have a game in Beauce, Quebec, another 15 hours away on the bus. The Beauce Jaros are the roughest, toughest team in the North American League. "They have this guy named Wally Weir who wears a toque during the games, not a helmet," Bruce says. "The rule is, if you knock Wally's toque off, you have to fight him. So Wally gets a lot of room that night. We do a ton of poke-checking. There is no chance I'm going anywhere near the corner with Wally Weir. We win the game and skate backward out of the arena because we figure Wally and the rest of them will jump us."

Boudreau scores 25 goals and 60 points in just 34 games with Johnstown that season, while making the greatest hockey movie ever. He signs with the Maple Leafs at season's end and spends the next year with the Dallas Black Hawks of the Central Hockey League. He leads the league in goals, propelling him to the NHL.

In just his second NHL game (March 7, 1977), the Leafs are playing the Philadelphia Flyers at the Spectrum. This is prime Broad Street Bullies era. Mayhem is a nightly occurrence. Darryl Sittler and Paul Holmgren get into a fight at the end of the second. Benches empty. "I'm standing watching most of it with my teammate Paul Evans, who I grew up with," Bruce says. "Darryl comes over and he's livid. He's screaming at me, 'Go get [Bobby] Clarke right now!' So I look over and Clarke is surrounded by Bob Kelly and Bill Barber. So I look back at Darryl and like a scared little boy, I just start shaking my head no."

Bruce made some questionable decisions as a young man. This was not one of them.

The next year he scores 29 points in 40 games in his second NHL season with the Leafs. The streaking and all those other bad choices finally seem to be behind him.

"But sometimes things just happen," Bruce says. "After a few seasons bouncing up and down, the Leafs' new coach Mike Nykoluk tells me I am going to be their second-line centre the next year. I'm super motivated. I train hard all summer. And when I get to camp, they start me on defence. I get cut after four days. That was pretty much it for the NHL."

Bruce spends most of the rest of his playing career in the minors. Back where he started. Starring in real-life *Slap Shot*. On a road trip from Oklahoma City to Dallas, the team bus gets caught in an ice storm and slides off the road into a ditch. "The cops come and are trying to figure out how to break up the ice to get us out. First they slide cardboard under the wheels. That doesn't work. So these two sheriffs pull out their guns and start shooting at the ice to break it up! They must have fired a dozen bullets. All these Canadian kids are sitting on the bus watching, going, 'This is nuts!'"

One playoff series when Bruce is with the New Brunswick Hawks, a fight breaks out between the two coaches: Eddie Johnston (Moncton) and Pat Quinn (Maine). "They had been yapping away at each other, and they end up at centre ice whaling away in their suits, blood everywhere. The next game, they build a big partition between the benches so no one could go after each other."

Bruce's hockey journey takes him to stops in Minnesota, Johnstown, Toronto, Dallas, New Brunswick, Cincinnati, St. Catharines, Baltimore, Iserlohn (Germany), Chicago, Halifax, Springfield, Newmarket, Phoenix, Fort Wayne and Adirondack. Along the way, he becomes one of the highest scorers in minor-league history, with 548 goals.

Yet most of you don't know Bruce for any of this. Not the streaking, the *Slap Shot* cameos, the prodigious scoring. It's not until his second life as a coach that Bruce Boudreau truly becomes a legend. And if you had to pinpoint *the* moment it happens, it's probably a between-periods rant to his Washington Capitals in 2010. Captured in all its expletive-filled glory by HBO cameras filming a documentary series.

"We're on a three-game winless streak and down 1–0 to Florida," Bruce says. "We just killed a five-on-three, and the guys walk in like someone had shot their dog. I ask the HBO crew to leave the room. They say, 'No, we have permission to stay.' So I say,

'Okay then. I don't know what's about to come out of my mouth, but here we go.'"

With apologies to any kids reading, the iconic sixty-seven-second speech that follows deserves unedited word-for-word treatment. Thirty-five years later, Bruce (blue) streaks again.

"Look, I have never seen a bunch of guys look so fucking down when something bad happens. What are you guys, like prima donna perfect that you can't fucking handle adversity? So shit's not going right. It's not fucking working the last ten days. Fucking get your heads out of your ass and fucking make it work by outworking the opposition. You kill two fucking men [down] and then we stand around and watch it while they fucking score here. Fucking, you come to the bench like fucking this. And when the power play, it's not working, so you're trying to stickhandle. You're looking like this and not standing. Outwork the fucking guys! If you want it, don't just think you want it. Go out and fucking want it! But you're not looking like you want it. You look like you're feeling sorry for yourself. And nobody fucking wants anybody that's feeling sorry for themselves. You got twenty fucking minutes. You're down by one fucking shot. Surely the fuck we can deal with this."

And he walks out of the room.

I wish there was footage of the HBO producers, who were likely leaping into each other's arms like they'd just won the Stanley Cup. Because in documentary scene terms, they had.

But Bruce is in big trouble. Not with his GM, his owner or Gary Bettman and the NHL. With Mom.

"She is so embarrassed," Bruce says. "She tells me she can't go to work because I swore so much on TV."

And yet it endears Bruce even more to a hockey nation that already loved his straightforward, old-school approach. "When I was a player, I had some bullies as coaches," he says. "I would sit out twenty straight games and they wouldn't say a word to me. Or they'd make us leave our equipment on after a bad loss and bag skate [us]. I always said I would never be like that. I wanted to communicate, and always tell players exactly where they stood. Even if there were a few f-bombs thrown in."

Holding every player accountable is a Boudreau principle. But he realizes early he has to handle superstars like Alexander Ovechkin a little differently. If he does a video session where he shows his players making mistakes, he would include Ovie, with a caveat. "I would always let him know in advance if he was going to be the star of the video," Bruce says. "I would never surprise or embarrass him. Same with J.T. Miller in Vancouver. He always wanted me to use him as an example, but I would always talk to him before, so he knew it was coming."

Early in Bruce's Washington tenure, GM George McPhee orders him to start strictly enforcing curfew on the road. McPhee is concerned the young Caps are enjoying the nightlife a little too much. Bruce wants no part of this, but his boss insists.

One night, Bruce calls all the players' rooms before 11 p.m. curfew but can't reach Ovechkin. "I call Ian Anderson, our team services guy, and say, 'We have to find Ovie! I have to report to George that everyone is in their rooms.'"

At 10:58, Bruce's phone rings. It's Ovie. "All I can hear is this loud electronic music blaring in the background," Bruce says. "You can barely hear him. I say, 'Ovie, are you in?' And he says, 'Yeah, Coach, I'm in.' And I go, 'Great, see ya tomorrow!' I didn't want to know anything else."

Bruce yells at Ovechkin only once in four and half years as the Capitals' coach. On November 1, 2011, they are playing the Anaheim Ducks and trailing 4–2 in the third. Ovie is having a bad night. The Capitals score to get within a goal late. With the net empty, Bruce calls a time out. "Ovie asks, 'Where do you want me to play, Coach?' I am still livid with him, so I say, 'Right on the fucking bench. That's where you are gonna play.'"

The two exchange a few more expletives, and Ovie stays on the bench. The Capitals tie the game without him. And in overtime, Bruce puts Ovie back out. He sets up Nicklas Backstrom for the game winner. But afterward, all anyone wants to know is what happened between the coach and his superstar on the bench. Bruce is fired later that month.

"I guess I get fired because I told Ovie off on the bench," Bruce says. "The funny thing is we're playing Anaheim, and their GM Bob Murray thought I was a tough ass who had balls for benching Ovie. So he hires me the next day!"

There is no lingering bad blood between Ovie and Bruce. "He runs up and hugs me every time I see him," Bruce says.

Could anyone have bad blood for Bruce? He's still beloved by the fanbases of every team he's coached. But there has never been a scene quite like his last game behind the bench in Vancouver in 2023. The Canucks are struggling, and reports have already leaked out that they are going to dump Bruce and hire Rick Tocchet.

On January 21, 2023, the Canucks are playing Edmonton at home. Bruce knows it's over. So does the crowd. In the dying seconds of a 4–2 Oilers win, the entire arena picks up a chant they've been doing since Boudreau arrived: "Bruce, there it is!" (to the tune of Tag Team's "Whoomp! (There It Is)." They give him a long standing ovation as he leaves the bench.

"It's so touching," Bruce says. "The players surround me and tap their sticks. It means everything. A coach never gets a chance to say goodbye to all his players together. But I know I'm getting fired, so I get to address the players. I would say of the twenty-three guys in there, fifteen are crying. I'm crying, saying goodbye."

Bo Horvat and J.T. Miller come into Bruce's office and present him with the wrestling belt the team had been giving to a player after every game. Bruce, a massive wrestling fan, is the one who brought the belt in. They want him to keep it. And then he waits.

"All of my assistants think they are getting fired too, so we just sit around having a couple of drinks, waiting. The team services guy is there because we know he's the one who will get the call to tell me to come downstairs. At twelve thirty, he gets the call, and they say, 'Tell Bruce to meet us in the room at nine a.m. tomorrow.' And we all cheer."

Bruce Boudreau is a hockey lifer. It's all he knows. He spends the next two years watching games and doing work for the NHL Network and TSN. For Trade Centre 2023, we do a bit where he recreates the famous Capitals rant to pump up the TSN commentators. We beeped out the f-bombs this time. Family show.

"Hey, guys, listen up for a minute here. I've never seen a group of people look so BLEEP down. What are you, prima donna perfect where you can't BLEEP handle a little bit of adversity? This is the NHL. You guys are BLEEP too good to be doing nothing! Pounder, you've let that BLEEP nomination go to your head. Button, this isn't junior. Let's get this BLEEP going here. Duthie, let's get our BLEEP in gear here. You haven't done a thing for two weeks. You sit on your BLEEP and you pretend to make BLEEP phone calls. You're better than this. LeBrun, Johnston, crack some BLEEP trades. We're sitting here on our BLEEP doing nothing. We need information! Gino, what are you doing? You're sitting there, you don't even have a chair. Get the BLEEP up and do some work! Look, I know BLEEP Duthie is hosting and you're not working with much, but surely the BLEEP we can do better than this. Let's get 'er going!"

The man is a national treasure.

For the record, we chose not to recreate the streaking scene.

PATIENT #1

Roberto Luongo Plays Two Periods, with a Hospital Visit in Between

---

Roberto Luongo is down. This is hardly new, or news. Luongo spends much of his career on his back, stomach, ass . . . face. Stopping pucks in every way imaginable is one of his trademarks.

But this is different. This time, he's in agony.

GORD MILLER ON TSN: Now Komarov comes walking in, shoots from a sharp angle, Luongo the stop . . .

RAY FERRARO: Oh, he's hurt!

MILLER: And Luongo is down! Roberto Luongo drops, falling awkwardly after making the first save.

It's his shoulder. He feels like he's been shot. Luongo has rarely gotten hurt in his long Hall of Fame career. He's one of the most durable goalies ever. So the crowd in Sunrise, Florida, falls silent. This can't be good.

It's March 3, 2015. The trade deadline just passed, and it's the biggest game of the season for the Panthers. They are two points back of Boston for the final wild card spot in the Eastern Conference. And they're playing a reeling Leafs team that has lost 16 straight games on the road (this is their infamous "18-wheeler off the cliff" season). It's a must-win game. And watching their star goalie crumble to the ice late in the first period is a nightmare.

"It kills," Luongo says. "I can't move my right arm."

But after a long discussion with Panthers trainer Dave Zenobi, he stays in for the rest of the period. The Panthers score in the dying seconds to take a 1–0 lead. But when the horn goes, Luongo is doubled over as he skates off the ice. In the Panthers' room, team medical staff peel off his number 1 jersey and shoulder pads and feel around the shoulder. Luongo winces when they hit the spot.

"You have to go to the hospital and get it looked at," they tell him, fearing there might be a fracture. They give him a shot of Toradol and help him out of his gear and into his suit. One of the Panthers' team doctors drives him to the Cleveland Clinic, about 15 minutes away. Backup Al Montoya takes over for the second period.

At the clinic, Patient #1 gets X-rays taken of his shoulder. There's no rush. Luongo's night is over. Florida's hopes now rest on the (non-wounded) shoulders of Montoya. With no TV or radio in the clinic, Luongo has no idea what's happening in the game for nearly an hour.

Back at the rink, the third period starts with Florida up 2–1. It's about to get weird.

Just 22 seconds in, Toronto's Jake Gardiner fires a point shot that goes off the back boards and right to Nazem Kadri. Montoya does the splits trying to slide over to make the save, but Kadri scores as he runs right into the spread-eagled goalie. While the Leafs celebrate, Montoya gets up gingerly. He shuffles awkwardly in the net.

MILLER: Al Montoya is talking to referee Justin St-Pierre. Now, the Panthers have reported that Roberto Luongo will not be back tonight . . .

FERRARO: We've always joked about this scenario. Who will be the next guy in?

By the look on Panthers coach Gerard Gallant's face, it's not so freakin' funny, Ray! These are the pre-EBUG (emergency backup goalie) days, so it's pure Panther panic.

Montoya skates to the bench and has his own chat with the trainer, Zenobi.

MILLER: If Montoya can't continue, NHL rules state that the Panthers will be given a 'reasonable amount of time' to find a goalie. If they don't, someone's got to play goal for Florida. It might be a forward or a defenceman who has to put on the pads. We'll be back after this.

Solid dramatic commercial throw, Gordo. Right on Gord's cue, Panthers forward Derek MacKenzie gets up from the bench and runs toward the room. Another forward, Scottie Upshall, follows close behind.

"We just figure we are the two best guys for any mission," Upshall laughs. "If that means putting on Sweet Lou's pads and making kick save after kick save for our team, that's what we are ready to do. Back to our street hockey days of Road Warrior pads and frozen tennis balls! We go to the room and start playing rock, paper, scissors to decide who is going to go in. I lose in a best of five."

FERRARO: I'd tell you where I'd be, and that would be hiding under the bench! There's going to be a few guys here that wouldn't volunteer for this job in a hundred years. Can you imagine? The Panthers are in a playoff race here. These are vital points for them. And you wonder why coaches don't have any hair!

High above the ice in a team suite, Panthers goalie coach Rob Tallas is having a déjà vu. Two years earlier, the Panthers had to call up Jacob Markstrom from San Antonio after an injury to José Théodore. But Markstrom's gear doesn't make the flight. He's stuck at the airport waiting for it. Minutes before warm-up, the Panthers have only one goalie, Scott Clemmensen.

"We call the league and ask Gary Bettman what we're allowed to do," Tallas says. "I ask if I can dress for warm-up and come in if our goalie gets hurt. Gary clears it. I do warm-up and sit on the bench for a while until Markstrom gets there. So when Montoya gets hurt, I know exactly what the rules are. And I head right down to the dressing room."

The delay lasts 11 minutes (leading to a rare in-game panel fill on TSN, forcing me to wipe the pizza off my face and put my jacket back on, which is unprecedented). Montoya finally skates back to the net. He can barely move.

"He had torn his groin [muscle] right off the bone," says Upshall. "The Leafs are licking their chops and shooting from everywhere. And our one-legged Cubano is still in there making saves."

Tallas runs into the dressing room and finds . . . chaos. "I look to my right and Derek MacKenzie has half his gear off and is strapping on goalie pads," Tallas says. "Scottie Upshall is standing there talking to him. Our owner is on the phone with Gary Bettman. It's madness. So I turn to Derek and say, 'No, no, no. You can't go in. You're not allowed.' It's in the rules to protect the players. I found this out when the Markstrom thing happened. They could get hurt and end their career."

There is a large digital clock in the room that is synched up with the game clock. Suddenly, it starts moving again. "I look at Scottie and yell, 'Scottie, the game is back on!'" Tallas says.

If you're keeping score, the Panthers are now down two goalies and two forwards. Upshall curses and sprints out of the room.

MacKenzie throws off the goalie pads and scrambles back into his gear. And Tallas straps the pads on. He's 41 and hasn't appeared in an NHL game in 14 years.

"I'm terrified," he says. "I don't even put goalie skates on anymore. I just use regular skates. So I'm not even thinking about making saves. I'm worried about my first three strides and not falling headfirst as soon as I step on the ice."

Back at the clinic, Luongo is out of X-ray and in the waiting room. He's told he has a small fracture in his shoulder. He pulls out his phone for the first time since he left the rink.

"The way I scroll through Twitter is to go back so I can read things in the order they happened," he says. "So I'm looking at the Panthers account and some of the other accounts I follow and I see 'Montoya is down.' And then, 'Confusion on the bench, looks like Derek MacKenzie might be going in,' and then 'Rob Tallas is getting dressed. He might be going in.' You've heard of doom scrolling? This is it. I'm like, 'What is happening?!' So I turn to the doc and say, 'Dude, we gotta go back, now!' We jump in the car, and I'm yelling at him to go faster and faster."

Coming soon: *Fast and Furious 17: Fort Lauderdale Drift*.

As Luongo and Doc Vin Diesel tear down a Florida highway, the whistle has blown and Montoya is back at the bench. Gallant argues with the refs about how much time they should be given to figure this mess out.

FERRARO: I just can't believe this, I've gotta be honest with you. I've been around the NHL since December of 1984. I've never seen this. There's a stream of traffic in the Panthers' tunnel.

And then, like Clark Kent just before he finds the phone booth and his tights, there is Luongo. Wide-eyed in his dress shirt and pants, talking to the trainer. "First I run into the locker room and see Tallas putting on his gear, and his face is white as a ghost," Luongo says. "He's terrified. So I go out to the bench and I tell the trainer, 'I have a little fracture and can't lift my arm. But because of the Toradol, the pain isn't too bad. I can still move, so I can play. They seem desperate, so they say, 'Okay.' So I run and get my gear back on." Tallas has now appeared in full gear by the bench, ready to go in. Or throw up. Or both.

While Luongo is getting re-dressed, the Leafs score to make it 3–2. Montoya looks helpless. He can't move. With nine minutes left, there is a whistle as Kadri takes a tripping penalty. And with an entrance that really could have used the John Williams *Indiana Jones* theme behind it, Luongo emerges from the tunnel and jumps back on the ice.

> **MILLER:** Now Roberto Luongo is coming back into the Florida goal! How about that! Luongo was in street clothes and he's coming back in for Florida!
>
> **FERRARO:** Okay, that is remarkable. It really is.
>
> **MILLER:** He was in a suit five minutes ago!

They don't even know he went to the hospital.

"I think when Lui heard his two fourth-line assistant captains were fighting for the chance to put on his gear, it gave him a jolt of energy . . . or laughter," Upshall says. "When he comes out of that tunnel, it's a huge relief. We know he'll make it look easy. Even with one arm."

> **FERRARO:** When you talk about a commitment to your team, Luongo and Montoya have just shown it here!

I hope when Luongo tells this story to his grandkids, he'll say he stood on his head for the last nine minutes as the Panthers came back to win it in overtime. And they carried him off the ice like Rob Lowe in *Youngblood* after he scores the winner and beats up Racki.

But hockey isn't Hollywood. The Panthers don't come back. They lose 3–2 and would miss the playoffs. Luongo does make five saves, to finish a perfect 19 for 19 on the night. Hockey's first (and likely last) shutout-not-shutout-with-a-hospital-visit-in-between, ever.

"Definitely one of the wildest nights of my life," Luongo says.

POSTSCRIPT: *The Panther-Leafs game, in part, leads to the NHL bringing in the emergency goalie system. A system that would see an accountant (Scott Foster) and a Zamboni driver (David Ayres) thrown into games. The NHL introduced new rules in 2025 to ensure professional goalies are always available. But Tallas doesn't believe that is enough. He has proposed the NHL let teams call up their minor-league goalies on a rotating basis, with no salary cap implication. Luongo, meanwhile, retires in 2019 after two decades in the NHL and joins the Panthers' front office. He and Tallas would finally get their Hollywood happy ending in 2024, when the Panthers win their first of back-to-back Stanley Cups.*

LOST BOY

Mike Johnson's First NHL Road Trip Nightmare

The rookie is in full panic mode. Near tears. Sweat pouring off his brow.

The best week of his life, the one he dreamt of all those years playing minor hockey in Toronto and college at Bowling Green, has turned into a nightmare. And it has nothing to do with his game. This is no costly late penalty. No missed empty net. It's way worse. This is a reputation ruiner. Before he's even had a chance to earn a reputation. He may never recover from it.

He throws his bag over his shoulder and sprints toward the fence, scrambling upward like a scene from some prison escape movie. Except he's trying to get *in*. Barbed wire lines the top of the fence. For a moment, he ponders tearing his suit, and likely his flesh, by trying to climb over it. But it's impossible.

The rookie is out of time. And options.

"I'm screwed," Mike Johnson says to himself. Or maybe he screams it aloud. That part is a blur. Doesn't matter really, as no one is there to hear him. He's lost and alone.

Just a couple of hours earlier, MJ (as most know him) was on top of the world, racing up the ice at Maple Leaf Gardens, wearing the blue and white of his beloved Leafs. His first home game. One hundred family members and friends screaming for him every shift. Surreal.

It's March 1997. And it's been a whirlwind week for MJ. He just finished his fourth and final year at Bowling Green State in Ohio. An undrafted free agent, he signs his first pro contract with the Leafs on a Saturday and is immediately called up to play his first NHL game in Tampa on Sunday.

"The first game is just awesome," MJ says. "I play eighteen minutes, get an assist, four shots, play some power play and penalty kill, and get cut for nine stitches above my eye. When it's over, I say, 'I can do this! I can play in this league!'"

The 22-year-old doesn't know a soul on the Leafs. There are a few quick hellos in the dressing room in Tampa, and some bench chatter during the game, but he doesn't get a chance to have a real conversation with anyone. The team leaves Tampa right after the game to fly back to Toronto. MJ flies alone to Detroit where he left his car. He drives to Bowling Green to gather his stuff, then back to Toronto for his first home game as a Leaf, against the Philadelphia Flyers.

It's a massive night. His friends hold up a banner that reads MIKE JOHNSON FAN CLUB and go nuts every time he steps on the ice. But the game itself doesn't go quite as well as his debut in Tampa.

"We play Philly and the Legion of Doom line and lose 6–3," MJ says. "Eric Lindros has four goals and two assists. Mikael Renberg has two goals and two assists. John LeClair has three assists. I go minus-two and don't touch the puck. Welcome to the NHL."

Still, he's buzzing. MJ has made it. He's a Maple Leaf.

There are multiple baptisms into NHL life. And MJ is rattling them off. First game, first point, first stitches, first home game. Next up: first road trip. His first chance to fly charter, eat the fancy food and hang out with the guys he's been watching on TV for years. He can't wait.

The Leafs are leaving a couple of hours after the Flyers game for a flight to Pittsburgh, where they play the following night. MJ is spending a few minutes with his family and friends after the game when the Leafs' travelling secretary asks if he needs a ride to the airport.

"No, just tell me where to go," he responds casually. After all, he's lived in Toronto his entire life. He knows where the airport is. Duh. He'll just drive and park there, like the vets do. So the travelling secretary jots down the directions on a slip of paper.

427 to Renforth Drive. Renforth to Silver Dart Drive. Look for the ESSO avatar.

Easy. The Leafs' plane is set to take off at 11:45 p.m. MJ spends a few more minutes with his group, then jumps in his old Acura Integra. It's 10:30. He figures 25 minutes or so to the airport and he'll be nice and early to begin his new pampered NHL charter life. *"Should I have the steak or lobster tonight?"*

Traffic is fine (a Toronto rarity, even at 10:30 p.m.), and MJ is on Renforth Drive, right next to the airport by 10:55. Right on schedule. But there's one little issue. He can't find Silver Dart Drive, the street he's supposed to turn onto to lead him to the terminal.

Remember, it's 1997. MJ's car has no navigation system. There are no cellphones with Waze. It's just the kid and his slip of paper. With directions that no longer make any sense.

"I'm driving up and down Renforth, and I can't find Silver Dart Drive anywhere," MJ says. "So I'm getting unsettled. I don't have anyone's number, not even the PR guy. So I can't even stop and call someone. I've got nothing. But how hard can it be? There aren't many places that can have an airport hangar. I have to be close."

Up and down Renforth he goes. Five minutes go by. Ten. Fifteen. Unsettled quickly turns to desperate.

"I start to wonder if I should drive to Pittsburgh. But my old car isn't sounding great either. Maybe I should call my parents and ask them to buy me a regular plane ticket to Pittsburgh. I have no money. I don't even own a credit card yet. These are the thoughts running through my head."

11:10. 11:15. 11:20. He starts expanding his circle of search, going farther up and down the road. Now he's in some residential neighbourhood. A lost boy.

"I'm getting more and more rattled and terrified," MJ says. "You can't be the last guy on the plane on your first flight. Missing it? I can't even ponder that possibility. What are the guys on the plane, who I don't even know, saying?! My plane is taking off in fifteen minutes! I'm now in full-blown panic. I'm almost crying. I'm driving twice the speed limit, hoping I get pulled over so at least a police officer can give me a ticket and show me where to go. I jump out of my car at a red light and I'm banging on cabbies' windows asking where Silver Dart Drive is. I'm going nuts."

Fruitless, all of it. 11:45 now. 11:50. Midnight. And then suddenly, the little cartoon light bulb suddenly goes on above his brain.

"I've been so focused on Silver Dart Drive, I never really looked up," he says. "I've driven up and down Renforth fifty times, but never really looked to the horizon. So I finally do and there is this giant ESSO sign, the size of a blimp, right in front of me! You can still see it today. It's incredible that I missed it."

Turns out Silver Dart Drive does not run directly off Renforth. The travelling secretary's scribbled note skipped one small critical connector road.

The Integra screeches onto Silver Dart Drive. MJ, still panicked and not thinking straight, heads toward the first building he sees, parks and starts sprinting toward what must be the hangar next to the airport runway. But there is no entrance is sight.

Desperate, he runs toward the fence. And starts climbing.

"It's ludicrous," he says. "I'm in my suit from the game, carrying my other suit bag, trying to jump a barbed wire fence to find my team's plane. I get to the top but can't get over the barbed wire. I jump back down, leap back in the car and peel out of there. Finally, I see an actual gate for the terminal."

Hope, at last. He ditches his car and sprints inside. As he's running through the door, the Toronto Raptors are walking out, after arriving home from their own road trip.

"That is the one moment where I forget for a second how screwed I am," he says. "I'm like, 'Hey, that's Damon Stoudamire! Cool!'"

He quickly gets a Tie Domi–level face punch back to reality. (That's not really a metaphor, by the way. MJ believes Tie Domi may actually punch him in the face if he ever gets on this plane.) There is a guy in a vest who looks like the kind of guy who would know where the Leafs' charter is.

"Is this where I get on the Leafs' plane?" Mike asks, gasping for breath.

"Yup, this is it," the man replies.

Finally! Salvation. He's found it. Maybe MJ and his new teammates will all have a good chuckle when he gets on the plane. They'll tousle his hair, grab him a beer and save him a seat for the card game.

"But the plane just left," the man continues.

Oh. Insert multiple expletives. You know that *Simpsons* episode where they freeze-frame the moment Ralph Wiggum's heart breaks after Lisa rejects him? This is that moment for Mike Johnson.

"Oh my God, they're gone! All my hopes and dreams come crashing down. I've just missed the team charter on my first road trip in the NHL. I'm done. I'm twenty-two, but at this moment, I'm a terrified child. I'm completely lost."

That painful realization feels like it lasts an eternity, but MJ figures it's probably just 20 seconds or so. As his mind ponders whether to scream, cry or curl up in the fetal position on the floor, he notices the guy in the vest is on his walkie-talkie. "Hang on," Vest guy says. "They are coming back for you!"

To MJ, this feels like a worse outcome than missing the plane. "You are telling me they are going to come back to Toronto to get me, and I'm going to have to face those guys?!"

Sort of. Turns out the plane was still taxiing down the runway, seconds from taking off. A few minutes later, the 747 pulls up back in front of the hangar. And the rookie gets set to take one of the greatest walks of shame in NHL history. He jumps in the cab of a pickup and they drive him out to meet the plane.

"I feel like I'm walking up to the edge of the *Titanic*," MJ says. "I take these stairs up off the back of the pickup like a dead man walking. I'm terrified of the door opening. I don't even know anyone to find a familiar face."

He climbs the stairs and the door opens. The first face he sees is the flight attendant. She shakes her head with a look of disgust. "I didn't really need that from her at that moment," he says. "Things are bad enough. So I walk in, turn the corner into the aisle, and I am instantly assaulted with a barrage of words I cannot repeat."

C'mon. Repeat a couple for us. Earmuffs, kids.

"It's a chorus of 'you motherfucking piece of shit, college puke, fuck you!' And I'm like, 'Sorry guys, wrong directions.' And I dive into a seat in the first row. I don't even know where I am supposed to sit. I've never been on a team plane before. I feel like I'm ducking to avoid the insults that are flying. It goes on for thirty seconds. Feels like ten minutes. I slink into the chair, and we start moving to take off again."

Assistant GM Bill Watters is the first to come over and ask what happened. MJ tries to explain the bad directions, the fact he had no one to call. He feels like he's begging for mercy.

"Don't worry about it," Watters says calmly. And MJ instantly feels a little relief. Coach Mike Murphy comes over next to get the details, wearing a wry smile.

"Well, that's a helluva story for your first road trip," Murphy laughs. "It's gonna cost you, but don't worry, you are playing tomorrow."

The only player who says a word to him on the plane is Craig Wolanin, a veteran defenceman at the last stop of a long career. He tells MJ a story about how he missed a flight once. "Thank you," MJ whispers. The gesture means more than Wolanin will ever know. For the rest of the flight, and the bus ride to the Pittsburgh hotel, MJ sits alone, in silence.

He finds out later he also got backup goalie Marcel Cousineau in trouble. "I guess they saw Cousy talk to me briefly at the Gardens, so when I wasn't on the plane, they all turned to him and yelled, 'Where the fuck did you tell this kid to go?!' And Cousy is like, 'I don't even know this guy's name! I didn't say anything!' He comes up to me later and says, 'Kid, you are killing me!'"

MJ gets fined $1,000. Doesn't sound like much now, but for a kid who has a total of roughly $0 in his bank account, it hurts. But there is a bright side. "It actually works out because it's an icebreaker," he says. "It gives me something to talk about with the guys at lunch, and on the ice the next day."

Less than five minutes into the game that night in Pittsburgh, Steve Sullivan feeds MJ on a two-on-one, and the rookie buries it. His first NHL goal. He adds an assist later. The Leafs lose 6–3, but the kid has had a good night.

Most importantly, he makes the flight home. In fact, in 11 NHL seasons and 15 more travelling around as one of the best analysts in hockey, he's made every plane on time. And hasn't had to climb a single barbed wire airport fence. Trauma is a teacher.

A footnote MJ discovers later: He wasn't the only player the Leafs were waiting for on the tarmac that night. Defenceman Dmitri Yushkevich didn't show up for the flight either. He had been scratched against the Flyers and wasn't happy. He ends up flying to Pittsburgh the next day with general manager Cliff Fletcher and plays against the Penguins too. It makes MJ feel a little better. Just a little.

"I've had a good life," he says. "But that was probably the single hardest hour of it up to that point. My absolute worst nightmare."

That Christmas, in his stocking, MJ receives a map book from his family. With Silver Dart Drive highlighted and tabbed.

TERRY RYAN: THE MOVIE

The Cinematic Life of a Newfoundland Legend

Jason Momoa holds a knife to Terry Ryan's throat.

"Please, please, have mercy," Terry pleads. "Please!"

Terry is going to die. Of this, there is no doubt. Momoa is going to slit his throat. But he is about to get a brief stay of execution.

"Hold on," says director Brad Peyton.

Peyton is about to shoot scene 1 of episode 1 of season 1 of the new Netflix series *Frontier*. But first, he pulls Terry aside. "I need you to sell this," Brad says quietly. "I need you to cry. Not like you are begging for your life, but like you are begging him to kill you, because you are suffering so badly. I need blood, snot and tears. How much time do you need?"

"I don't know," Terry answers. He's as green as they come. It's also his opening scene. As in, the first one of his acting career. "Maybe thirty seconds?" he says meekly, with no clue what the appropriate answer is.

"Everybody shut up for two minutes!" Peyton yells to the crew. Then he looks back at Terry. "Make these two minutes count."

"What should I think of?" Terry asks, desperate for advice.

"Something . . . not good," Peyton responds and walks away, leaving his novice actor in a mini panic.

Terry shuts his eyes. He tries to send his head to horrible places. But it's not working. He can't find terror, desperation, sadness. Though he's had plenty. Instead, his mind is smothered by the disbelief that he is really here. That Terry Ryan, the guy everyone labelled an NHL bust, the hockey prodigy who felt he let his entire province down, the husband who lost his marriage, the father who lost his family's home, the guy who had almost given up on life . . . has somehow been given another shot. That he is on the set of a big-time show, doing a scene with freakin' Aquaman! That his best buddies are all here watching, just behind the camera, cheering him on like he just won Game 7 in OT. That this life that has punched him in the face and knocked his teeth out, over and over . . . is now picking him up off the ice and lifting him on its shoulders. That he finally feels like he's a "fucking somebody" again.

And right then, Terry Ryan starts bawling.

Uncontrollably. Wave after wave of happiness tears spill down his beaten, bloodied, made-up face and his British Redcoat character's . . . red coat. The director, Peyton, seizes the moment, puts everyone in place and yells, "Action!"

"Please, please, have mercy," Terry cries.

"This is your own doin'. This is not your land," Momoa's character says, his voice action-hero cool. He sharpens his knife on flint. Terry whimpers as he sobs, his breath trembling.

"You shouldn't be here," Momoa continues. "But don't worry . . . I'll be seeing ya."

And Momoa fake slits Terry's throat. Fake blood gushes as he falls forward to his gruesome fake death. And to his wonderfully real new life.

It's almost too perfect. That this moment—this quick-edit mental montage of Terry's entire life—happens here. On a TV show set, in his beloved Newfoundland. For Terry's entire existence has been pure cinema. Action, comedy, drama, tragedy.

The opening scene of *Frontier* could easily be the opening scene of *Terry Ryan: The Movie*—a genre-defying biopic, waiting to be pitched. And unlike *Frontier*, every scene really happened.

SCENE 2
A Hockey Arena Bathroom in Quesnel, British Columbia, 1992

Fourteen-year-old Terry is staring in the mirror, psyching himself up for his first hockey fight. Think opening scene of *8 Mile*, but with a scared teenage Newfoundlander in shoulder pads.

"You have to do this. You have no choice," the voice inside Terry says. He beats his chest with his fist.

A week earlier, Terry played his first game for the Quesnel Millionaires, a Junior A team in British Columbia. He is lined up against guys as old as 20. One of them jumps him off a faceoff and beats the crap out of him. An early message that no matter how big a star you were in minor hockey in Newfoundland—and there had never been a bigger one—you're out west now, playing against men.

In the days before the rematch, a teammate shows him how to chip his helmet, to make it jagged, so it will cut the hand of his combatant. "This is barbaric," Terry thinks. He's just out of peewee. But you do what you have to do to survive. Which brings us back to that scene in the bathroom. Terry stole a bottle of hot sauce from the table at breakfast. He pours it in the plugged sink and soaks his hands in it. Then puts his gloves back on and heads to the ice.

"Let's fucking go!" he says to the guy who jumped him, as soon as he gets on.

"I'm not fighting a fourteen-year-old," his opponent replies, suddenly not as tough as the last game.

Terry doesn't give him a choice. They drop the gloves. When Terry isn't throwing wild punches, he's rubbing his hands all over the guy's face. The hot sauce is so strong, it reminds Terry of smelling salts. He whales away at his blinded-from-the-sauce opponent. The packed arena goes crazy for the kid from the Rock.

Cut away to a starstruck teenage girl in the crowd, smiling and cheering at the rookie's balls. She would take Terry's virginity later that night.

(That scene will probably be deleted.)

SCENE 3
A Conference Room in the Crowne Plaza Hotel in Edmonton, Alberta, June 1995

It's Terry's NHL draft year. He's interviewed with every team except two: the New York Islanders, who have the second overall pick, and the Tampa Bay Lightning, who have the fifth. He walks into the Islanders interview and there are two empty seats, one at each end of the table. Terry takes one of them.

"We like everything about you," says one scout.

"Love your combination of skill and toughness," says another. Terry beams.

The door opens. Islanders general manager Mike Milbury walks in and throws his stuff at the opposite end of the table, facing Terry. There is no handshake, no greeting. Milbury remains standing.

"I think you skate faster with the puck than without it," Milbury says. Terry is confused. He thinks he's being ripped, but isn't quite sure.

"Okay, Mr. Milbury," he answers quietly.

"I think you got lucky with Wade Belak," Milbury continues. Terry and Belak had a legendary scrap that season in the Western Hockey League. "If you fight him ten times, you'll lose nine of them."

Terry stares at Milbury, trying to figure out where this is going.

"It's a good thing you played with Daymond Langkow all year," Milbury says. "You wouldn't have all those points without him."

Now Terry has his back up. "Well, it's a good thing he fucking played with *me*," he fires back.

The Islanders' scouts awkwardly shuffle their feet. The room, relaxed just minutes ago, is now thick with tension.

"Okay, tough guy, I'm going to give you a scenario," Milbury says. "You and Langkow are in Tri-Cities, and you've been out having a good time. You end up taking a girl back to her house. It's 10:50, your curfew is eleven, and it's a ten-minute ride home. But she spreads her legs and says, 'Fuck me, Terry.' What do you do?"

Terry's mind starts working at hyper-speed. What kind of messed-up question is that? What answer is the GM looking for? He's trying to do math. *Ten-minute drive ... curfew eleven ... girl wants to sleep with me. Jesus.* Terry takes a sip of water.

"Well, MIKE," he says boldly. "I fuck her for five minutes and then I speed home."

The scouts at the table bow their heads, trying to hold in their laughter.

"Get out of here," Milbury says. Terry stands up and leaves.

He's met outside the door by Lightning GM Phil Esposito, who seems to have overheard the end of the exchange with Milbury, his old teammate in Boston. "What did you just say to him?" Esposito says. Terry repeats the scenario and his line.

Esposito laughs. "Great answer!" When they sit down in the Lightning's conference room, Espo keeps the absurd sexual content rolling. "How far apart did Napoleon sleep from his wife?" he asks. So many riddles today for Terry.

"A bone apart?" he answers.

Esposito nods and chuckles, then cuts to the chase. "I'm not going to draft you, Terry," he says. "You're not a good enough skater. But we're picking fifth and I'm very interested in Daymond Langkow. Tell me what kind of guy he is." Terry gives his buddy a glowing referral.

"Perfect," Esposito says. "I appreciate that. I have no more questions, and we have lots of time left. So if you want to hear a story from me, I'll give you anything you want." And for the rest of the interview, Phil tells Terry all about the 1972 Summit Series.

Cut to the draft the next day. The Lightning take Langkow fifth overall. The Islanders do not draft Terry. They pick Wade Redden, who ends up being traded to Ottawa the next season. Terry hears his name a few minutes later. He goes eighth overall, to the Montreal Canadiens, the team he grew up loving.

SCENE 4

A House in Mount Pearl, Newfoundland, July 1995

Terry's high school friends are having a party for him before he heads to Montreal for his first NHL training camp.

"Would you ever have the guts to fight Tie Domi?" one of Terry's buddies asks. Terry is pretty sure he will never get that chance. He figures the Habs will be sending him right back to junior, like most 18-year-old rookies in 1995. But there is a girl at the party named Gillian Chipman whom Terry is trying to impress.

"Damn right I would fight Domi," he says, puffing out his chest.

Cut to the Habs' camp. Terry is flying all over the ice, desperate to make an impression. He's not scoring, so he decides to fight a young Canadiens tough guy way out of his weight class. Donald Brashear obliges. Terry holds his own. Impression made.

"We love your effort," Habs coach Jacques Demers tells Terry. "We are going to send you back to junior, but would you like to play a game at the Montreal Forum against the Boston Bruins first? You'd have to miss your junior home opener."

"Yes!" Terry answers, before Demers has finished his sentence.

The Habs give Terry two tickets to the game. He's young, dumb and broke, so he tries to scalp them outside the Forum and gets caught. He receives a stern lecture, but they still let him play. It's Terry's first and likely only game before he gets sent back. So he fights again, this time against Steve Leach, right in front of the Canadiens' bench. His last punch knocks Leach down but breaks Terry's knuckles. The crowd at the Forum erupts. Demers puts Terry right back on when he gets out of the box. Mark Recchi fires the puck out of the corner, off Terry's skate and in. He's scored a goal at the Forum.

It earns him one more game: Saturday night against Toronto at Maple Leaf Gardens. The Habs go out for beer and pizza after the Bruins game, and Terry tells the vets, "I'm going to fight Tie Domi."

They laugh. "Sure, kid."

There is a pay phone down in the bowels of the Gardens, right where the players go on the ice. Just before warm-up, in full gear, Terry picks it up, dials 0 and calls his parents collect. "Mom and Dad, I'm going to fight Tie Domi tonight," he says.

"No, you are not!" his mom says from Mount Pearl. Terry smiles, hangs up and walks up the steps to take the ice. He notices Habs and Leafs players chatting near centre, something he'd never seen in junior. Domi is there, so he cozies up to him.

"Hey, you want to fight tonight?" Terry says.

"Fight who? Stevenson . . . Odelein . . . Brashear?" Domi replies.

"What would you think about fighting me?"

"I'm not fighting an eighteen-year-old kid from Newfoundland," Tie says, chuckling.

"How do you know me?" Terry says, shocked Domi is aware he exists.

"I do my homework. That's why I'm Tie Domi." He winks and skates away.

Midway through the first, there is a skirmish inside the Leafs' blue line. Terry purposely gives a hard, one-handed shove to Leafs defenceman Mathieu Schneider, just to get Domi's attention. It works. They square off.

Domi knocks Terry down on the first punch but lets him back up. They exchange blows for 30 solid seconds. Terry gets the worst of it but hangs on. In the penalty box, he's elated. "I can't believe I got to do what I told all my buddies I would do!" he thinks to himself. He imagines Gillian Chipman, watching longingly from Mount Pearl.

Domi yells some friendly barbs from the other penalty box. He suggests Terry go to the Brass Rail, a famous Toronto strip joint, after the game. Terry goes and takes his high school buddies, who flew in for the night, with him. There is a table set aside for them. "Mr. Domi arranged it," the manager tells him.

They would fight twice more in the next two years. But scrapping with Domi never helps woo Gillian. She would marry one of Terry's good friends.

SCENE 5

Opens with a montage of Terry dominating with the Red Deer Rebels in the Western Hockey League playoffs in 1996, scoring 18 goals in 16 playoff games, without getting in a single fight. The play-by-play commentator says, "This kid is unreal! He's headed to his second Canadiens camp next fall and has a great shot to make the team." But Terry doesn't make it. He gets sent down to the Habs' farm team in New Brunswick.

A Coach's Office in Fredericton, October 1997

New coach Michel Therrien sits behind his office desk, smoking a cigarette. Terry sits opposite him. It's their first meeting. Therrien does not say a word. The two sit in silence for 10 minutes, staring at each other. Then Therrien says, "Get out." Terry is perplexed. He's always been a popular player with coaches. He doesn't know how to handle it.

A few weeks later, Therrien benches Terry for an entire game. In the last minute, he taps him on the shoulder and says, "Go fight Jeff Ware." Now Terry's angry. He takes it out on Ware, leaving him beaten and bloodied. At the end of the scrap, Terry rips his own helmet off and fires it into the glass. He calls his agent after the game and says, "I'm leaving. I'm never coming back here."

Terry doesn't leave. The Habs own him. He scores 21 goals and gets in 30 fights under Therrien that season, and is named the team's rookie of the year. But he's not the same person. He hates his coach. He hates himself. Depression becomes his most frequent combatant.

Not much changes the next season—43 points, a ton of fights that bring crowds to their feet. And emptiness inside. That summer, Terry calls Montreal general manager Réjean Houle, crying.

"Reggie, why did you guys pick me eighth overall if you weren't going to give me a real chance?"

"I don't know if I would have," Houle replies. (He didn't become GM until after Terry was drafted.) "You aren't a good enough skater."

It hurts, but Terry appreciates the honesty. He respects Houle. Maybe he isn't good enough. He just wishes he'd been given a chance to find out for sure. He loved being a Montreal Canadien. But he knows he's done with them. That summer, he messes up his ankle training. And he's never really the same player. He spends the next three seasons bouncing between five different teams in three minor leagues, on an ankle constantly shot up with cortisone.

"I lose a step that I don't have to lose," Terry says. "And I know my NHL dream is over."

SCENE 6
A Ball Hockey Rink in St. John's, Newfoundland, Summer 2001

Terry isn't done with pro hockey just yet. But his summer fun is ball hockey with his buddies where he's a superstar. He would later win multiple Canadian championships. But this scene opens with a super slo-mo shot of Terry falling. His teeth smash the concrete. "I look like Jim Carrey in *Dumb and Dumber*," he says. The nerves are exposed. He needs serious dental work but decides it can wait a few weeks. He has an invite to the Dallas Stars' camp. He figures the Stars will take care of his teeth. He visits the team doctor as soon as he arrives.

"Doc, can you get me fixed up?"

"Sorry, Terry, you aren't signed with us."

Shit. He hadn't thought of that. Everything was taken care of with the Habs, but Terry is on his own now. He has a decent camp but injures the ankle again. The Stars send him to the Idaho Steelheads in the West Coast Hockey League. But the Steelheads' season doesn't start for a few weeks. Terry is in agony, only able to drink milkshakes and eat soup.

His first day in Boise, he goes straight to trainer Kip Dribnak and tells him the story. "I can't help you," Dribnak says. "You just told me you did it playing ball hockey at home. That's not covered."

"For fuck's sake, Kip. What if I take a puck in the face and lose all my teeth?" Terry says.

"Well, obviously then we'd fix them," Kip replies. The wheels start turning in Terry's head.

"I'm going to do it to myself," he tells his Steelheads teammates. They start wagering on whether Terry is actually crazy enough to knock his own teeth out.

A few days later, the players are hanging out by the pool in the apartment complex they live in. One of the guys' kids has a Nerf hammer. Terry has had a few beers and decides it's time. He tries to chip away at the damaged teeth but fails miserably. They are stronger than he figured. "Get me a sledgehammer," he says to teammate Bobby Stewart. Bobby put his money on Terry, so he's happy to oblige.

Terry holds the hammer in both hands in front of his face and swings it toward his mouth. But he panics at the last second and tries to pull up. Too late. It misses his teeth and smashes his lower lip. The lip rips open, leaving what would become a lifelong scar. Blood is everywhere.

"Fuck it," Terry says. He grabs the sledgehammer again and drives it into his teeth, taking out the entire top row. His face is destroyed. And he has one more problem. How does he convince the team this happened on the ice?

The next morning, he gets to the rink early with Stewart. His hat is pulled low over his face, his mouth covered with his hand. He says hello to Dribnak and the staff without making eye contact, then quickly gets dressed and on the ice before anyone else. He has tucked his teeth inside a Cooperall girdle under his pants. Within seconds, Stewart fires a slap shot just over Terry's head and off the glass. Terry goes down like he's been shot. He jams his knuckle into his mouth, making it bleed, which isn't hard with fresh wounds from the night before. Then he pulls all the teeth out of his girdle and throws them on the ice.

"Kip!" Terry says, showing his empty mouth to the trainer as he skates off.

"Wow, you are one unlucky son of a bitch!" Dribnak says, apparently buying all of it.

Ten thousand dollars' worth of dental work later, Terry has a brand new smile, paid for by the Steelheads.

SCENE 7
GM Centre in Oshawa, Ontario, 2015

Terry is staring in a bathroom mirror again, pumping himself up. Just like that 14-year-old kid before his first scrap. *"You have to do this. You can't back out."*

But this time, he will not be dropping the gloves. He put them away when he retired from pro hockey 12 years ago. Tonight, Terry will do something much scarier and more dangerous than fighting. He will be the opening act for popular Canadian comedian Gerry Dee.

After he retired, Terry wrote a book called *Tales of a First-Round Nothing: My Life as an NHL Footnote*. Gerry Dee reads it, loves it and invites Terry to Toronto to discuss a hockey show he's thinking of creating. Though that never materializes, Gerry asks Terry to open for him at one of his shows.

"But . . . I'm not a comedian," Terry says, dumbfounded.

"Just tell one of your stories," Gerry says. And so here stands Terry. Alone on a stage, in front of thousands. Trying not to throw up. He tells the story of his last shift in the NHL, a wild fight with Cam Russell. The crowd eats it up.

He ends up doing a few more shows with Gerry. The Milbury story, the teeth story, the Domi story—they all make it into the act. But Terry knows stand-up comedy is not his next career. And it's hard to laugh when his life is crumbling around him.

SCENE 8
Union Station, Toronto, 2015, 3:00 a.m.

Terry walks aimlessly through the halls and tunnels of Toronto's transit hub, taking naps here and there where he can. He will never use the word *homeless* to describe this month of his life. He feels it's disrespectful to those who truly live on the streets. But right now, he fits the definition.

He has nowhere to sleep. He showers at GoodLife Fitness, thanks to a card from his gym back in Newfoundland. Or at the rinks, when friends invite him out for pickup hockey. Gerry Dee had given him $500 for each of the comedy shows. He's forever grateful. But now he desperately needs to find real work.

The laughs, on stage and in his book, are a mask. A series of bad investments have left Terry broke. His marriage is ending, though he remains close with his ex, Danielle. They have a beautiful daughter named Penny-Laine. She's Terry's world. And he's trying to help raise Tison, Danielle's son from her previous marriage to B.J. Young. B.J. had been Terry's teammate in junior, and his best friend. He died in a car accident in 2005. Terry married Danielle three years later.

He was supposed to take care of them all. He'd come to Toronto hoping to earn money to send home. He gets a few odd jobs working crew on TV sets, something he had done back in Newfoundland on *Republic of Doyle*. But it's not much. Eventually, he gets off the streets and into a $30-a-night bed in the tiny attic of a house occupied by foreign students who don't speak English. It's the worst time of his life. He heads back to Newfoundland, lost.

Flash-Forward a Few Months Later...
Portugal Cove, Newfoundland

Terry is crying. He stands, holding Penny-Laine's hand, staring out at the ocean from the driveway of his home. It's a simple house, but it has a pool and sits on four beautiful acres, overlooking the Atlantic. He was going to build something special here. Something forever. Now a SOLD sign sits on the lawn. He's come to say goodbye.

He couldn't make the mortgage payments. He bought the house for $300K. At one point, he'd been offered $500K for it. Now he's had to accept $325K. Then the story gets around town that the bank is going to foreclose if Terry doesn't sell. The buyer drops his offer to $275K at the last minute. Terry has no choice but to say yes.

The dreams of that first-round pick who fought Tie Domi in his own barn as an 18-year-old, who had the world by the balls, are all long gone. Life has done what Domi couldn't. Knocked Terry out.

SCENE 9
A Movie Set in Keels, Newfoundland, October 2015

Terry is sitting on the grass, staring out at the Atlantic. A bottle of Jack Daniels beside him, half a joint in his hand. He takes a long, deep breath, relieved that he finally has a job. And hope.

Danielle is thinking about moving to Alberta with Penny-Laine. Terry has to show he can support them so they'll stay. He'd worked overnight shifts at a Lotto outlet for the first month home, making minimum wage, startling co-workers who once wore his jersey.

Then finally a break. He gets a gig as a gofer on the set of *Maudie*, a biopic of Nova Scotia folk artist Maud Lewis, starring Sally Hawkins and Ethan Hawke. On his first day on the set, he leaves his book on Hawke's chair, something he could be fired for.

On this warm October evening, shooting is done for the day, and most of the crew have left. Terry hears someone approaching. Ethan Hawke sits down next to him. "I loved your book," Hawke says.

"You... actually read it?" Terry answers, shocked.

"No wi-fi out here. Good luck for you."

"What do you mean by that?" Terry says.

"Your book, there is depth there. It's poignant. You are a character. I think you should audition for something."

Weeks later, Terry takes Hawke out on the town in St. John's. Things are looking up. He has another job lined up as a set designer on a new Netflix series coming to Newfoundland. Ethan and Terry hit the pubs on George Street and talk more about movies, life and ... shooting your shot. "Fuck it," Terry says. That night, half-cut, he calls Allan Hawco, a Newfoundland writer/actor/producer he knows from *Republic of Doyle*. He asks if he can come in for an audition for a part in that new Netflix show.

Cut to the waiting room for the audition. Terry can feel all the real actors staring at him, thinking, "Why is that washed-up hockey player here?" When he gets in and starts reading to the camera, he's awful. So with nothing to lose, he pulls a false tooth out and starts reading his lines that way. The casting people are suddenly intrigued.

Terry still isn't sure how much of it was his toothless delivery and how much was just some Newfoundland friends doing him a favour—but after one more audition, he gets the part of a British soldier, about to be executed by Jason Momoa in the opening scene of *Frontier*.

SCENE 1 (AGAIN)

And so we return to the moment our movie opened, with Terry covered in fake blood, having nailed his line and his death scene. It changes ... everything.

His buddies who came to watch, the ones who had seen him struggle with life after hockey ended, celebrate with him. One line or not, Terry is an actor now. He's in a union. He is a "fucking somebody" again.

Jason Momoa becomes his friend. He wants to learn to skate. Terry takes him to an old local barn every Sunday. When Momoa's assistant has to go home to California for a few months, Momoa looks at Terry and says, "Want to be my assistant?" They fly to Europe. Momoa gets Terry small parts in a couple of other movies, sets him up with some of the industry's best stuntmen to teach him that trade. Terry is now making enough money to pay off his debts. To take care of his family.

Back in Newfoundland, he gets a visit from Paul Bissonnette. Biz wants to tape an episode of his wildly popular podcast, *Spittin' Chiclets*, with Terry. One of the many stories Terry tells on the pod is the one we've just told, about Ethan Hawke, Momoa and Terry's journey back from the abyss.

Life works like hockey sometimes. A lucky bounce, puck goes in, long slump ends. Suddenly goals come in bunches. Jared Keeso, a massive hockey fan and the creator and star of *Letterkenny*, happens to be listening to Terry on *Spittin' Chiclets*. A couple weeks later, Terry gets a call. "Do you want to be on *Letterkenny*?"

They need two Newfoundlanders to taunt the bench in a hockey scene. After the shoot, Keeso tells Terry he has another idea he would be perfect for. A few months later, Terry is cast in Keeso's new comedy, *Shoresy*. He'll play a first-round NHL draft pick from Mount Pearl. Bit of a stretch. His character's name is Ted Hitchcock. The joke is that if you say it fast, it sounds like "10-inch cock" (1995 Phil Esposito would have liked that one).

Shoresy is a hit. Terry is a star. That step he lost? He's got it back. And then some.

We do this interview at an airport hotel in Toronto. A bantam hockey team in town for a tournament is hanging out in the lobby. They stare and whisper, and then finally come up and ask for autographs and photos. With Terry Ryan, Canadian folk hero.

SCENE 10

Wait, what? The movie should end right there, shouldn't it? The can't-miss-but-did-miss kid finds redemption in his second act. The first-round bust who felt like he'd let his family, his friends, his whole province down becomes a Newfoundland icon, again. His stories, now folklore. Roll the damn credits!

But that's not Terry Ryan. There's always one more twist. One more tale they'll tell on George Street forever. And that's exactly where this scene starts.

St. John's Newfoundland, January 2024

It's the Saturday night of Terry's 47th birthday weekend. He's out with his boys, tying one on. Life is good now.

Friday was daddy–daughter night. He took Penny-Laine to the Newfoundland Growlers game. The Growlers are St. John's East Coast Hockey League team. They are playing Friday, Saturday and Sunday against the Adirondack Thunder. Penny is 13 now. She loves the Growlers. Goes to the games with Dad all the time. They hear of a flu bug running through the team but don't think much of it.

Saturday, Terry starts drinking mid-afternoon. Midnight will officially be his birthday. Shots for everyone! He's at a popular George Street pub called Green Sleeves when his phone rings. It's Zach O'Brien, a Growlers legend and one of Terry's best buddies.

"T-Bone, we're in bad shape. Everybody's sick," O'Brien says. "We need you tomorrow."

Terry laughs and hangs up. Birthday gag. But a few minutes later, one of the Growlers' coaches, Adam Pardy calls. "We're serious. Do you want to play tomorrow?"

Terry still doesn't believe it. He hands the phone to his friends, to get them to confirm it's no joke.

"You are playing for the Growlers tomorrow afternoon," they tell him. "You need to get the fuck home!"

If the game had been three days earlier, the Growlers would have been able to take players from the Newfoundland Senior Hockey League. But after January 10, they aren't eligible. So Ted Hitchcock is real, again.

Terry grabs his phone and wakes up Penny-Laine. "I'm going to play for the Growlers tomorrow!"

He texts Paul Bissonnette to tell him, not knowing Biz is a guest analyst on *Hockey Night in Canada* that night. During the intermission of the late west game, Biz tells the nation that Terry Ryan is making a comeback tomorrow at 47.

Back home, Terry drinks two litres of water to thin the booze in his blood. Then he eats a sandwich and goes to bed, though he's too nervous to really sleep. The game is 12 hours away.

He drives to the rink with Penny-Laine late in the morning. She has her hand on Terry's forearm the whole way. Terry's only fear is embarrassing her. "I was a pro hockey player and you never saw that," he tells her as they drive. "I'm doing this for you. Just like I always tell you, all you can do is try your hardest. If it doesn't go my way, that's the breaks."

"I love you, Dad," she says.

Terry knows most of the Growlers. They are as pumped as he is that's he playing. He signs a one-day contract with the Toronto Maple Leafs, the Growlers' parent club. That makes him smile. *Look at me now, Tie!*

When he stares into the stands during warm-up, it hits him.

"For many of those fans, the last time I played pro, I was a failure to them. I was their hope. And all I did was disappoint them. I stopped telling people I was a hockey player out of shame. Now I go out there and they're going nuts for me. I look up as I walk out and I see Penny-Laine with her soccer friends, and she mouths, 'I can't fucking believe you are playing for the Growlers.' I've never heard her curse before. And I mouth back, 'I can't fucking believe it either.'"

His parents are there. So is Danielle. And all his childhood friends and hockey buddies. His hands are shaking. He can barely hold his stick.

There is a 2003 movie called *Big Fish*, where a dying father tells his son wild stories from his life that the son doesn't believe. Then the father dies, and all of the characters from his stories show up at the funeral.

This is what Terry thinks of as he's skating around the ice. This is the living wake of his hockey career. One last fish story that no one would believe, except they are all here to see it.

In the room, Growlers coach Matt Cooke announces the starting lineup. "Terry, you're going."

"He didn't even have to give me a shift, so that means a lot," Terry says.

He gets a hit in on that first shift, but not much else happens. When he sits back down on the bench, his friend Zach O'Brien turns to him and says, "Well, T-Bone, I can't believe I'm saying it, but you're going to be on my Hockey DB page."

Terry stays glued to the bench for the next two periods. And he's fine with it. He's had his moment. But with the Growlers down 5–1 early in the third, the crowd goes full *Rudy*.

"We want Terry! We want Terry!" The chants echo through the arena. Terry feels bad. He knows Matt Cooke is in a tough spot. But one of the other players says, loud enough for everyone to hear, "Read the room." Cooke already has. He looks down the bench at Terry and nods. "You're up."

Terry plays a regular shift for the next few minutes, even gets a scoring chance. The thought of starting a fight had crossed his mind before the game, but he quickly dismissed it. What if he gets pummelled? What if the Thunder score, and he hurts his team? Fate has handed him this unlikely second-chance Hollywood ending. The last thing he wants is to end up looking like a selfish showboat.

"Fuck that," he says to himself. "This is a great moment. I'm just going to play hockey."

But with six minutes left, Thunder forward Zach Walker runs long-time Growlers defenceman James Melindy, a beloved local firefighter, and a friend of Terry's. Melindy's helmet gets knocked off. Terry is on the ice when it happens, and instincts take over. He confronts Walker. They drop the gloves.

At 47, Terry Ryan has one last dance. They both land a couple of blows before Walker wrestles Terry to the ice. The Growlers lose 6–2. And no one cares. Terry is named Growlers Player of the Game. He skates out for a victory lap. The crowd goes crazy.

After, he finds Penny-Laine. They embrace. "I can't believe it," she keeps saying. Neither says much more. Neither has to. They walk down the hall, arms around each other.

It took a long time. And a lot of pain. But Terry Ryan finally has his happy ending.

Fade to black.

Now you can roll the credits.

SHARKNADO

The Perfect Storm That Led Macklin Celebrini to NHL Stardom

In his grandparents' backyard in Burnaby, British Columbia, a five-year-old boy is smacking Wiffle balls like he's Juan Soto. His uncle Randy is pitching and can't keep his nephew in the yard. One after another, the balls fly over the fence onto the neighbour's property.

"Hey, Uncle Randy," the boy says. "Someday people are going to pay to watch me do this."

The kid's father, looking on from the backyard deck, shakes his head and laughs. How can his son have this much swagger at five? He types the boy's words in his phone, just to remember them.

A year later. Now it's a soccer game. Relentless sideways Vancouver rain has left all the parents standing on the sidelines numb and shivering under their umbrellas. The boy, now six, weaves through defenders and scores a beauty. He immediately pulls his jersey off, sprinting around the field like he just won Canada the World Cup.

Dad, a former pro soccer player, can't even get upset with his son's showboating.

"The joy in his face, I'll never forget," he says. "We're all standing there freezing, and he's running around the field shirtless and oblivious to the rain and cold. Just pure passion." He types that moment in his phone too.

He would remember it 12 years later when he sees that same expression, that same joy, on his son's face in a hockey rink in San Jose. Forty seconds into overtime against Detroit, Macklin Celebrini takes a pass at the blue line, beats a couple of Red Wings, cuts in front and goes shelf for his first NHL game-winning goal. For the record, he does not take off his jersey this time.

"Someday people are going to pay to watch me do this."

Wrong sport, kid, but right idea.

There is no one recipe for creating a hockey phenom. We all know the stories of Wayne Gretzky spending endless hours on Walter's backyard rink. Or Sidney Crosby perfecting his pass and shot by destroying the dryer in his parents' basement. That's the folklore. But it's only part of the equation.

The true greats don't have *the* "it" factor—they have several. The gift of being born with it, the means to develop it and the burning desire to never stop chasing it.

Rarely have those elements combined so perfectly as they have with Macklin Celebrini. His road to becoming a first overall NHL draft pick and a budding superstar in San Jose seems like the perfect storm. Or if you're sick of that overused George Clooney doomed-fisherman-film metaphor and prefer silly Ian Ziering disaster-comedies: a Sharknado.

First comes the gift.

Genetics help. Dad Rick Celebrini won four national soccer titles at the University of British Columbia before playing pro in the Canadian Soccer League. Mom Robyn was captain of the UBC women's soccer team. But the "born with it" part isn't just about natural ability. It's a rare cocktail of talent, confidence and a burning hatred of losing. At *anything*. Rick realizes early that Macklin may possess this rare hat trick.

"When he's three, I would be in my bare feet trying to keep the soccer ball away from him in the backyard. He would grab onto my shorts and make this grunt, this snarl, as he tried to take it from me. He wouldn't stop, no matter how long it took. He had to get that ball."

(Just for comparison: When I was three, I tried to get the ball once from Dad, but I got distracted by a butterfly. When it flew away, I cried until Mom gave me a Pop-Tart.)

It also helps having an equally passionate older brother, Aiden, to compete with, at . . . everything.

"We have battled it out our whole lives," Macklin says. "Hockey, soccer . . . every sport. We were playing mini-sticks in the basement once, and I'm beating Aiden, and he's not happy. It turns from hockey to full MMA in a hurry."

Little Mack doesn't lose at anything, much. But like his big bro, it doesn't go well when he does.

"When I was in atom, we were playing a tournament in Toronto, and we lose in the semis," Macklin says. "We're at the airport afterward getting some food, and I vividly remember sitting with Mom, and I just won't stop crying. There happens to be a member of the Canadian women's team there. She gives me her hockey card, trying to cheer me up. But I want no part of it. I just keep bawling. I'm probably a little exhausted, but I just can't stand the idea that we lost."

This never goes away with the greats. One of Sidney Crosby's agents told me a story once of Sid coming to Sunday dinner at his house as a rookie. Sid loses a game of bingo to the agent's nine-year-old son. His instant reaction is to slam his fist on the board, sending bingo markers flying. He's immediately apologetic, blushing and laughing as he picks the pieces off the floor. But for that second, Sid was pissed he lost.

"The competitiveness . . . they can't turn it off," Rick says. "Every single drill I've ever seen Mack do, from a young age until now, he always has to be first."

This magic combo meal of hunger/talent/confidence that Rick saw in his little Wiffle ball slugger only grows as Macklin starts getting really good at hockey.

At nine, he gets picked to play for the British Columbia team in the Brick Invitational tournament. Most of the kids don't know each other. Before their first practice, the dressing room is silent. Nervous stares all around. So Macklin stands up and says, "All righty, boys, listen up. We have one rule in this dressing room. There's no fucking swearing!" The kids all crack up. The coach tells Rick this story months later, saying it broke the ice and got all of them chatting.

So little Mack has all the qualities you want in a hockey player. But he also has two ultimate intangibles: a father who knows exactly how to develop a star athlete, and a legend to show him what it takes to become one.

A lot of pain, a little fate and Shaq's abs bring Rick Celebrini and Steve Nash together.

The Canadian basketball icon injured his back early in his NBA career. He starts seeing physiotherapist Alex McKechnie at a clinic in Burnaby, BC. But McKechnie gets hired by the Los Angeles Lakers after he fixes Shaquille O'Neal's abdominal issues. Nash needs a new guy. So he calls Alex's partner and protégé, Rick. It leads to a friendship that would change both their lives.

"In all brilliance is simplicity," Nash says. "Rick is brilliant at simplifying the movement of the human body."

The summer Nash re-signs with Phoenix in 2004, he rents a place in Vancouver and works with Rick six days a week. They train twice a day, jump in the ocean in the middle and talk endlessly about movement. How to teach the body the right way to move to prevent injury and maximize performance.

"Just one example: I used to drive left, pull up right," Nash says. "One day Rick asks me, 'Why?' I sprained my ankle in the tenth grade, took no time off, and went from a kid who would dunk off my left foot to finishing off my right foot. He changes that by breaking down the movement patterns. He teaches my body the ability and confidence to go that way again. And for the rest of my career, I feel comfortable pulling up left or right. It changes my entire game."

Rick and Steve work together for the rest of Nash's career and become best friends. Near the end of Nash's Basketball Hall of Fame induction speech, he says, "Rick Celebrini, many of you don't know him, but he has been a big brother, a mentor and a world-class physical therapist who taught me how to move, taught me how to play and taught me how to embody the spirit this game was meant to be played with. He's the godfather to my youngest, Luca, and he means everything to me."

Macklin is born into the middle of this relationship. As a kid, he tags along to the gym sometimes. Sees how hard Nash works every day to get better. "He has a huge influence on me my entire life," Macklin says.

And as Rick perfects his methods of teaching movement with Nash, his own kids—Aiden, Mack, Charlie and RJ—become his students.

"When they were little, we played these silly games up at the soccer field," Rick says. "I'd kick the ball and pretend it's a treasure chest they have to bring back. But pirates are firing at them, so they have to dodge and duck and dive. Just really fun stuff. You have to foster joy and passion first. And as they get older, you can focus more on the movements of the sports they are into."

When Mack starts focusing on hockey, Rick starts focusing on perfecting his stride.

"We do a lot of things at a very young age that other kids don't ever do," Macklin says. "It's a lot of off-ice movements Dad comes up with—lunges, how you load your hips, keeping your knees aligned with your toes, not having your feet rotating inward or outward, keeping them facing forward. Everything is connected, so it helps you shoot harder, skate better. Dad had seen a lot of injuries from guys moving the wrong way, so he figures if we can do this early and get it ingrained, it will prevent so many problems later."

In 2018, Rick becomes the director of sport and performance with the Golden State Warriors. As if growing up watching Nash isn't enough, now Macklin sees the work ethic of Steph Curry and Draymond Green up close.

"These guys spend so much time working on their games," Macklin says. "They don't want to be anywhere else but on the court. That's where they are happiest. And that's how I feel on the ice. If you don't really enjoy working at what you love to do, you'll never put in the time to make it happen."

"The first time I meet Mack, he's eleven," says Green, a four-time NBA champion. "Rick brings him to the facility, and I'm watching him carry around this hockey stick, working on his game. Not because Rick is telling him to, just because he loves it. I can't believe it. We're in a basketball gym. Every kid that comes here, even if they don't play basketball, tries to grab a ball and shoot or mess around with it. Mack just keeps moving from one area to another with his stick, working on different skills. You know I like to talk, so I say to him, 'I hear you are going to be the first draft pick someday.' And he says, 'Yes, I'm going to be the number one draft pick.' But he doesn't say it like some cocky kid. He says it with the quiet confidence of someone who is ready to put the work in to make it happen. It's such a rare trait at that age. Sometimes you just know when someone's got it. Whatever *it* is. I know right there and then: Mack's got it."

The Warriors are on a road trip to Chicago while Macklin is playing junior with the Chicago Steel. Green asks Rick if he can make the 45-minute drive with him to see Mack play. "All my teammates freak out when they find out Draymond is coming," Mack says. "They get really nervous and we don't play very well. But it means a lot how much interest he's taken in my career."

"I grew up in Detroit a Red Wings fan," Green says. "The Yzerman years. So I always followed hockey. But with my basketball career, I lost track of it. Macklin has pulled me back in. I love watching him."

We'll never know for sure how much all this helped Mack. The way Rick shaped his movements, growing up watching and inhaling the habits of legends like Nash, Green and Curry. Maybe he's so talented he would have made the NHL if he were a plumber's kid.

"You're right, we'll never know, but I feel like it gave me a huge advantage," Macklin says.

"Having Rick as a father is a cheat code," Green says. "But when people say 'perfect storm,' I don't see that. What I see is a family that was taken apart from each other so that a dad could put them in a better position by taking this job with the Warriors. It could have torn the family apart for the years that Robyn and the kids stayed in Vancouver. But instead, I watched them grow closer. Watched Robyn cater to each child: Aiden's got a thing, Macklin's got a thing, Charlie's got a thing, RJ's got a thing. Watched how they all navigated the distance apart. I see the work ethic Rick and Robyn instilled in their kids. That's the part that's special to me."

"Robyn is the unsung hero of our story," Rick says. "Taking care of all four kids for the years I'm in California, getting them to all their games and practices. She is the glue that kept us together. And allowed all of our kids, not just Macklin, to chase their dreams."

And the chase is on. Aiden, 20, plays hockey at Boston University. Charlie, 15, is the top-ranked tennis player for her age in Canada. RJ, at 12, looks as good on the ice as Mack did at his age.

"These kids have an amazing mom and dad in Robyn and Rick," Nash says. "Those are great ingredients for any athlete. And when I watch Mack, he has this incredible explosiveness you can't teach. But the most important thing is that he wants it so bad. That's the true gift. When you give a brilliant guy like Rick an athlete with explosiveness and an incredible desire, the result is going to be off the charts. That's what we're seeing with Macky."

Nash takes an overnight flight from Europe just to see Macklin get picked first overall in the 2024 NHL Draft in Vegas. That's the last little piece of this perfect puzzle. He becomes a San Jose Shark, a half hour from where Rick works. Mack drives to see Dad regularly for treatments, training and . . . just to hang out.

He still does all the movements Rick taught him. He goes through a careful program before every game. In the summer of 2024, he trained with the Hughes brothers. Canucks star defenceman Quinn Hughes is fascinated by what he sees and asks to learn Mack's entire routine.

Macklin Celebrini is still 18 as I write this. Halfway through a brilliant rookie season. Still learning. Still having "Welcome to the NHL" moments.

"We were playing the Senators early in the season and I'm talking to Brady Tkachuk during a TV time out," Macklin says. "I'm thinking, 'This is pretty cool.' Then the next shift he just blows me up with a hit. And I'm going, 'Oh my God. This is no joke.'"

There is a bucketful of factors that ultimately decide if a player is going to be good, great or historic. Some of those Macklin controls. Some he doesn't. All we know for now is there has rarely been a teenager better built for this stage.

People are going to pay to watch him do this. For a long time.

TOUCHING RANDY

Brad May and the Ducks Annoy Their Coach and Win a Cup

Brad May jumps over the boards and races toward the puck, adrenaline pumping through his body. At 35, he feels like a rookie again.

It's March 1, 2007. Anaheim at Los Angeles. May's first-ever shift with the Ducks.

It has been a frustrating season for the veteran forward. He had surgery for a dislocated shoulder and didn't play a single game with the Colorado Avalanche. But now he's just been traded to Anaheim, his fifth NHL team, at the deadline. The Ducks are stacked and poised for a run at their first Stanley Cup. And in his 17th season, May knows this could be his last shot at a ring. So he's eager to make a great first impression. To show coach Randy Carlyle and his teammates that he can add toughness, character and a spark to their lineup. And it starts right now. With this first shift. He's flying up the ice, ready to prove th— "ARRRGH! OH CRAP, I PULLED MY GROIN!"

May grimaces and skates gingerly back to the bench. He tries the leg a couple more times but can barely make a stride.

"I can't believe it," he says. "My Ducks debut, and it's over in thirty seconds. I feel embarrassed, ashamed. These guys traded for me, thought I could help them, and I'm done on my first shift."

It's horrible timing. But when Carlyle calls May into his office the next morning, he's hopeful the coach will reassure him that everything will be fi— "THIS IS BULLSHIT, MAY!"

Carlyle is scowling across his desk at his wounded new player. "What are you going to do for the Anaheim Ducks?" he asks.

"Well, Coach, I'm going to work really hard and—"

"Bullshit, May. My dad was from Sudbury and he worked his whole life in the mines. Working hard is not special. It's expected."

"Okay, Coach, well I will also—"

"Burkie [Anaheim general manager Brian Burke] thinks you are going to be okay, but I just don't see it. Get out of here."

May limps out of the coach's office, head down and spinning. "I'm like, 'Oh shit. I just failed the first test interview with the coach,'" May says. "Randy sets the tone right away that this is his show, and I'd better be on my toes and earn my place here."

But it's tough to earn your place with an ice pack on your groin. So all May can do for now is get to know his teammates and try to fit in.

That's never been a problem before. May has been beloved on every team he's played for. In writing this book, I had half a dozen guys say, "You have to talk to Brad May. He's the best ever." Teammates always adore their tough guys. And May is some tough, racking up more than two thousand penalty minutes in his career. But he's more than a scrapper. He's a glue guy, albeit a mischievous one.

When May was with the Buffalo Sabres, the veterans all lived in the same neighbourhood: Williamsville, New York. Every Christmas, they have a contest to see who can decorate their homes the best. Guys spend thousands of dollars trying to outdo each other. The young single players are all invited over on Christmas Eve to judge.

One year, Brad, his wife and his mother-in-law (oddest crime crew ever) sneak over to teammate Dave Hannan's house very late on Christmas Eve and steal all Hannan's lights and outdoor decorations, including a large inflatable Santa from the front lawn.

"Dave comes into the room for the next practice, and he's all stern faced," May says. "He goes, 'I don't know about you guys, but my kids had a terrible Christmas. Someone stole all my decorations. My kids were all crying.' I know he's screwing around because he knows it's one of us and he's trying to get a reaction. But then we go out for practice, and I've had a buddy string up all Dave's Christmas lights around one end of the rink. I put his inflatable Santa in the penalty box, with lights flashing. I got him so good."

But now May's the new guy in Anaheim. And it's his turn to get got . . . good.

A few days after May's painful debut, the Ducks hold a team golf outing at Teemu Selanne's club. May isn't sure what he's supposed to do. "I feel like I can play golf, but I'm supposed to be injured and I don't know if I should be out there swinging a driver in front of Randy. Not after that first meeting."

He plays anyway. In fact, once the round is over, a few of the guys decide to go back out and play a few more holes. Brad tags along. They decide to do an eight-man scramble, with two teams of four. But they need stakes. A typical $10 or $20 match isn't really enough juice for a bunch of ultra-competitive hockey players.

That's when Ducks forward George Parros chimes in.

"Let's play Touch Randy."

Excuse me?

"What the hell is Touch Randy?'" May says.

Well, it seems coach Carlyle is not the most cuddly guy out there, especially around the team. It's just not the way he interacts with his players.

"Look, I know you just got into it with Randy and are on his shit list," Parros tells May. "It would be hilarious and so awkward if, *when* your team loses, you have to make some sort of physical contact with him in front of the rest of the boys. Debt to be paid before our road trip."

May's team loses the golf match. Of course.

"I'm laughing, because the whole thing is hilarious, but I have no idea how I'm going to touch a guy who just chewed me out yesterday," May says. "So I'm nervous the entire next day knowing I have to find a way."

The other three guys in May's losing foursome find a way to tap Carlyle on the arm or shoulder. Already the coach looks equal parts annoyed and perplexed. But May just can't find the right moment. He's on eggshells already, rattled by his first-shift injury and Carlyle carving him after.

The only rule of Touch Randy, besides the touching Randy part, is that the touch has to be witnessed. So by the time May boards the plane, all eyes are on him. Time is running out. May walks by the coach, already in his seat at the front of the plane. Last chance before takeoff. May puts his hand firmly on Carlyle's shoulder and says, "Hey, Coach."

"I keep walking and I'm scared to even look back," May says. "I just sit down and hope he doesn't chew me out again."

He doesn't. And Touch Randy instantly becomes the go-to game for the Ducks for the rest of the season and playoffs.

"Every shooting game in practice, every card game on the bus, the loser would always have to touch Randy," May says. "Guys would go up and tap him on the ass with their stick during practice. And you could see him stare at them like, 'Get out of my personal space!' It would drive him nuts. But to this day, I don't think he knows. It's the funniest thing any team I've ever been on has ever done. And it brought the boys even closer together. Definitely made me feel part of the group."

May's groin heals, and he works his way out of Carlyle's doghouse. He becomes a key part of a tough and terrific bottom-six forward group that helps push the Ducks deep into the playoffs.

They keep winning and winning. And touching and touching. Until one night when the subtle Randy touches turn into full-fledged hugs. Because the Ducks have just won the Stanley Cup.

"Just an unreal moment," May says. "Randy was a hard-ass, but I think with that group of guys who were that good, he had to be that way to keep everyone in line. Especially down in Southern California. With the lifestyle there, it's easier to drift and not be as intense and competitive as you need to be. Nothing was ever good enough for Randy. That's how he kept us sharp. We all respected that. It helped us win a championship."

"Me, Shawn Thornton and Travis Moen would fill the Cup with beer, chug a little and then dump it over someone's head," Parros says. "And Randy is the first person we do it to. That's our favourite Touching Randy ever. We had fun with Randy playing that game, but we loved him."

Touching story. (Sorry, had to.)

THE MASKED MARVEL

Sarah Nurse Becomes a Superstar in COVID Chaos

Life-changing moments can happen at the strangest times.

And February 27, 2022, isn't just strange for Sarah Nurse, it's *Twilight Zone* weird.

She's on the ice in Beijing, China, getting ready to play a huge hockey game. In an empty rink. In the middle of a global pandemic. A game that would come to symbolize the bizarre COVID Olympics. A game that would alter the trajectory of Sarah's career.

It's warm-up. Sarah is up against the boards, ready to take her turn in a routine line-rush drill. But a teammate has just been pulled because of a problematic COVID test. Suddenly two superstar forwards are missing a winger. Her coach grabs her by the jersey and gives her a little push. "Sarah, go!"

And man, would Sarah go.

The 2022 Games are peak COVID, and thus the opposite of everything the Olympics are supposed to be. No fans. No Athletes' Village. Constant testing. It's kinda like prison, but with medals.

"It's terrifying," Sarah says. "When we get to Beijing, we keep hearing stories of athletes just disappearing and being kept isolated in ten-by-ten rooms for days. Even if you don't have COVID, but just have traces in your system, you could be taken away."

The Canadian women's hockey team is split into groups of four. They stay in apartments together. The only times they leave are to go to testing, to the rink or to eat—alone in private cubicles. The food is so bad, they survive mostly on Corn Flakes, protein shakes and white rice. They barely see any other athletes.

"It's really bizarre," Sarah says. "We're allowed to go outside, but it's winter, so we basically stay in our apartment the entire time. I play a lot of *NHL 22* those two weeks. It's the first year women are in the game, so we play as ourselves and try to manifest gold that way."

In the video game, and in real life, Canada looks great. They cruise through their first two games against Switzerland and Finland. Sarah plays on a line with Blayre Turnbull and Rebecca Johnston, and she produces early—two assists against the Swiss, a hat trick versus the Finns. Not bad for someone who came into the tournament having barely played in three months.

Back in October, Sarah's skate caught a rut in the ice. She felt a pop in her knee. Torn MCL. Fortunately, she returns to the team just in time for the Games. "I really have no expectations at all for this Olympics," Sarah says. "I'm just thrilled to be playing hockey again."

Sarah has always been a steady player for Canada, but never a star. She played on the fourth line in her first Olympics in 2018, winning silver. "I've been that fourth-line player who gets very limited minutes. I've been that second-line centre who is a complementary player. But I'd never been one of *the* guys on our team."

Canada's next opponent is Russia . . . sorry . . . the Olympic Athletes of Russia (renamed because of drug sanctions). Rumours are swirling that the Russians arrived in China with COVID-positive players and have refused to be tested, or have had inconclusive tests. There's not a lot of communication at an Olympics where you barely see anyone, so no one is sure what the truth is.

But during warm-up, it's a Canadian player who gets pulled off the ice. There are issues with first-liner Emily Clark's morning COVID test. (It would turn out to be an error in testing.) So as Canada starts its three-on-two rushes, Marie-Philip Poulin and Brianne Jenner are without a winger. That's when coach Troy Ryan calls Sarah's name.

"I'm thinking, 'Oh God.' I've watched these players be superstars for Canada, and now I'm with them. I'm freaking out." And the game hasn't even started yet. It won't, for 90 minutes.

The Canadian team doctor has heard about the Russians' possible COVID exposure and refuses to let Team Canada take the ice. There is a long delay and heavy negotiations before it's decided that both teams will wear N95 masks during the game. The images of Canadian and Russian players battling on the ice with masks under their cages quickly go viral.

"It's so weird," Sarah says. "It's really hard to breathe, and we get so hot the masks are sticking to our faces. It almost feels like we are waterboarding ourselves."

Just two minutes into the game, on her second shift ever with the top line, Nurse intercepts a pass and goes shelf to give Canada the lead. It's a shame no one sees see the grin under the mask.

"I can't believe this is happening," she says. "I still can't believe I'm playing with Marie-Philip Poulin, let alone scoring. At the Olympics. Wearing an N95 mask." Sarah adds an assist later as Canada rolls 6–1.

Clark is back in the lineup for Canada's next game, a showdown with archrival Team USA. So Nurse figures it's one-and-done on the top line. She's game-planning with her regular linemate Turnbull in the dressing room when they are handed the lineup sheet. Sarah is staying with Poulin and Jenner.

"I feel like I'm playing well, and the puck just seems to be following me around, but this validates it for me. I'm like, 'Okay, I'm not delusional!'"

Midway through the second period, with the Americans leading 2–1, Nurse breaks into the US zone on her weak side, puts her shoulder down and drives into the defender. She does a spinarama move and feeds Jenner, who buries the tying goal. "I had seen Brianne make that play so many times. I had always looked up to her, so for me to make that pass to her in the biggest game of the Olympics, the biggest stage in our sport, I kind of feel like this is the moment I arrived."

Canada wins 4–2 and clinches the top seed for the playoff round. The new line is clicking. And Sarah is racking up points. She gets four assists in a quarter-final romp over Sweden. Four more in the semis against Switzerland. All of a sudden, she is one point shy of tying Hayley Wickenheiser's all-time record of 17 points in one Olympics. She has no idea until Turnbull mentions it before the gold medal game.

"Do you realize you are one point from Wick's record?"

"Wick's record . . . for what?" Sarah responds.

It's all happened so fast. And now the record, and more importantly, the gold medal, will come down to a pressure-packed rematch with the Americans. Yet Nurse feels strangely calm.

"There are no nerves at all," she says. "I just feel so confident and comfortable with myself and my linemates. And I can feel the confidence our teammates have in us. It's like I have waited for this opportunity my entire life. Now that it's finally come, I'm ready."

Canada comes out flying. Natalie Spooner scores in the opening minutes. But a video review shows Sarah had been offside, 30-odd seconds before the goal is scored. "I don't even know what happened," Sarah says. "I'm on the bench asking, 'Why was the goal called back?' And my teammates are saying, 'You were offside." And I'm like, 'Shoot. Okay, I'll get it back for you, promise.'"

Moments later, Sarah ends up in front of the net off a botched faceoff play, and redirects a shot from Claire Thompson into the US net. A woman of her word. Later, she assists on Poulin's second goal of the game.

History. Her five goals and 13 assists are the most points by any woman, ever, in an Olympic Games. But it's an afterthought for now. There is gold to be won.

Canada is in control throughout, but the Americans score with 13 seconds left to cut the lead to 3–2. Nurse's line goes out for those final 13 seconds. "We huddle before the faceoff, and Pou and Jenner are so serious, so stoic. That's how they approach the game, and it works great for them. But that's not me. I look at them and say, 'Guys, in thirteen seconds, we are going to have a gold medal!' They just stare at me with the most serious faces and skate away. I'm like, 'Oops, wrong crowd!'"

Maybe you aren't supposed to say it out loud, but Sarah is prophetic. They win the faceoff cleanly, dump it into the American end, and it's over. After the crushing disappointment of losing to the US in the 2018 Olympics, Sarah is a gold medallist. The first Black woman to win gold in hockey. In a tournament unlike any we've ever seen.

When she gets back to Canada, everything has changed.

"I take my dad to a Leafs game," Sarah says. "We didn't have the money to go to games when I was growing up, so it's something I love to do with him. We board the train from Hamilton to Union Station, and I start hearing people whispering and staring at me. Suddenly everyone is coming into our car from the other train cars to talk to me about the Olympics and take photos with me. I used to get recognized a bit, but never anything like this. They are all congratulating me. It's overwhelming. And it's not about me. It's just amazing that this has happened for women's hockey."

A few weeks later, she's on vacation in Mexico with her Canadian teammates when she gets a call from her agent. Remember that video game Sarah spent countless hours playing in Beijing, trapped in her apartment? EA Sports wants her to be on the cover of the 2023 edition, the first woman given that honour.

Sarah, like the rest of us, hopes there is never another Olympics like the 2022 COVID Games in Beijing. The video of the Canadians and Russians playing in those N95 masks will forever be a reminder of how crazy a time it was. And yet that day, and the mistake with her teammate's test sample, ends up changing Sarah's life. She is now one of the faces of women's hockey—with Team Canada and with the Professional Women's Hockey League, where she stars with Vancouver.

And that smile just keeps getting wider. No longer hidden behind a mask.

O-DOG AND THE PEACH PIT AFTER DARK

Jeff O'Neill Stays Out Too Late in LA

Jeff O'Neill wakes up and isn't sure where he is. He blinks, trying to shake the morning brain fog. Wait... Los Angeles! Right.

His Hartford Whalers are here to play the Kings. Oh yeah. He went out last night. Like, *out* out. Hit half the bars in town. When you play in the Eastern Conference, you only get to LA once a year. And when you get in two nights before the game, the light is rarely greener.

"Where are we?" the guy they call O-Dog (O for short) says to the woman smiling at him from across the room. It's all coming back now. A new friend from the night before. "A condo in Studio City," she replies.

"What time is it?" O asks, as the haze slowly clears. "I have to be on the bus for practice at ten."

The smile vanishes from the woman's face. "You have no chance," she says.

Freeze this frame for a moment. To truly understand the level of fear about to rush through O's body, you need to know where he has just been. Springfield. That's not the name of one of the clubs from the night before. Springfield, Massachusetts. The minors.

"It's the only time in my entire career I get sent down," O says. "For me, it's doomsday. I've seen guys go down there and never come back up. If I don't get my shit together, my NHL dream might be done."

He plays one game for the AHL's Springfield Falcons and then gets lucky. Whalers forward Robert Kron injures his ankle. O gets called right back up to Hartford. "Every time I see Robert to this day, I give him a huge hug because he saved me. And the first thing the team is doing when I get back is flying to LA."

You would think the trip to Springfield would have been a wake-up call for the 1994 fifth overall draft pick in just his second NHL season. A slap-in-the-face reminder to be on his best behaviour if he wants to have a long career. But back then, you couldn't take the dog out of O-Dog.

"I don't always make the smartest decisions in those days," he says. "The team is all going out in LA, and for some reason I still can't explain, I decide it's a good idea to go back to acting like a big wheel and stay out all night. Like a complete idiot."

Now press play again. Back to the condo in Studio City. Just in time to see the blood drain from O's face.

"No, no, you don't understand," he tells the woman, who is suddenly the most important person in his life. "You have to get me to the Hilton by LAX by ten or my career is done."

"I'll drive you," she says. "But we aren't going to make it."

Two minutes later, they jump in her old Camaro and tear up side streets to the freeway. It's a standstill. The legend of LA morning traffic is real. "I start swearing because I know I'm done," O says. "My first practice back up from the minors and I'm going to miss the bus. The Whalers are going to send me home. It's game over in my second season."

But the new friend is a good friend, because she isn't giving up. "I have one detour I can try, but it's a shot in the dark," she says. The Camaro exits the highway and starts darting through

Hollywood side streets. She's Sandra Bullock in *Speed*, just without the bus or the bomb. (Although O believes missing his bus would blow up his career.) Twenty minutes now until the bus leaves. Fifteen. Ten. Five . . .

Somehow, she pulls it off. At 9:58, they are just a block away from the hotel. O is soaked in sweat, but realizes he's actually going to make it. "Please don't pull up right in front of the bus," he pleads, knowing coach Paul Maurice always stands outside until all the players are on. Too late.

"She pulls this *Dukes of Hazzard* tire squeal right up beside the bus," he says. "I get out, and Paul and [assistant coach] Randy Ladouceur are staring at me. I just put my head down and climb on like nothing happened."

Career saved, thanks to Danica Patrick and her Camaro. O takes his seat and exhales.

"Good night, O?" a teammate asks from a few rows back. Laughter fills the bus. O just shakes his head, too traumatized to answer. The coaches don't ask any questions. There is no curfew on a night off. You're good, as long as you are on that bus at 10.

But there is most definitely a curfew the night before games. One that O always adheres to. Or . . . almost . . . always.

"I never ever go out the night before a game," he says. "Except once. When LA gets me again."

It's early February 2002. The Hartford Whalers are now the Carolina Hurricanes and are about to head out on their California road trip. O gets a call from his friend and former teammate Nelson Emerson, who is now with the LA Kings. A bunch of Kings players have been invited to a party at the Playboy Mansion. Emerson knows O is coming to town and asks if he wants to tag along.

"We have a game the next day in Anaheim, so I shouldn't," O says. "But how many times do you get invited to the Playboy Mansion? So I say, 'Screw it, I'm going.' The Kings are going straight there after their game against Washington, so I buy a ticket to the game and sit in the Staples Centre and watch. An NHL player, alone in the stands, watching an NHL game. I'm such a loser. But I figure it's the only way I won't be late."

As soon as the buzzer goes, he heads downstairs to meet the handful of Kings going to the party. They jump in a car and head to UCLA. Apparently, no one gets to drive right up to the Playboy Mansion. You have to take a shuttle bus from the university campus.

"Not going to lie, the girls on this shuttle bus are absolutely beautiful," O says. "And they aren't even the Playboy Bunnies. When we get there, it's pretty much exactly what you'd imagine it would be. There are LA Lakers out on the dance floor, Playboy Bunnies everywhere, Hef [Hugh Hefner] holding court."

There is also one Hollywood actor who keeps staring at O, to the point of making him uncomfortable. Many years later, it would make more sense. "I'm the only guy to ever go to the Playboy Mansion and the only person that hits on him is Kevin Spacey."

Around midnight, the guilt of being out late before a game starts to get to O, and he decides to bail early. "It's really cool that I got to go, and it was a fun night, but I had to get the hell of out there," he says. But here's the thing. The Playboy Mansion isn't just hard to get into—it's also hard to get out of. The shuttle they took to get there is nowhere to be found. O finds a bench outside the front door and sits down, hoping he can get a taxi. There's one other guy on the bench. It's actor Joe Tata, better known as Nat from the original *Beverly Hills 90210*.

"I sit there forever, just me and Nat from the Peach Pit," O says. If this were an actual *90210* episode, Nat would slide O a milkshake and offer him some gentle advice about how it's probably best not to miss curfew to hang out with Playboy Bunnies. Except this is the Peach Pit After Dark. (Yeah, I watched every episode. Don't judge me.) And Nat is hanging out with the Bunnies too.

"Finally I get a cab and leave Nat alone on his Playboy Mansion bench. I don't get back to the hotel until two thirty or three. Curfew is eleven. I am like Tom Cruise in *Mission: Impossible* going through that hotel. I'm climbing along walls and ducking into staircases to make sure Paul Maurice didn't stay up to check on me."

That night against the Ducks, O plays guilty. And great. "I had been practising this one-handed Eric Lindros move where you fend off guys with one arm and kind of scoop the puck with the other. I decide this is the night to try it in a game for the first time. And I score probably the best goal of my NHL career."

So in summary, O misses curfew by four hours, scores a beauty and the Canes win 4–1. There's a lesson in there, kids.

No, delete that. This is not a good lesson.

"I look back on it as a forty-eight-year old man and think how stupid I was," O says. "Going out all night that first time after just getting saved from the minors, then breaking curfew just to check out the Playboy Mansion. So dumb. Fun. But dumb."

"Next week on 90210, Dylan and Brenda break up, and Brandon worries after Nat said he was going to a party and doesn't show up for work the next day at the Peach Pit . . ."

THE PRANKSTER

Todd Simpson Torments His Teammates

The Phoenix Coyotes are standing around the ice, bewildered. Practice has been stopped. Collective confusion is written, in all caps, on their faces.

There is a strange purple substance all over them. Their hands are covered in it. It's bleeding down their arms, staining their gloves and jerseys. It's like Barney the Dinosaur just blew up all over them.

"Holy shit," Todd Simpson says, to no one but himself. "Maybe I went too far."

FIRST RULE OF PRANK CLUB: TO BECOME AN ELITE PRANKSTER, YOU MUST FIRST BE A PRANKEE.

As a rookie with the Calgary Flames in 1995–96, Simpson returns to the dressing room after practice to find his boots nailed to the bench (a hockey classic). Years later in Chicago, Matthew Barnaby steals Simpson's car and keeps it for a week. He sends Simpson clues cut out from newspapers and magazines, like serial killers send cops in bad movies.

And in 2000, Simpson rejoins his Florida Panthers in Pittsburgh after an injury. He stays out on the ice late after the game-day skate, getting back in playing shape. As he gets dressed after, he realizes someone has cut out the belly button and two nipples of his shirt.

"I walk into the team meal with my nipples and belly button showing though these three holes," Simpson says. "Everyone is laughing, including me. I'm trying to figure out who did it. My number one suspect is Mike Sillinger."

SECOND RULE OF PRANK CLUB: GET EVEN.

Simpson spends the rest of the day plotting his revenge. Since he isn't playing that night, he waits for the team to go out for warm-up and goes straight to Sillinger's locker. Like most veteran NHL players, Sillinger has lost a few chiclets. He wears a bridge with four false teeth when he isn't playing. Simpson steals the bridge from Sillinger's stall, drops it into a pre-addressed FedEx envelope and walks outside the arena. The FedEx driver he arranged in advance is waiting to pick up the package.

"I have the teeth in my hand for about a minute total, then walk right back inside to the press box to watch the game," Simpson says. It's Jason Bourne–level prank planning.

After the game, Sillinger is getting dressed and realizes he's . . . toothless. "Who stole my teeth?" He bellows across the room. Puzzled shrugs are the only response. "C'mon guys, give 'em back." Still nothing. "Fine, you better look after them. They're worth two thousand dollars."

The Panthers are on their way to Ottawa, and Sillinger spends the bus ride to the airport going up and down the rows, interrogating suspects. "I wanted to have a steak tonight boys. Maybe some corn on the cob. I need my chompers."

He makes zero progress. By the time they get to the hotel in Ottawa, he's given up. "All right, boys, whoever has them, just make sure you give them a good brushing before bed. I like my teeth clean!"

The next morning, Simpson gets confirmation from FedEx

that the package has arrived at its destination. Mike's wife, Karla Sillinger, has signed for it at their home in Florida. "So I know she has them," Simpson says. "And I know she would have called him right away and said, 'Why did your teeth just get delivered to me?' But Silly doesn't know that I know."

On the bus ride to the rink in Ottawa, Sillinger sits down next to Simpson and makes a point of telling him his wife is away with the kids.

"So I know he thinks it's me and he's bullshitting me," Simpson says. "He wants me to think they never got there. We are just starting a long road trip, and he wants me to think my plan went wrong to make me panic. I figure he's going to get Karla to ship them back, and then he's going to plant them on me, or get some other form of revenge. But I don't let on that I know anything. This goes on for two more days. Finally, he gives up and admits she has them. We both burst out laughing. Silly is a great guy. He appreciates the gag."

Simpson pulls countless small pranks during his decade in the NHL. But one season in Phoenix, he decides to take it next level. You know in movies (and real life) how bank robbers pull off the heist and then get foiled when dye packs explode all over their money? Well, police also use a powdered substance that does the same thing, turning into a bright purple ooze when it comes in contact with sweat or moisture. During his time in Florida, mischievous teammate (and accessory before the fact) Ray Whitney tells Simpson you can buy this powder at a nearby police equipment store.

Backstory: Whitney's dad, Floyd, a police officer, first used the powder on Travis Green when Ray and Travis were playing junior in Spokane, Washington. Revenge for a "leaner" that Travis had placed against his hotel door. (A bucket of water that soaks your feet and your carpet when you open the door.) Floyd placed a little powder in Travis's laundry bag, which left him with a purple wardrobe Prince would envy. Ray carries on the proud family tradition by putting the powder in a bunch of teammates' white socks years later. But telling Simpson about it is like giving the Joker a nuclear weapon.

Simpson starts planning his prank opus on the Panthers. But he gets traded to Phoenix before he has a chance to pull it off. "You don't want to start pulling pranks as soon as you get traded to a team," he says. "So I hold on to it for a year, waiting for the right time."

There are warning labels on the powder, so Simpson decides to start small. One day, he arrives early before practice and puts a tiny bit of the powder in Shane Doan's jockstrap. A sweaty jock is pretty much guaranteed to activate the substance. Surely it won't be enough to cause any permanent purpling of Doan's . . . errr . . . little Doaners.

Simpson keeps a close eye on Doan during practice. If something is happening down below, it's buried by his gear. He lingers after, trying to get a peak at Doan when he comes out of the shower. "Like a real creeper," Simpson says. But Doan takes forever showering, and Simpson starts to feel conspicuous. So he leaves.

"I sneak a peek at him naked the next day, and everything is perfect down there," Simpson says, still sounding creepy. He's disappointed there is no prank payoff. Maybe he was too cautious. Time to go all in.

He shows up early again and this time shakes a healthy portion of powder into the left glove of all the Coyotes players, including his own. The only gloves he leaves alone are Doan's and the two goalies'. So if it works, they'll all suspect one of them, likely Doan. (Doan is beloved by Simpson and everyone else on the Coyotes. You always prank the ones you love.)

One Coyote, Landon Wilson, goes out on the ice early, and within minutes he's back in the dressing room. "What the hell is going on?" Wilson says. "I have purple shit everywhere!" It's all over his arm and sweater. The team is perplexed, but they shrug it off and head out on the ice anyway. After a few minutes of warm-up, coach Bob Francis blows his whistle and calls them together.

Claude Lemieux is late on the ice, because he's already noticed something is amiss. When Francis starts yelling at him for being late, Lemieux takes off his glove and shows Francis his hand and arm, covered in purple. The rest of the players start taking off their own gloves. Some are rubbing their faces, taking off their helmets. Purple is now spreading everywhere. It's in their hair, running down their necks and pants. This is the moment Simpson realizes he may have over-pranked.

"I'm like, 'Oh crap.' This is way worse than I thought."

But Francis has a practice to run. He could care less if everyone on his team looks like they've gone to war with an army of eggplants. The Coyotes have a full skate.

"It's absolute chaos out there," says Mike Johnson, a Coyotes forward at the time. "The best part is Bob Francis is getting so angry at all of us for getting so distracted by this purple everywhere. Every time we stop between drills, guys are taking their gloves and helmets off. Claude Lemieux takes his skates off at one point. Coach is snapping."

They manage to get through practice and head back to the room, where the purple carnage can be fully measured. "It's just a disaster," Simpson says. "All over the jerseys, all over everyone's gear. Except for the goalies and Doaner. So I start blaming him. And everyone else chimes in too. He knows he's been set up."

The Coyotes' training staff need to bring in professional cleaners to try to get the purple out of the equipment. Remember, the purpose of this powder is so the bad guys can't clean it off the money they've stolen. It doesn't come out easily.

No one is angrier than Lemieux. He suspects Simpson from the outset. "This is going to cost you so much, Simmer," he says.

"I have an expensive carpet at home. I have five-thousand-dollar sheets on my bed. And if it gets in my Mercedes, you owe me two hundred and forty-five thousand."

Simpson admits nothing. He does feel awful for the trainers, who work endlessly trying to end the purple plague. Quietly, he cuts them a cheque and swears them to secrecy.

Months later, there are still remnants of Simpson's purple rain. A kid gets called up from the minors, and the trainers give him a pair of gloves that hadn't been used in a while. When he comes off the ice, it's another magenta mess.

For the rest of Simpson's career, former teammates kept asking him before faceoffs, "Simmer, the purple prank . . . was that you?" He just smiles. He would come clean to Doan eventually. Then Doan comes clean . . . on how he came clean. "He tells me his junk was totally purple that day in the shower!" Simpson says. "He stayed at the rink until five o'clock that night using rubbing alcohol to get it off. He didn't want to give whoever did it the satisfaction of knowing."

Simpson's time in Arizona ends on October 3, 2003. He's in the dressing room before a skate when he's told he's been claimed off waivers by Anaheim. He packs his stuff and says his goodbyes, and the Coyotes head out onto the ice for practice.

It's an emotional day. Simpson is one of those teammates everyone loves (except Claude Lemieux on certain days). When the Coyotes return to the room after the skate, they find one final parting gift from their now ex-teammate. Simpson has taken everyone's keys off their key chains, thrown them together in one bag and placed them on a shelf underneath the chalkboard. There is a goodbye message on the board:

Thanks for everything, boys. Enjoy the drive home. Simmer.

"This guy has just had his life turned upside down, he has to figure out how to move his family to Anaheim and start over there, but he still takes the time to go into every guy's pocket and remove their keys," says Tyson Nash, a Coyote at the time. "Back then, every key looks identical. It's not the fobs and technology we have today. We're trying to figure out house keys and mail keys. Every guy is out in the parking lot trying different keys on our cars. I couldn't get in my house. We were still swapping keys for weeks after!"

You know that meme of the guy walking coolly away from the action-movie explosion? That's Todd Simpson, heading off to Anaheim, to wreak havoc on a new group of unsuspecting teammates.

**LAST RULE OF PRANK CLUB:
LEAVE ON A HIGH NOTE.**

THE ELEPHANT AND THE MOUSE

Brendan Morrison Gets a Harsh Introduction to Salary Arbitration

I know. That title sounds like a children's fable. And it is, apparently. We'll get to that. But this is also a true story. Not of mice, but of men. Men sitting across a table from each other in the most awkward, uncomfortable setting in the hockey business: salary arbitration.

Wait! Don't flip to the next chapter. Don't go back to dog videos on TikTok. I know the mere mention of salary arbitration makes eyes glaze over. But this is the story of the wildest salary arb argument you will ever hear. And Brendan Morrison has a front row seat for it. Because it's his case.

Brendan is a British Columbia native who became a star at the University of Michigan, putting up 284 points in his four years as a Wolverine. He gets taken in the second round of the 1993 NHL Draft by the New Jersey Devils before getting traded to his hometown Vancouver Canucks at the deadline in 2000 for Alexander Mogilny. He signs a two-year contract with the Canucks that summer for $775,000 a season.

Vancouver is a young team on the rise, and Brendan is a perfect fit. By his second full season there, he is centring a line with star wingers Todd Bertuzzi and Markus Naslund and putting up solid numbers. He scores 23 goals, adds 44 assists and is plus-18 over 82 games in 2001–02. Time for a sizable raise.

Filing for salary arbitration is a standard move for players. Most of the time, a contract will get done before it gets to the hearing. Brendan and his agent, Kurt Overhardt, are confident this will be no different. But Canucks GM Brian Burke has other ideas.

"I have a rule on my teams," Burke says. "Once a player files for arbitration, we're going. All these players file and settle on the courthouse steps. That ruins the whole summer for everyone. That's why it's such an affront to me when Brendan files. He is the first and only arbitration case I've ever had as a general manager. So I call Kurt and say, 'Fuck you, Kurt.' I'm gonna kick this guy's ass now."

Suddenly, Morrison is on a plane to Toronto for his hearing the next day.

"I still figure we'll get something done last minute," Brendan says. "But Kurt and I go out to a movie that night, and when we get out of the theatre, there's a text from Burkie that reads, 'If this goes to arbitration tomorrow and Brendan gets one more penny than what we feel he's worth, we will let him walk.'"

Brendan is rattled. He loves playing in his hometown and has no desire to leave. But if the Canucks really walk away from whatever the arbitrator decides, he will become an unrestricted free agent and likely make much more money elsewhere.

Morning comes. Still no deal. So Brendan, Overhardt and Roland Lee, a lawyer with the NHL Players' Association, walk into a room in a Toronto office building. They sit down across a table from Burke; his assistant, Dave Nonis; and their lawyer, Daniel Dumais.

"It's a crazy set-up," Brendan says. "The room isn't very big, so it's very intimate. I can reach over the other side of the table and touch Burkie and Nonis and their lawyer. The arbitrator sits at the end of the table, running the show."

Arbitration works like a mini trial. First, the team makes its case for what they think the player should be paid. Then the player's side does the same. Both make closing statements, and the arbitrator eventually settles on a number he or she believes is fair. In Brendan's case, the Canucks offer a two-year contract at $1.75 million per year. Brendan's camp is asking for $2.7 million per, over the same term.

The Canucks begin. And instantly, Brendan feels like they've pulled his jersey over his head and are feeding him fists to the face. "It's really tough to listen to, because they are basically trying to tell me how bad of a player I am right in front of me even though they told me at the end of the season how excited they were about my future in Vancouver," Brendan says. "At one point they say, 'Brendan kills penalties for us, but the only reason he does is because we don't have anyone else who can do it.' I just put my head down and bite my lip. I almost start to laugh. The whole thing is so strange."

Oh, and it's about to get much stranger.

Roland Lee does most of the talking for Brendan's side, focusing on how important a role he plays for the Canucks. He centres their top line, going against other teams' best defensive pairings. He produces on the power play and logs big minutes on the penalty kill (because no one else can, apparently). And he takes key faceoffs all over the ice.

Now it's time for the Canucks' closing statement. Dumais, the Canucks' lawyer, has an epic tale to tell. I'll add in italics what Brendan is thinking as he listens.

"Mr. Arbitrator, this case reminds me of the story of the elephant and the mouse," Dumais begins.

Sorry, the ... what?

"There is an elephant and a mouse travelling through the jungle together."

Wait, is this bedtime when I'm ... five?

"The elephant and the mouse come across a raging river. There is a drawbridge but it is broken. So the mouse looks at the elephant and says, 'How are we going to get across?'"

I can't wait to see how this relates to my power-play production.

"The elephant says, 'Don't worry, little mouse, I will carry you across.' So the mouse jumps on the elephant's back, and they head across the raging river."

Is this The Jungle Book? *Where is Baloo the bear?*

"The elephant is big and strong and he makes it to the other side of the river, with the little mouse safely on his back. *[Pause for dramatic effect.]* And this, gentlemen, is the exact story of the Canucks line of Naslund, Bertuzzi and Morrison! Naslund and Bertuzzi are the elephant ... and Morrison is the mouse!"

As he delivers his punchline, Dumais slams his fist on the table for emphasis. Brendan, in semi-shock, almost bursts out laughing.

"I have tears in my eyes, because I can't believe what I've just heard," he says. "I'm thinking, 'Holy crap, did this actually happen?' But I'm also angry. Is this what these guys really think of me? A freaking mouse riding on Markus's and Bert's backs?"

The hearing ends, mercifully, and both sides walk out. As he's leaving the room, Brendan feels a hand on his shoulder. It's Burke. "Mo, just want you to know this is just business," Burke says. "This is not how we feel about you. We think you are a great person."

But also a frightened, clingy rodent.

Brendan flies from Toronto to Michigan for a Wolverines alumni golf tournament. He gets a call two days later from Overhardt. The arbitrator has announced his decision.

Brendan is awarded a two-year contract worth an average of $2.3 million per season. It's right in the middle of what the two sides argued for. And despite what they had threatened the night before the hearing, Burke and the Canucks accept the deal. "Everything is kumbaya after that," Brendan says. "I never took it personally. But it is definitely one of the weirdest moments of my career."

He ends up signing one more contract in Vancouver and plays eight seasons there, lasting four years longer than Burke does. Burke ends up in Anaheim, where he wins a Stanley Cup with the Ducks in 2007. And the following summer, when Brendan is a free agent again, it's Burke and Nonis who sign him in Anaheim.

"Burkie and I have talked about it a few times, and we always laugh about the mouse and the elephant," Brendan says.

"Wasn't the best story to use in a court case," Burke laughs. "I had no idea it was coming. I love Brendan. But I'm still pissed off we went to arbitration. It ruined a weekend of my life for no reason."

Brendan retires in 2012 after 14 seasons in the NHL. He still lives in Vancouver and hosts a popular fishing show. In his office hangs a framed caricature he received from Overhardt a few months after the arbitration case. It's an artist's sketch of an elephant in a river with a mouse on its back. The mouse is wearing Brendan's number 7.

13 AND 21

Remembering John and Matty Gaudreau

On August 29, 2024, hockey lost two of its best friends. John and Matty Gaudreau were killed when they were struck by a car while riding bikes near their childhood home in South Jersey. John was 31, Matty 29. Few loved the game, and each other, the way the brothers did.

John was Johnny to most of us, but always John to his family. He was the kind of rare talent who could live up to a nickname that was ... his actual sport—Johnny Hockey. His younger brother, Matty, was also a terrific hockey player who never minded living in John's long shadow.

We all felt the loss. And we didn't even know them. Their family, their friends, their teammates ... they felt like they'd lost part of themselves.

John wore number 13. Matty, 21. So here in chapter 13, 21 friends and family members will tell their favourite John and Matty stories. I hope their kids read this someday and smile. This is who their dads were, in the words of those who loved them.

> *John and Matty are born 16 months apart in New Jersey.*
> *Younger brothers of Kristen, future older brothers of Katie.*
> *Sons of Jane and Guy Gaudreau—a long-time hockey coach*
> *who can't wait to get his boys on the ice.*

Jane Gaudreau: Guy takes John skating for the first time when he's a year and a half. He's so excited to get his boy out there. But then I get a message at work, telling me to call Guy at the rink. I'm worried something is really wrong. I call and ask, "Is everything okay?" Guy says, "No. It's John. I just don't think he has it. I tried to put Skittles down and get him to skate toward them. But he just isn't into it." I say, "Guy, he is eighteen months old. Maybe wait until he's potty trained to decide if he'll make the NHL."

Guy Gaudreau: The boys are inseparable from the beginning. As soon as they can both run, they are competing at everything. Every sport, every game.

Jane: Every night they race to be the first one upstairs at bedtime. One would grab the other's leg to trip him and pass him. Then one would hide the other's toothbrush so they could be the first one in bed.

Charlie Vasaturo: John, Matty, myself and Jamie Hill are best friends from when we are three or four years old. We'd play mini-sticks endlessly. Always me and Matty, the oldest and youngest, versus Jamie and John. Best of sevens, unless John loses, then best of whatever until John wins. There are still dents in the walls. The Gaudreaus would come to pick them up, and we'd all start crying because we didn't want to stop. Or John and Matty would hide. They were so small, they would lie down side by side on one stair, refusing to leave.

Guy: And it never ended. They would come home from Boston College at 19 and 20 years old, and they would play mini-sticks against each other in the house.

Jane: John is the sensitive one. Matty is the protector. Even though he's younger. When John starts second grade, he comes home upset because he isn't on the list to use the class computers. I tell him to talk to the teacher, but he's too shy. "Can't you call her, Mom?" He's upset all week. Finally, he comes home excited and says, "Mom, I am on the computer list!" I'm thinking, good for him for getting over his shyness and going to the teacher. Then when I meet the teacher a few weeks later, she says, "Both your sons are very nice." I say, "Oh, you met Matty too?" She goes, "Yes, he came to me and told me I had to put his brother John on the computer list because he's really upset." Matty was in kindergarten. That was the beginning of a life of Matty looking out for John.

John is the worrier. We're at a hockey tournament in Canada once, and his little sister, Katie, who is a dancer, is swinging from the railings of the stands. It's not high. I'm keeping an eye on her. Then I notice John misses a shift. Guy is coaching, and he's trying to get my attention. When the period ends, he yells across the ice, "Tell Katie to stop! John won't play because he's worried she's going to fall!"

Guy runs the hockey program at Hollydell Arena, in Sewell, New Jersey, where his boys start their hockey careers. Eric Robinson, now a Carolina Hurricanes forward, is another of their childhood friends.

Eric Robinson: We spend our entire summers doing hockey camps. We play capture the flag, where each team has a flag at their end of the rink, and the other team has to take it and bring it back to their end. Matt and John want to win so bad, they figure out a plan. They open the gate at their end when no one is looking, and John sneaks off the ice and crawls all the way to the other end. Then he sneaks back on, steals the flag and starts skating back. Matt would be cheering wildly and our team would be going, "How did he do that?" They are so close, even then. You never thought of Matt without John or John without Matt.

Guy: Like all brothers, they fight. At 14 or 15, they go to this showcase tournament. After a game, John's underwear gets wet. Matty is still in the shower, so John steals Matty's underwear, gets dressed and leaves.

Jane: Matty is so mad. He comes out in front of all the parents in the hallway and is yelling, "You stole my underwear!" John's going, "No, these are mine." Matty's yelling, "No, I had the blue ones!"

Only a brother would take his brother's dirty underwear because his are wet.

Eric Robinson: A bunch of us would always sleep over at their house in high school. Coach Guy is trying to help them put on weight. He keeps saying, "You have to be heavier if you want to play at the next level." So he would feed us this feast of eggs and bagels. We are all stuffed and feeling sick. Except Matt and John. They're laughing because they're feeding their eggs to the family dog. Coach Guy thinks he's bulking them up, but really their dog is just getting fat.

Guy: They are always skinny. I'd make them chocolate milkshakes every morning because I know they wouldn't give the dog those. John goes to play in the USHL in Dubuque, Iowa, at 17. The first thing the NHL does is come weigh every player in that league. John is 132 pounds. So they load up his jockstrap with pucks to get him to 135.

Madeline Gaudreau (Matty's wife): I think Matty and John shoved pucks and weights in their pants pretty much every year of their careers to try to cheat the scales. They could never keep weight on. When Matty plays pro in Bridgeport, they ban him from doing cardio. All his teammates hate cardio, so they are so mad at him.

Katie Gaudreau (John and Matty's younger sister): They would play in this summer tournament at the rink, and I would run the clock. One game this guy on the other team hits John in the back and gets a penalty. Matty comes to defend John, they all get into it, and both of them end up in the box too. I'm mad at this guy because these are my brothers. I ride or die with them. He gets a 2 and 10 [misconduct], but I put the penalty up on the board wrong. So he starts yelling at me. I start crying, because I'm 13 and a bit of a drama queen. Well, John and Matty lose it. They are screaming at him, "You don't yell at our sister!" There's no divider, so they end up fighting this guy in the penalty box because he was mean to their sister. They all get kicked out. That's just the way they protected me their whole lives.

In 2011, John and Matty are trying to decide which university they will attend. They don't even consider going to different schools.

Kevin Hayes: I'm relaxing on a boat after my freshman year at Boston College, when our coach, Jerry York, calls. "I need you at the school tomorrow at seven a.m.," he says. "We have a recruit coming with his younger brother, and I want you to show them around campus." I'm in the coaches office the next morning, and these two tiny kids walk in wearing the exact same outfit—cargo shorts and USA Hockey polos. They look 10 years old. I'm thinking, "What the . . . ? These guys are going to help us win?"

So I take these little kids around campus for two and a half hours. They don't say 10 words the entire time. When they leave, I think I failed miserably. There is zero chance they are coming to Boston College. I find out later, Johnny says to his parents after, "Just let Matty pick. Wherever he wants to go, I'll go." Matty picks BC, so they both come.

I'm in some classes with Johnny. He's so shy at first. I can't figure him out. One day, he has this paper in front of him and he's writing on it the entire class. I'm thinking, "This kid makes a lot of notes!" So at the end of class, I say, "Dude, what were you writing?" He shows me the paper. He's drawn the most perfect picture of his iPhone. Complete with all the apps that were on his screen. So yeah, Johnny was a student of ... hockey.

In no time, he is everyone's favourite guy at BC. The kindest guy ever. All he wants is to make people happy.

Matty is two years behind John, so even though he makes the choice for them to go to Boston College, he goes to play for the Omaha Lancers in the United States Hockey League first.

Vince Pedrie: This kid shows up in Omaha and must weigh 140 pounds, tops. I'm thinking, "How can this kid play in this league?" But as soon as Matty steps on the ice, you see his hockey IQ is through the roof.

Boston College makes it to the NCAA championship game against Ferris State that year. Matty and I watch the game at our billet's home. With about three minutes left, Johnny scores this dazzling goal to put BC up 3–1. They win the national championship. Matty is going crazy. He calls Johnny. They are so happy, sharing this moment. Listening to them dissect Johnny's goal and celebrate together is something I'll never forget. They have the most incredible bond I've ever seen.

Madeline: I'm going to Millard North High School in Omaha, and my best friend, Jessica, is dating the captain of the Lancers. She says, "I want to introduce you to this new kid named Matty." I agree, and we meet in the school library. Which is funny, because if you know Matty, he's never in a library. He keeps coming back to the library when I'm there, pretending he's studying. Then once we started dating, he never came back to the library.

There is just something different about him. He's patient, caring. He celebrates all my little accomplishments and big ones. He's truly one of a kind.

From the beginning, he warns me about how close he is with

John. He says they are a package deal. And they were. We're not just a couple. It's always the three of us. John would get scared to sleep alone, and would sleep in the same bed with us all the time. Always in the middle. One night I lock the door, and he stands outside, knocking and quoting *Friends* for an hour until I give in.

Matty joins John at Boston College the next fall. He and Madeline would date long distance during his entire time there.

Chris Calnan: Matty and I are teammates and roommates our first year at BC. It's tradition that we do a showdown at practice the day before every game. It's a sudden-death shootout: You score, you keep going; you miss, you're out. Before the first BC football game, there's one just for freshmen. Whoever loses has to go to the football game tailgate wearing Timberland boots, this superfan T-shirt and really short cutoff jean shorts. So it's going to be extremely embarrassing. Of course, I lose. I'm terrified. I'm in our dorm room cutting off my jeans to make these tiny shorts. I turn around, and Matty is cutting his jeans off too. I say, "What are you doing?" He goes, "Dude, I don't care. I'm with you."

So we walk to this tailgate looking like a couple of idiots in our jorts and boots. The fact he would do this, after knowing me only a couple of weeks, just so I wouldn't be humiliated alone, is incredible. Just a special human being.

In late 2012, John goes to Ufa, Russia, to play in the World Junior Hockey Championship.

Boone Jenner: I'm playing for Canada. I've heard rumblings about this kid Johnny Gaudreau on the American team, but I've never seen him play. I don't know him from a hole in the wall. Then we play the US in the semis, and he tears us apart. He scores two goals and they beat us 5–1. I'm like, "Oh. So that's Johnny Gaudreau." He's just incredible. They win gold. The tournament ends up being his coming-out party. He might have reminded me once or twice when we end up together in Columbus.

Fifteen months later, after his college season ends, John signs with the Calgary Flames.

Guy: He signs his contract and wins the Hobey Baker that same night. The Flames fly us on a private jet to Calgary, and John plays his first game against Vancouver. Right up until that minute, I never thought he'd be able to play in the NHL. They're so big and fast. The Flames lose 5–1, but John scores the only goal and is the best player on his team that night. I'm thinking, "Holy Smokes, he can play in this league!"

Sean Monahan: I've been in Calgary a year when he gets there. He's this really shy kid, but once he lets you in, he's hilarious. We grow up together in Calgary. We would eat the exact same pre-game meal at the same restaurant, Villa Firenze, for eight years. Johnny's pre-game meal is epic. All he eats is this massive plate of pasta, about 12 pounds of it.

Boone Jenner: I've never seen anything like it. It's piled a foot high. No white sauce, no red sauce. Just pasta, maybe butter, and a huge Coke. The first time I see it, I'm like, "There is no way you are finishing that." He does. Every time.

Matthew Tkachuk: His entire pre-game routine is legendary. He plays soccer in red Louis Vuitton sneakers. He doesn't stretch. He just goes in the hot tub and dunks himself for 30 seconds, then throws his gear on in two minutes and goes out and dominates. His skates are tied so loose, I don't know how they don't fall off.

Erik Gudbranson: He would send a new pair of skates home to his dad to break in. Guy wears them for a year and then sends them back for Johnny to wear the next season. When he tells me this, I'm laughing, dumbfounded. He loves his gear beat up. You can fold Johnny's skates and stick them in your pocket. They are like slippers.

Matthew Tkachuk: He scores this shootout goal in Minnesota that is the most insane thing I've ever seen. He makes about 12 moves, the goalie goes down, and he ends it with this little chip shot over him. Anyone else would have stickhandled into the corner. We're on the bench in awe every night.

While John is becoming a star in the NHL, Matty is still at Boston College, cheering on his brother and, occasionally, pretending he's him.

Ryan Fitzgerald: I play with Matty all four years at BC. A crew of us live together. We are all 21, but Matty is 20. He's using John's ID. We go to a bar in Boston to watch John play for the Flames. Matty gives his ID to the bouncer. The guy looks at him, puzzled, and says, "You're Johnny Gaudreau?" Matty goes, "Yup!" He repeats, "You're . . . Johnny?" Matty says confidently, "Yesssir." The bouncer stares at him, looks back at Johnny's game that's on TV in the bar, and says, "I'm going to ask you one more time. Look me in the eye and say you are Johnny Gaudreau." Matty just proudly sticks out his chest and says, "Yes, I'm Johnny Gaudreau!" Finally, the bouncer, says, "Well, no you're not, because Johnny Gaudreau is playing on the TV right behind me." Matt shakes his head and says, "You got me. Guys, we need a different bar!"

Matty has this ability to be really confident about things he has no business being confident about. During winter break we stay at school for practice but they shut down the dorms. They put us up in a hotel that is a big pilot hub for Logan Airport. So we're sitting at the bar and this old-timer pilot sits down next to me. He starts making small talk. Matty's on the other side of me, not in the conversation. After a few minutes, Matty chimes in out of nowhere. "How come there are life vests instead of parachutes on planes?"

The pilot goes, "What?"

Matty says it again. "Why not parachutes instead of life vests?" This old guy explains very nicely that the plane is going too fast and it's not practical, that it just wouldn't work.

Matty's like, "No. I think parachutes would be a good idea."

Fast-forward an hour. Now it's Matty and the pilot, several beers deep, going back and forth about this parachute versus life vest debate. The pilot is banging on the table, saying, "No, no, no! You don't get it! Parachutes won't work!" Matty's so stubborn he won't give it up. They ended up exchanging numbers and being friends on social media. At the end of the night, we're going up the elevator, and Matty looks at me and says, "Yeah, parachutes would be a pretty stupid idea."

On March 17, 2015, the boys' older sister, Kristen, gives birth to her first child, a girl named Kamryn.

Kristen Gaudreau (John and Matty's older sister): I knew they'd be great fathers because you've never seen two guys so excited to be uncles. Whenever they had time off hockey, they'd come to see Kamryn. We do a family Disney trip when she is one, and it becomes a running joke that every time Matty holds her, she happens to not have a diaper on and she pees on him. Every shirt he has on ends up soaked. But he keeps saying, "I don't mind. I'll keep holding her." John hates rides, so that's his time. We'd be flying around on some roller coaster, and there would be John, watching from the side, so happy to be holding his niece . . . and not on the ride.

As Matty finishes his college career, John has quickly become the face of the Flames, racking up points and endearing himself to teammates.

Matthew Tkachuk: Johnny's already a superstar when I get there as a rookie. The young single guys on our team go down to Cabo for our bye week. I look up to Johnny and am just in awe of everything he does. So whatever he says, I'm doing. One day he goes, "Chucky, let's go have some fun." He takes me to Mango Deck, this famous Cabo bar. We're having the time of our lives. I'm pretty sure I threw up on someone's Rollerblades at one point. Then Johnny says, "Let's go on Instagram Live!" So he grabs my phone and we start interacting with people. It's just an insane scene. And I've had way too many Jell-O shots. Eventually we go back for a nap. I wake up and have three missed calls from [Flames GM] Brad Treliving, a couple from [assistant GM] Craig Conroy and a bunch from other Flames officials. I call Tree back first and say, "What's going on?" He goes, "Chucky, I want you and Johnny to have a great time, but I'm begging you, stay off social media." He makes it pretty clear if I wasn't with Johnny, I would have been in big trouble. Probably would have been sent down to the minors. But they let it slide because I'm with Johnny Gaudreau. Ever since that day, Johnny's been my hero for saving me. Wherever he goes, I'm always going.

Kevin Hayes: John is the most competitive person I've ever met. He is obsessed with his summer softball league in Jersey. One time, I ask him how it's going and he says, "Bro, it's going unbelievable. I lead off every game with a bunt. I steal second and third and score every time." A professional athlete bunting to start a rec league softball game! Unreal.

He's great at everything, but just an unbelievable cornhole player. He's so good, he gambles with ghost peppers. Whoever loses has to eat those extremely hot peppers. Of course he crushes me, and I have to eat one. It ruins me for three hours.

Boone Jenner: He gets me at cornhole too. I tell him I haven't played much, and he says, "Don't worry, me neither." So we have this really close game. Then he says, "Let's play for 20 bucks." And he beats me 21–0. I find out after that he enters cornhole tournaments back home.

Rasmus Andersson: One day my rookie year, we are doing this three-on-two drill in Ottawa. Our D had a rough game the night before, so Billy Peters, our coach, wants us to be really aggressive on the lines, not letting the forwards in. Johnny's line with Monny [Sean Monahan] and Lindy [Elias Lindholm] is against my pairing. I'm trying to be aggressive, Johnny tries to dangle me, and I accidentally hit him. He goes down. I'm like, "Oh fuck." He stays down for a few seconds and I'm in full panic. I'm 15 games into my rookie year, and I just hurt our superstar. Johnny leaves the ice. I can't even function the rest of practice. I have to apologize. So after, he's lying on the training table and I say, "Johnny, I'm so sorry man. I didn't mean to." He doesn't answer. He goes silent for days! Finally, I go up to him and say, "Johnny, come on, it's been four days." He looks at me and goes, "Three more days." After a week, he finally says, "We're good now. Just never hit me again." But he says it with a wink and a smile. And I know he's been playing me the whole time. We laugh about it a ton in the years after. Once you become friends with Johnny, you have a friend for life.

Erik Gudbranson: I've moved around the league so much it's hard to make meaningful friendships. When I sign with Calgary, the very last guy I talk to is Johnny. I can't figure him out. They do hotel rooms alphabetically, so Gudbranson is next to Gaudreau. We're in Florida early in the season staying at the Ritz-Carlton on the ocean. We end up at our doors at the same time. So I say, "Go grab the two beers in your fridge and come to my room." And he quietly says, "Okay."

We talk until five thirty in the morning. We're cut from the same cloth. All that matters are family and friends. We sit on my balcony until the sun comes up. He looks out at the ocean and says, "What's better than this? We're in a hotel that's too nice for us. We get to sit here, listen to the waves come in, have a couple of beers, get to know each other. What could be better?" And he was right.

Have you heard of love languages? How different people express love? Well, Johnny, if he liked you, he'd try to piss you off every day. We'd be out for dinner and he would constantly give it to me. Then I'd snap, and to remind him I'm bigger and stronger, I'd chase him down and put him in a public garbage can upside down.

Johnny has this amazing ability to love. He didn't do it with everyone, but if he cared for you, it was real and he showed it.

Matty graduates from BC and is finding his own way through pro hockey. He gets signed by the New York Islanders and bounces between the American Hockey League (Bridgeport Sound, Stockton) and the East Coast Hockey League (Worcester, Reading) for three seasons.

Madeline: Other players would constantly say things to Matt, like, "You aren't as good as your brother." And announcers can't say his name without saying he's Johnny's brother. But it never bothers him. He's so proud to be John's brother. He would watch all of John's games. And John would fly home when he had a break and drive four hours to watch Matt play in Worcester.

Guy: Jerry York [former Boston College coach] said he's never seen a tougher player than Matty for his size. John is able to put on a little weight later in his career, but Matty never breaks 145 pounds. He is fearless, plays so hard, fights anyone he has to fight. But you just can't do that at his size. It takes a toll. He breaks some bones. I try to tell him to change his style. But it's just who he is.

In 2018, Guy has a heart attack while running a half-marathon. John jumps on a flight from LA to Philadelphia, not knowing if his dad is going to be alive when he lands. Guy recovers, but it deeply affects both his boys. John immediately buys a beach house in Avalon, New Jersey, for the family.

Jane: John tells us, "This is where we're going to spend every summer. All of us. Life is too short, and we need to spend as much time together as we can." When the Flames didn't make the playoffs, he'd get to the house a month before summer and he'd call us and say, "Are you coming down? When are you coming?"

Rasmus Andersson: He would call me in the middle of the summer and say, "Come to my place in Jersey." I'd say, "Johnny, I'm in Sweden! I can't just come to Jersey for the weekend. I just got home after an eight-month season." He'd say, "Just come. Bring your family, stay for a few weeks." He wanted family and friends with him, always.

Andrew Mangiapane: He loves it so much there. He invites me down and teaches me how to crab fish. We paddle out on these boards to the middle of the bay and set the traps, then paddle back later that night. We catch tons of crabs. He cooks them all up for us, and they taste amazing. He never looked like that type of guy, but he loves it.

Meredith Gaudreau (John's wife): My family is renting a beach house in Avalon. I hear that a hockey player bought the house next door. But I think it's some old retired player. One night my sister Tyler is having friends over for her birthday. And our new neighbour is having his friends over. They end up coming by our place. I see John for the first time and say, "I'm in trouble. I'm going to marry this guy."

I have zero idea who he is. And he never says anything. A few weeks after we start dating, I'm at his house and his dad is watching ESPN. They are ranking the top forwards. I see him and say, "John, is that you on TV?!" He says, "No." He's so humble. He never says a word about himself. It isn't until I come to Calgary that I realize he's this huge star. I'm blown away. I remember telling my mom, who was the same as me when it came to hockey knowledge, "Mom, Johnny is actually really good. I think he's one of the best players." And she goes, "Sure he is, Mer. Sure he is."

The first time I go over to his family's house where he grew up, I see this room with twin beds, football wallpaper and kids' stuff all over the room. And I figure out... this is where John and Matt still sleep. John's been in the NHL for five years! They just never wanted to be apart.

Jane: When our oldest, Kristen, moves out, we have all these empty bedrooms, and we say, "Boys, don't you want your own space?" They say, "Why would we?"

Sean Monahan: Johnny tells me he met a girl in the summer. I ask if she is coming to live with him, and he says, "I think she might." None of us have even seen John with a girl before. When Meredith comes into his life, he becomes a different person. We're stuck in the playoff bubble during that first COVID season, and we both buy rings. As soon as we get out, we propose 13 hours apart.

Meredith: I am the girl who would cry when John would leave for a road trip, no matter how short or long. I barely sleep when he's gone. I wait up to talk to him after every game no matter what time zone he's in. I wake up and text him "hi" as soon as I open my eyes. He answers me instantly: "Hey Reg." We call each other Reg or Reggie, from Reggie Dunlop in *Slap Shot*. His dad and all his uncles still call me Reggie.

Sean Monahan: My favourite memory is when John finds out he's going to be a dad. We're in Calgary, and me and my wife, Brittany, go to dinner with John and Meredith at Villa Firenze. They've just found out they are pregnant an hour before. When they tell us, I've never seen him so excited.

Meredith: We only had girls on our side of the family, and I get a little nervous. Maybe he wants a boy? We're in the delivery room, and I hear them say, "It's a girl." I look over and John has tears in his eyes. You can see he is absolutely in love with her. She's now the spitting image of John. She was the real love of his life.

Boone Jenner: John is terrified of flying. He usually pulls his toque down over his eyes for takeoff and landing. But when Meredith goes into labour with their second in February of '24, he can't wait to get on that plane. The team leaves early from Anaheim so he can get back in time. He races straight to the hospital. And sends me a GIF of a boy playing hockey, so I know it's a little boy. Johnny Hockey number two.

Matty retires from hockey in 2022. He is eager to settle down with Madeline and start a family like his brother. They buy a house in Jersey, five minutes from Guy and Jane. Matty starts coaching, following in Guy's footsteps. The last year and a half of Matty's and John's lives are full of friends' weddings and little moments that those who loved them now cherish.

Keith Yandle: Hayesy [Kevin Hayes] gets married in Cape Cod in the summer of '23. We're there for the whole week, and every night me and Johnny get a bonfire going for the entire crew. The house we rented is right on the beach. The night of the wedding, the after-party is going to be back at the house. The wedding is unbelievable—everyone is dancing, and Johnny keeps hitting me, saying, "We gotta go! We gotta get that bonfire set up!" I'm like, "Johnny, everyone's here, we can't leave." But he keeps saying, "No, no, it's windy, we are going to need more wood. We have to go!" So we leave the wedding early and get this absolute monster of a bonfire going. But the wind knocks it out. We're struggling to get it going again, and I see little Johnny walking down these steep steps from the house with a big propane tank over his head. It has disaster written all over it. I'm like, "Johnny, we can't put this in the fire." I actually have to hide the tank so he won't do it. We finally get the fire going, but he's looking for the tank half the night. He wants everything to be perfect, so everyone can sit around the fire all night telling stories about Hayesy and his wife, Katya. That's Johnny.

Brady Tkachuk: You've probably seen the video from the party at the wedding. "All Night Longer" comes on by Sammy Adams. It's a staple for the Boston guys, so I figure it's only fitting that I pull Hockey up on my shoulders [the Tkachuks call John simply "Hockey" or "Hock"]. Someone posts the video the next day and it goes everywhere. It's a pretty awesome moment. He looks so happy.

But my favourite Johnny memory is from the World Championship a few months before. We have dinner and grab a couple of beers on a patio. We talk about family for hours. We're expecting our first at that time, and Johnny is telling me how great it is to be a father. He goes on and on about his daughter, Noa, and his baby boy, Johnny. How he can't wait to share his love of hockey with them. He gets me so excited to be a dad. Our son, Ryder, is born just two and a half weeks after we lose Johnny and Matthew. I wish they got to meet him.

Rasmus Andersson: Johnny is the best man at Mangy's [Andrew Mangiapane's] wedding. We both have our young daughters with us. One day where there is nothing planned, we just go to the bar and talk for hours. We haven't seen each other much since he went to Columbus. In retrospect, I'm so happy we got that time. At the wedding party, we look at each other, and he says, "Time to get this thing going." So we rip off our shirts and hit the dance floor.

Sean Monahan: That same summer, 2023, we take a yacht from Fort Lauderdale to Key West. Just the four of us—Brittany and me, Johnny and Meredith. It's so much fun. I think I know how to fish, but he teaches me a lot. He also plays me. I hook something and he tells me it's a shark. I fight it for 30 minutes. He's cheering me on, yelling, "You got this, Monny!" I'm exhausted trying to reel it in. Turns out my line was caught on the bottom. He knew it the whole time.

Kevin Hayes: Johnny and I go over to play for USA at the 2024 World Championship. Our wives aren't coming until later in the tournament. We check into our rooms in Ostrava. The rooms have two tiny single beds squished together to make one slightly less tiny bed. Johnny texts and says, "What room are you in?" Two minutes later, there's a knock on my door. It's Johnny and his full set of luggage. He says, "I just figured we'd room together until our wives get here." So for 13 days, we share this little room with no air conditioning and all our luggage. He leaves his own room completely empty. Two grown-ass NHL players, sharing one tiny bed. And you know what? I'm so lucky we had that time.

Cole Caufield: I don't know Johnny until that World Championship. But I idolize him. We go bowling, and he's unbelievable. We start calling him Johnny Bowling. We play this game on our iPads called *Wolves*, where our names are our real names backward. So I'm Eloc and he's Ynnhoj. That's why I write *Eloc* on my sticks now. He's so good to us young guys. When he passes away, I feel so helpless. I need to honour him. So I change my Canadiens number to 13.

Madeline: Matty and I first get pregnant in February of 2024. We had been trying for almost a year. But we have a miscarriage. Matty is so upset. But not long after, we're in Omaha, visiting my dad after he had a heart attack. I keep telling Matt, "I think I'm pregnant again." And he keeps saying, "No, you're not." When we get home, I take a test. Matt is outside doing yard work. We live by the woods, and any free time he has, he's always in the back working. I show him the test and he drops everything and hugs me. He's so happy. We don't get our hopes up until we go to our first appointment. We hear the heartbeat, and he starts crying. We do a gender reveal with the whole family down at John's beach house. But the OB accidentally puts the gender in my email. So I know it's a boy. But I keep hinting to Matty that it's a girl because everyone has girls first in the family. Meredith does the reveal. I've never seen Matt so excited.

Ryan Fitzgerald: The first time I see Matty since he knew he was going to be a dad is my wedding in mid-August. He keeps joking with me that his little guy is going to be a 6-foot-4 power forward. We don't get our wedding photos back until after the accident. At first, it's so strange and hard to see him in all the photos. But I'm so glad I have them now.

Eric Robinson: We're all at Jamie Hill's wedding the weekend before the accident. That morning, my wife, Allison, takes a pregnancy test and it's positive. We're freaking out, but we don't want to tell anyone yet. At the party, I go to the bar and I'm being all slick, getting a beer and a Shirley Temple for Allison. I sit down, and in two seconds Matty says, "Allison's pregnant?" I'm like, "No, no, this is a vodka–cranberry." He smiles. "I just got Madeline the same drink, bud. Congratulations." He gives me a big hug and promises he won't tell anyone. He's so excited we're going to be dads together. I can't believe he busted me in two minutes.

Charlie Vasaturo: The night before Jamie's wedding, John and I stay over at Jamie's house. John likes simple, dumb humour. So he buys two cans of fart spray and five of these little electronic crickets, the size of a paper clip. We're relaxing watching TV, and every time Jamie leaves the room, John whips out his fart spray. Jamie returns and is like, "You guys are disgusting! Take it outside!" I have my head buried trying not to laugh. Jamie finally goes to get Febreze to make his house smell better, and we plant the crickets. We put one in his air vent, one behind a painting. This is the kind of sicko John is: These things make cricket chirps randomly every 5 to 45 minutes. And they last for three years! All night Jamie keeps going, "Did you hear that?" We're stone-faced, going, "We didn't hear anything." For months after I get messages from Jamie saying, "I found another one." I think he's still searching for the last couple. And John is probably laughing somewhere.

Andrew Mangiapane: About a month after John passes, Meredith gives me a pair of his dress socks and one of his ties for good luck. She says, "I know you are starting on a new team, and this way, John will be with you when you walk into the rink." I start wearing them. I just assume they are clean. A few weeks go by, and I start noticing this growth on my foot. My wife, Claudia, tells Meredith, and she says, "Oh no. I forgot to tell you John had some athlete's foot issues." Turns out John wouldn't wash his socks if he had a point streak going. They were good luck socks. So that's John's last gift to me. The little guy's still pulling pranks, even after he's gone.

Jane: When the accident first happened, I was so angry. I would ask why did both of them have to be taken from us? It was too much. But after a while, the thought that they were . . . they are . . . together . . . the way they were for so much of their lives . . . gives me some peace.

Kristen and Katie: John and Matty were the best brothers. They loved their family and friends so much and would do anything for them. We miss them every day. We will remember all the great times and never stop sharing their memories with our kids . . . and theirs.

Matty and Madeline's son, Tripp Matthew Gaudreau, is born December 26, 2024.

Madeline: Matty was truly born to be a dad. He has left me the biggest piece of him—our Tripp. Going through this without him has been heartbreaking, but the moment I meet Tripp, I feel a

Matty and John's first coach was their dad, Guy.

John and Matty with their mom, Jane.

John and Matty played together in high school and again at Boston College.

The Gaudreau family: Katie, Matty, Jane, John, Guy and Kristen.

John with Guy and Jane after his 100th point of the 2021–22 season.

John, baby Johnny, Meredith and Noa on the ice in Columbus in April 2024.

Madeline and Matty Gaudreau fell in love in high school and never looked back.

John and Sean Monahan, teammates and best friends in Calgary and Columbus. They even got the same dogs—Bailey is John's, Winston is Sean's.

Madeline and Matty, Meredith and John.

Madeline Gaudreau and baby boy Tripp, born in December 2024.

Meredith Gaudreau with Johnny, Noa and baby boy Carter, born in April 2025.

sense of peace—something I haven't felt in a long time. He is born with two angel kisses, one on each eye—I know they are from Matty and John. He looks just like his dad and already acts like him. I know Matty was holding him before I did. Tripp has the best guardian angels, and I know his daddy will watch over him for the rest of his life.

John and Meredith's third child, Carter Michael Gaudreau is born on April 1, 2025.

Meredith: I can't think of a single thing I would have changed about John and our relationship. I couldn't have asked for more, other than more time. A lifetime. I love and I miss him more and more every day of my life.

There is nothing more I want than to give our babies a life full of love and happiness, the life John intended for them. Honouring their daddy every day and teaching our kids the lessons their daddy taught me—work hard, be kind, have fun and stay humble. We will continue to talk about Daddy every single day and kiss his pictures every single morning and night forever. We love you, Daddy, so much.

Even Noa, our oldest, is too young to fully understand everything that happened. But at the same time she is very smart. John always joked that she was going to be president. Despite losing her daddy one month before her second birthday, she has an awareness that something is different. Her mommy is different. Our life is different. She so innocently thought Daddy has been away playing hockey, but I can tell that thought is slowly shifting to a deeper understanding of her unfortunate new reality.

[Noa interrupts Meredith.]

Noa: Can I say something to Daddy?

Meredith: Of course. What do you want to say?

Noa: Thank you, Daddy.

BIRON'S BIZARRE BUFFALO BOOKENDS

A Goalie's First and Last Games for the Sabres Are Equally Unforgettable

---

There are games every hockey player will remember forever. Their NHL debuts, of course. Their final games in a city they've called home for most of their careers. Those moments are indelible, even if nothing significant happens.

So imagine if those two games turn out to be the wildest of your entire career.

Before Martin Biron's big break . . . comes heartbreak. One of his hockey dreams growing up in Lac-Saint-Charles, Quebec, was to someday make the Canadian World Junior team. In 1995, after a brilliant start to his junior career with the Beauport Harfangs, he comes agonizingly close.

On the last day of Canada's camp, just before Christmas, the phone rings early in the morning in Marty's hotel room. His roommate, Brad Larsen, answers and looks at Marty. "It's for you," he says.

Marty knows exactly what that means. He is one of Team Canada's final four cuts, along with Dan Cleary, Daniel Brière and Jay McKee (the latter two would end up being Marty's teammates in Buffalo years later).

"I'm crushed," Marty says. "It had always been a huge target on my list of goals, so it hurts a lot. I didn't play well in camp, and they took Marc Denis over me to back up José Théodore."

Marty's junior team is on Christmas break, so he heads back to Quebec to spend the holidays with his family. The night he gets home, he watches a Montreal Canadiens–Pittsburgh Penguins game on TV. Jocelyn Thibault makes 29 saves as the Habs shut out the Pens 1–0. Marty remembers saying, "I wouldn't want to be the next goalie who faces Mario and Jagr after they've been shut out."

The next day, Christmas Eve, he is getting ready to go to his grandparents' house when there is another phone call. His dad answers and yells to Marty upstairs that it's for him.

"C'est qui?" [Who is it?] Marty yells.

"Viens le prendre!" Dad replies. [As in, You'd better come take this one yourself.]

It's Larry Carrière, the assistant general manager of the Buffalo Sabres, who drafted Marty 16th overall the previous June. "I'm thinking I'm going to get told off for not making the World Junior team," Marty says.

Wrong, kid.

"Marty, we've had some injuries here, and you have to get on a plane to Pittsburgh tomorrow because we need you on the 26th against the Penguins," Carrière says.

Marty is in shock. He's still 18 and hasn't even signed a contract. He calls his agent, who explains that this is called an amateur tryout. He'll probably be there to back up for a couple of games, then head straight back to junior.

So on Christmas Day, Marty heads to Pittsburgh. He checks into the William Penn Hotel, down the hill from the Penguins' Mellon Arena. The Sabres aren't flying in from Buffalo until morning. They tell him the bus will pick him up at the hotel at 10 a.m. on their way to the morning skate. The teenager spends

Christmas night alone for the first time, with no clue what tomorrow will bring.

He wakes up excited and is in the lobby early, ready to meet his new teammates. Ten o'clock comes, no bus. 10:15, 10:30, 10:40 . . . nothing. Then suddenly, a man runs into the lobby.

"Marty, we called your room and you didn't answer! We need to get to the rink now!"

It's one of the Sabres' public relations staff, who has run down from the arena. The team arrived late and decided not to pick up their young goalie. They'd left messages for Marty to come to the rink, but the keener was already waiting in the lobby. (Pre-cellphone days—a communications challenge for all of us.)

So Marty sprints the few blocks uphill to the arena, lugging his bag of equipment over his shoulder. He gets there for the last few minutes of the morning skate, stays on to take a few extra shots and heads back to the room to meet the team. Except . . .

"They are all gone. The dressing room is empty," Marty says. "I'd never had a morning skate in junior. I don't know how this works, so I ask the trainer, 'What do I do now?' He tells me to go back to the hotel for my pre-game meal with the team. But when I get back, there is no one there either. They had all eaten already. So I still haven't met one guy on the Sabres, and I'm about to go play a game with them."

He heads to his hotel room, figuring he'll call his parents and watch TV before going back to the rink. No chance he's going to be able to nap before his first NHL game. Even if he's just backing up.

"I open the door to my hotel room, and it's pitch black, but I can kinda see there is somebody sleeping in the second bed. I'm like, 'Who is this stranger in my room?' I figure out pretty quick it must be a player, and I don't want to wake him. So I just lie down and stare at the ceiling. A half hour later, I hear him waking up, and he turns the light on and says, 'I'm Yuri Khmylev.'"

The veteran Russian winger doesn't speak much English, but Marty finally has a teammate to follow.

"I have no idea about anything," Marty says. "What time to get to the rink, what time any pre-game meetings are. Nothing."

When he does get to the rink, he spends a few minutes sitting in the stands, contemplating how he's gone from the devastation of getting cut from Team Canada to the elation of wearing an NHL jersey in just a couple of days. When he steps on the ice for warm-up, he still hasn't spoken to any of the Sabres coaches. He finds a place to stretch, not realizing it's right by the door where the Penguins come on. Suddenly the guys he was watching on TV two nights ago are skating past him.

"I see Petr Nedved, Larry Murphy, Jaromir Jagr, and I'm thinking, 'Is this real life?' Then there is a pause and suddenly a huge roar from the crowd. Mario Lemieux always comes out last, and as he steps on the ice, he taps my pads and says, 'Good luck, kid.' It's surreal. I've never felt so out of place."

The other Buffalo goalie dressed is Steve Shields. He is stretching right next to Marty. The Sabres players start shooting at the net, saying, "Tenders, let's go!" As in, get in the net. Well, it's the starter who takes the shots in warm-up, so Marty looks over at Shields, wondering why he's not moving. Shields looks back and says, "No, it's you! You're starting!"

Martin Biron is about to start his first NHL game against Mario, Jagr and the Penguins. And until this moment, he had no idea. "Maybe my English isn't good enough and I missed someone telling me. Now I'm a complete mess."

"I wouldn't want to be the next goalie who faces Mario and Jagr after they've been shut out."

He tries to regroup in the 15 minutes or so between warm-up and puck drop. But it's fruitless. Two minutes in, Jagr feeds Nedved for the first shot Marty faces in his NHL career.

"He has a bit of a partial breakaway and fires the simplest

shot. It's probably seventy-five miles an hour, but my head is still spinning so it feels like two hundred miles an hour to me. It goes over my glove and in. I haven't blinked and it's 1–0."

Three minutes later, the puck is behind the Sabres' net. Marty gets caught looking one way as it comes out front the other way. 2–0. "I see them celebrating and I don't even know what happened," he says.

The Penguins score twice more before the first period is over. Marty is on the bench to start the second.

"I'm a little shell-shocked," he says. "I've only been playing junior hockey a year and a half. I'd never faced guys like this."

Shields gives up two more goals in the second and it's 6–1 Pittsburgh. Sabres head coach Ted Nolan comes over to Marty before the third and says, "I'm putting you back in. I want you to get experience because you are starting again tomorrow night against Ottawa."

So much for a couple of games on the bench and back to junior. When Marty goes back in for the third, the game is essentially over. The nerves and PTSD from the first period fade. The kid finally relaxes and plays . . . great.

"When someone asks me about my NHL debut, I just say I pitched a twenty-minute shutout in the third against the Penguins, and Mario Lemieux never scored on me," Marty laughs.

This would remain one of Marty's claims to fame his entire career. Mario never scores against him. Ever.

"Jagr scored a million on me, but not 66."

The next night's game in Buffalo goes better. The Sabres still lose, 4–3, but Marty makes 30 saves. He appears in one more game in relief before being sent back to junior. It's three years before he's back in the NHL. He becomes a full-time Sabre in the 1999–2000 season and plays exactly three hundred games for them in nine years.

His final home game as a Sabre (though he doesn't know it

yet) is February 22, 2007, against the Ottawa Senators. And if his debut 11 years earlier wasn't crazy enough, Marty is about to go out with a bang. Actually, multiple bangs. To his face.

"I always wanted to get one fight in my career," he says. "I remember watching Félix Potvin beat up Ron Hextall, thinking, 'How is he doing this?' But Félix was wiry like me, so I figure if I ever get into a fight, I'm going to win too. I get into a few scrums in the AHL, try to fight Craig Billington once in the pre-season, and skate to centre ice once in Tampa to challenge John Grahame—he would have probably killed me—but a real fight never happens. Until the one I've been asked about pretty much every day of my life since."

Ottawa and Buffalo are huge rivals in 2007. The Sens would beat the Sabres in the Eastern Conference final later that spring, avenging painful previous playoff losses.

The game is intense from the outset. And five minutes into the second, Senators forward Chris Neil blindsides Sabres captain Chris Drury with a late high hit. Drury is down, blood everywhere.

"Chris Neil is a great guy, loved by everyone in Ottawa, but hated by everyone in Buffalo," Marty says. "I hate Chris Neil. And now my captain is lying on the ice, and we all know it's about to get crazy."

Drew Stafford goes after Neil immediately, and they drop the gloves. The trainer is on the ice tending to Drury. The two coaches are stoic at first, but when the replay of the hit is shown in the building, you can see all of Lindy Ruff's fuses blow at once. Full subcranial transformer explosion.

After Drury is helped off the ice and play is ready to resume, Bryan Murray puts out his skill players—a line of Jason Spezza, Dany Heatley and Mike Comrie. Ruff, smoke coming out of every visible orifice, immediately sends his tough guys over the boards— Andrew Peters, Adam Mair and Patrick Kaleta, who is playing his first NHL game. "I know at that exact moment there is going to be a brawl," Marty says. "I loosen up my glove and blocker and say to myself, 'Here we go!'"

Peters jumps Dany Heatley right off the faceoff. Mair jumps Spezza. It's on. Marty starts skating toward centre ice. One minor issue. The guy skating toward him from the other net is Ray Emery, maybe the toughest guy to have ever put on goalie pads.

"I know Ray is nuts and loves to fight, so I'm thinking my only chance is to nail him with one punch and take him down," Marty says. "And strangely, I'm thinking, 'This is going to be amazing. I'm going to win! Félix Potvin did it, and so will I!' And then as he gets closer, Ray has this big, terrifying smile on his face, and I'm wondering what I've gotten myself into."

As they come together, Marty makes a first-fight-ever mistake. He grabs Emery's left arm, leaving his right one free. "I go in like a left-handed boxer, reaching in with my right hand to grab him, and he just starts feeding me right hands. I'm trying to duck them but he just keeps nailing me in the back of the head. Now I'm down on the ice, thinking, 'What the hell am I doing messing with this guy?!' I can feel this golf ball growing on my head where he hit me."

Emery is now on top of Biron and eases up immediately. The fight is over. He's pummelled him. And at that moment, Marty—one of the smartest hockey people I've ever met—makes the most questionable statement of his career.

"Let's get up and go again, Ray!"

Emery gives him a look that says, "Wait, *I'm* supposed to be the crazy one!" Biron scrambles back to his feet, and the two prepare to square off again. But before they can, Andrew Peters charges in and grabs Emery for himself.

"I feel like I've been stood up at the dance," Marty laughs. "But I know I just got really, really lucky."

Emery wears that same grin as he and Peters exchange blows.

BIRON'S BIZARRE BUFFALO BOOKENDS

Now it's pure madness. Ruff and Murray are screaming at each other from their benches. The Buffalo crowd is in a full frenzy.

"I just watch the rest of it and pick up my gear," Marty says. "I don't even know the rules, but I guess we were the second or third fight so we get kicked out. I end up in the locker room, and all of the extra guys who didn't dress are in there. They are losing their minds telling me how awesome it was. So I just sit there in full gear eating pizza and wings the whole game, with a giant lump on my head courtesy of Ray's fist."

The Sabres win 6–5 in a shootout. Marty is hailed a Buffalo hero for taking on Emery. It turns out to be the grandest of goodbyes—his final home game as a Sabre. Four days later, he's traded to the Philadelphia Flyers.

So his Buffalo career is bookended by a bizarre debut and a brawling end.

The homes of most retired hockey players are adorned with photos of their greatest victories— hoisting the Stanley Cup, or arms in the air after a huge goal/save/win. But in the Biron basement, a huge framed photo hangs on the wall of Marty getting punched in the head by Ray Emery.

"To this day, that night is the number one thing people ask me about," he says. "It's one of those moments where there were eighteen thousand people in the rink, and two hundred thousand have told me they were there. If you listen to [Sabres legendary play-by-play voice] Rick Jeanneret's call, I do really well in the fight. He says, 'Emery and Biron are exchanging blows! They're going toe to toe!' And if you listen to the Senators' broadcast, they are like, 'Biron is getting destroyed!' Truth is, theirs is more accurate, but I like Rick's much better."

WALRUS AND WAFFLE MAN

The Artistic Comedy of George Parros

This generation knows George Parros as the guy who hands out NHL discipline. Elbow a guy in the head, George is likely calling. The previous generation knew George as a guy who handed out his own form of discipline: the bare knuckles kind. Nine NHL seasons' and 1,092 penalty minutes' worth.

But what neither generation knows, outside of friends and family, is that the Princeton grad can do other things with his hands. He's a bit of an artist.

"I always loved to draw," George says. "Just sketches and things. I still draw sometimes on long flights, just to entertain myself."

The skill came in handy during his playing days, when George was often in charge of entertainment for his entire team. He would constantly come up with games and contests to keep the boys amused (see: Touching Randy).

So on one long cross-country flight during a road trip with the Anaheim Ducks, George gets bored with the endless card games and comes up with a new challenge.

"Let's have a drawing contest," he tells his teammates. He makes this suggestion knowing a lot of hockey players have zero artistic talent without a stick in their hands. "That's what makes it so entertaining," George says, devilishly.

And so late at night, high above the earth, on a charter bound for somewhere, George rips out a bunch of pages from the notebook he travels with (both to draw on and to keep track of team fines—Fine Master is another of George's many roles on the Ducks). He distributes pens and pencils. And the Ducks start making art (loose usage of the term).

George calls out the categories: landscapes, dogs, various other animals. And while the winner is still to be determined, the loser is clear from the outset.

"It becomes apparent very quickly that Corey Perry is the worst drawer we've ever seen," George says. "He has no idea what anything looks like. There are no distinguishing features or shapes on any of his animals. Basically everything he draws looks like a snake."

Sadly for Perry, snake is not a category. George calls out his next subject: "Walrus."

Perry bears down. His pencil moves gracefully back and forth across the page. It's eerily reminiscent of da Vinci drawing *Vitruvian Man* during the first Milanese period.

Perry finishes and proudly shares his work.

"Corey's walrus is the most laughable drawing in history," George says. "He essentially draws a circle with this human face inside it. The whole team is dying. I'm like, 'Dude, there's not even any flippers or little arms on this thing.' So I try to help and draw a couple of flippers on his walrus for him. But it's not salvageable. It's a disaster."

Perry's walrus is the talk of the trip. So George decides to tuck it away in his notebook, for future abuse.

Around the same time, George is starting his own apparel line, Stache Gear, celebrating his notable facial trademark. It's a series of designer T-shirts and hats. They are sold exclusively at the Ducks' team store, with all proceeds going to two of George's favourite charities: the Childhood Leukemia Foundation and Garth Brooks's Teammates for Kids Foundation.

The clothing and hats all feature George's famous stache. Until he gets a devious idea.

"I don't tell Corey, but I take his drawing and ask them to make a T-shirt out of it."

A few days later, Ducks fans are walking around the Honda Center wearing Perry's signed walrus drawing (complete with George's added flippers) and the caption "Save the Walrus."

"It's the greatest inside joke ever," George says. "No one in the general public has any idea where it came from. It's just this bizarre "Save the Walrus" T-shirt with his atrocity of a walrus drawing on it. I think we might have even donated a little of the money raised to saving walruses."

The T-shirt sells out. That Corey Perry . . . always giving back. Even when he has no clue. "People were loving that shirt," George laughs.

The priceless Perry walrus sketch is not the only time George uses art to rib a teammate.

The Ducks are on the road in Vancouver when a hotel staff member tells the team services manager that one of the players has been eating waffles from the buffet. Apparently, they aren't included in the continental breakfasts the team has paid for.

It's hardly a scandal. The restaurant employee just wants to give the team a quiet heads-up that waffles aren't on their menu. But when George finds out, he tastes opportunity, smothered in maple syrup.

"Through rigorous investigation, I find out it's Jason Blake who ate the waffles," George says. "So I go to Blakey quietly and say, 'Listen, bud, security has you on camera stealing the waffles from the buffet and they are *not* happy. It's a problem.' And Blakey gets a little uneasy. He's upset that they are making a big deal about it. I don't think he even realized waffles weren't part of the buffet. So he's all pissed off, and it becomes a sensitive subject after that road trip. Of course, we all think it's hilarious."

So George decides it's time to bring out his artistic side again. He takes several wire coat hangers and twists them into a stick-man figure. Then he makes a trip to the grocery store and buys an abundance of frozen Eggos. "And I thread the waffles onto the stick figure and create . . . Waffle Man," George says. "I put a stick in Waffle Man's hands and hang him on the glass by our bench before practice. Blakey sees it and is just losing his shit. The guys are howling."

When I first reached out to George to ask if he'd tell me a story or two for this book, he said he'd text me some ideas as he thought of them. That way, I could remind him when we eventually get around to talking.

When you wake up one morning to a text that reads . . .

Perry drawing walrus

Waffle Man

. . . you know it's going to be a good day.

THE RIGA REDEMPTION

A Team of Canadian "Misfits"
Turn Disaster into Gold

I have this friend, Don, who loves the World Hockey Championship. He's travelled to a ton of them. Cheers hard for Canada every spring. He also likes to wager. Not big money. A few bucks here and there. And just before the 2021 Worlds in Latvia, Don sees some odds that make him ponder putting his Canadian passion on pause.

The host Latvians are 15-to-1 underdogs against Canada in the opening game of the tournament. Germany has the exact same long odds against the Canadians three days later. Those numbers feel crazy high to Don. The Worlds are often unpredictable, especially in the early games when teams have had little time together.

Don takes a hard look at Canada's roster and gets more intrigued. It isn't exactly an Olympic lineup. It never is at the Worlds. Team Canada is always picked from players who don't make the playoffs. And those selected need to be willing to give up three weeks of their summer, right after a gruelling six-month NHL season. There are always a lot of polite "Appreciate the invite but I'm going to pass" responses.

This year, especially. The planet is late in the second period of a pandemic. The NHL has just finished a bizarro regular season in a bubble (actually, it's not quite finished yet—more on that in a moment). Coming to these Worlds means a three-day quarantine in your hotel room upon arrival in Riga. And never leaving that hotel, except for games and practices.

It's a far cry from the usual player sales pitch for the Worlds: "Come play for Canada and bring your family for a vacation in Prague!" (Or wherever it is—the Worlds are always held in great European cities.)

"Nobody wanted to go," says eventual Canadian captain Adam Henrique. "When they first call me, I hem and haw for a while too. But I finally accept. We basically end up with this team of misfits."

The Misfits
Goalies: Adin Hill, Darcy Kuemper, Michael DiPietro
Defence: Braden Schneider, Jacob Bernard-Docker, Owen Power, Troy Stecher, Colin Miller, Mario Ferraro, Sean Walker
Forwards: Jaret Anderson-Dolan, Gabe Vilardi, Adam Henrique, Justin Danforth, Nick Paul, Brandon Hagel, Michael Bunting, Connor Brown, Maxime Comtois, Brandon Pirri, Nicolas Beaudin, Cole Perfetti, Liam Foudy, Andrew Mangiapane

The online comments back home when Hockey Canada announces the roster are harsh.
What a joke!
This is the best Canada can do?
Bye-Bye medal!
When Henrique gets out of his hotel quarantine and steps on the ice for the team's first practice, he wonders if the haters might be right. "It's a gong show," he says. "We can't even complete the three-man weave drill. We have a guy from Europe with ads all over his pants. I'm thinking, 'Oh my God, we could be in trouble.'"

My buddy Don decides to put together an unpatriotic parlay. He bets on both Latvia and Germany to upset Canada in regulation. Which is unheard of. And just for kicks, he tosses in a Finland win over USA, and Switzerland beating the Czechs. His $5 bet will pay $8,160.60 if it cashes.

Andrew Mangiapane has played meaningless hockey games before, but never quite like these.

The 2021 Stanley Cup playoffs have already started, and Mangy (as his teammates call him) and his Flames didn't make it. But yet, here they are, playing a trio of previously postponed regular-season games against the Vancouver Canucks. In front of no one.

"We're watching the playoffs, and then going out and playing the most meaningless games ever," Mangiapane says. "It's bizarre. We're looking at each other, wondering why we are even here. The strangest way to end the strangest season."

He can't wait to get it over with and do something he's never done before, at any level. Play for Canada. Mangiapane accepts his invitation to join the team in Latvia. He'll just be a little late. He scores the winning goal in a 6–2 Flames victory that mercifully ends the all-Canadian North Division season, then immediately jumps on a plane to Europe. He is in his hotel room, quarantining, when Canada opens the tournament against the heavy underdog hosts.

"I'm watching on my TV, eating some cheese and processed meats out of a cardboard box that they left at my door. And I'm like, 'What is going on?! We should be killing these guys!'"

Canada doesn't kill them. They don't even score. Latvia 2. Canada 0. Final.

Fans aren't allowed at the game, but afterward, hundreds of Latvians line the fence that has been put up around the arena, just to celebrate their heroes as they get on the bus.

The next day, Finland beats the United States 2–1, and Switzerland knocks off the Czechs 5–2. It's on for Don. He is three-quarters of the way to his own miracle on ice.

Mangiapane is still stuck in his room two days later when Canada loses 5–1 to the US. He's finally allowed out the next day but has to watch Canada–Germany from the press box. "Germany doesn't have their big guys either, so I figure we're fine," he says. "We weren't."

To the shock and dismay of Mangiapane, Henrique and the rest of Canada (well, except for one guy), Korbinian Holzer scores a late goal to seal a 3–1 Germany win.

Canada is 0-3. Don is 4-0. Cha-ching!

"I feel a little guilty cheering for Germany, but not eight-grand guilty," Don says. "The betting site refuses to pay me at first. They try to claim the odds were 'wildly inaccurate.' Which they were. That's exactly why I bet on them. I have to fight with them, but finally, they agree to pay up."

Don is thrilled. Henrique is despondent.

"That's the moment I say to myself, 'What the hell did I do coming here?'" he says. "I left my family. We're prisoners in this hotel. And I had been so proud to be named captain, to wear the C for my country. But now I'm thinking I'm going to be captain of the worst Canadian team ever."

TSN analyst Mike Johnson does an interview with a Swedish TV station. They ask if he is embarrassed to be Canadian. He most definitely isn't. But it's pretty clear the world is laughing at Canada.

Mangiapane is finally allowed to join the team, in their rec room at the hotel. When he walks in, it's a crisis centre. "Everyone is panicking . . . I'm panicking," he says. "There's no way I just played a bunch of meaningless games in Vancouver to come over here and play more meaningless games again because we're already out of it. But the entire team is so down, saying, 'We're done. We're finished.'"

Emotionally, maybe. Technically, no. The World Hockey Championship format is forgiving. There are 16 nations divided into two groups. The top four in each group make the quarters. So if Canada runs the table, they still have a shot at avoiding catastrophe. And it's not exactly a murderer's row ahead of them: Norway, Kazakhstan, Italy, before a tough one with Finland to finish group play.

"Everyone is pissed off—the coaches, the players, everyone," says Canadian coach Gerard Gallant. "But Mangy walks in smiling and brings some fresh energy. The schedule looks good, so we just say, 'Nothing to lose now. Let's go!'"

Canada beats Norway and Kazakhstan in its next two games, by the same 4–2 score. Hardly impressive, but Ws. A 7–1 win over Italy follows. Mangiapane is a force—four goals and three assists in the three games. Suddenly there is hope. "The mood has definitely flipped," Mangiapane says. "We start to think we might actually do this."

They still need to beat Finland to ensure a spot in the quarters. Canada leads 2–1 late, but with four minutes left, Arttu Ruotsalainen beats Darcy Kuemper to tie it. In overtime, Connor Brown finds Nick Paul in front with a wide-open net. But he can't finish. (Bookmark that.) Finland wins in a shootout.

Canada suddenly faces perhaps the strangest and most embarrassing scenario in its World Championship history. They need Kazakhstan and Latvia to lose their final games or they are out.

The Kazakhs fall to a loaded Russian team 6–0. One down. Team Canada gather in their rec room at the hotel to watch Latvia–Germany. Even if it goes to overtime, they're done.

"We're having beers with Team Great Britain, all these great guys who have regular day jobs and play hockey on the side, and we might be about to be knocked out just like them," Henrique says.

"A lot of the guys are worried the two teams are going to play for a sixty-minute tie on purpose to knock us out," Gallant says. That theory gains credence when Latvia presses hard to tie it late, trailing 2–1. But they don't score. Germany holds on. Conspiracy theory dead, Canada alive.

"The boys are celebrating, hugging each other like they just won in overtime," Gallant says. "The 0-3 start, all the negativity, it's gone. We just say to them, 'Now we have a chance to do something special.'"

Canada is rarely a significant underdog in any international hockey game. But they are in the 2021 quarter-final against Russia. Unlike the Canadians, most of the top Russian players are here. They go six and one in group play.

In the Canadian dressing room, someone brings up comments by a Russian player in the media that they have never even heard of most of the Canadians. The whole "They don't respect us, no one thinks we can win" thing is new to Canadian hockey. So they run with it. Anything for extra motivation. Not that this team really needs any.

The Russians lead 1–0 in the third when Brown feeds Henrique to tie it on the power play. Three-on-three overtime. If you've forgotten what happens next, put the book down for a moment and YouTube search some combination of the words *Stecher/Russia/Canada/Worlds/move/amazing*. They should all work. We'll wait for you, here.

[*Annoying hold music.*]

Welcome back. Holy onions, right? With no one backing him up, Stecher goes between his own legs to beat one Russian defender, fakes out another and feeds Mangiapane, who buries the winner.

"The move of his life!" Mike Johnson says on TSN, dumbfounded and definitely not embarrassed to be Canadian.

"We're celebrating and at the same time looking at each other, going, 'Where did that come from?!'" Gallant says. "We love Stech, he's a great defensive player, great shot blocker. And then out of nowhere he makes the most amazing move of the tournament and puts us in the semis."

"We're so fired up," Henrique says. "To go from that first ugly practice and those three losses to beating Russia is incredible. Mangy showing up changed everything. You could feel the chemistry building with every game. We had nothing to do except hang out with each other all day. And we all got really close."

Even the guy with the ads all over his pants, Justin Danforth, who joined Team Canada from the Kontinental Hockey League, has become a major contributor. "He works his bag off and becomes one of our best players," Henrique says.

The Misfits are suddenly two wins from gold. The 0-3 mess wiped clean. Mangiapane scores two more as they beat the Americans 4-2 in the semis, setting up a rematch with Finland in the gold medal game.

The Finns are the reigning champs and have eight players back from the team that beat Canada for gold in 2019. (The pandemic cancelled the 2020 Worlds.) They take 1-0 and 2-1 leads, but Canada comes back each time to force OT. Again. And a chance to write the greatest story in its World Championship history. The country had won 26 previous gold medals. But never one like this.

Remember that Connor Brown pass/Nick Paul empty-net overtime miss I told you to bookmark? It could have sent Canada home, had Germany not bailed them out. That would have been a shame. Because Brown and Paul have been spectacular for Canada, ever since the Riga Redemption Tour started.

And the theme of this rare Canadian Cinderella story is second chances, isn't it?

So, six and a half minutes into OT, three weeks into the "prison" hotel bubble, two weeks after being ridiculed around the hockey world, Connor and Nick decide . . . it's time to go home.

Gord Miller on TSN: *"Off the faceoff win it's Paul, along with Brown . . . Nick Paul to Connor Brown! Shoots it back across . . . They score! Nick Paul! The Golden Goal! And Canada has won the gold medal at the World Hockey Championship! Canada has authored the most unlikely story. To win the gold after losing its first three games. Down twice in the game, and this group of players who volunteered to come here . . . to be in a bubble . . . have taken home a gold medal for Canada!"*

The scene that follows is a more familiar one for Canadians. The bench empties. Gloves and helmets fly through the air. Giant pile of bodies in the corner.

"It's so surreal that we were able to pull this off," Mangiapane says. "Everyone had written us off, even when we made it to the quarters. We just said to ourselves, 'We're going to win this thing.' This was the dream, ever since I was a little kid. To wear that jersey. To win gold. To sing the anthem. But for it to happen this way? Incredible."

As captain, Henrique gets to hand the gold medals out to his teammates. "It's right at the top of the best moments of my hockey life," he says. "I still can't believe it all came together. No one expected us to do anything when the team was named. And after we lost those early games, *we* didn't expect to do anything!"

No country had ever won gold at any major international hockey event after losing four games in the tournament. Until Canada. Despite missing those first three games, Mangiapane finishes tied for the tournament scoring lead with seven goals.

"There are so many heroes," Gallant says. "Mangy showing up and changing everything. Nick and Connor—two character guys scoring that goal. Owen Power, eighteen years old, barely plays until Colin Miller breaks his arm, and then ends up being one of our best defencemen. Adam's leadership. I'm just so proud of all of them. I don't know if they'll call it a miracle. We *are* Canada. But it's our mini miracle, I guess."

───

After he won all that money betting against Canada, my buddy Don had pondered putting some of it right back *on* Canada. The odds of them winning gold after starting 0-3 were almost as long as Don's first parlay. But he didn't.

Instead, he turned his attention back to the NHL and threw $200 of his winnings on a random score for Game 7 of the Leafs–Canadiens playoff series. He had 3–1 Montreal. It hit, again. Another $8,000.

A week later, Don watches Connor Brown feed Nick Paul and goes nuts celebrating like the rest of the country. Sixteen thousand dollars richer and a gold medal for his team. Don might be the only guy who had a better tournament than Mangiapane.

BIG KO

Don Koharski on Doughnuts
and the Fight of His Life

The voice on the other end of the line is a little raspy. He has to pause, here and there, to grab a drink of water. The remnants of months of radiation for neck and tonsil cancer. But the laugh, which comes often, is unmistakable.

We've been texting for months. But he wanted to wait until he felt, and sounded, more like himself to talk. And today, Big Ko is good to go.

"My throat is still pretty raw, and I only started to eat real food a couple of weeks ago," he says. "Still have no taste buds. It's a great diet. I've never looked so good. I could ref ten more years in the NHL!"

Most who know Don Koharski call him Koho. But fellow referee Wes McCauley, who introduced us, calls him Big Ko. So he's Big Ko to me too.

It's been 16 years since he last refereed an NHL game. An entire generation knows him mostly from one 26-second clip, which still shows up regularly on *SportsCentre* Top 10 lists and *Coaches Gone Wild* shows. The 1988 standard-def WABC New York video is stamped 7 EXCLUSIVE. It shows Koharski and his officiating crew coming off the ice at the Meadowlands in New Jersey after a 6–1 Boston Bruins win over the Devils in Game 3 of the Eastern

Conference final. Devils coach Jim Schoenfeld chases Koharski down and cuts him off. Koharski stumbles to his right. The two then engage in a bleeped-out-expletive-filled back-and-forth that infamously ends with Schoenfeld yelling, "You fell, you fat pig! Have another doughnut! Have another doughnut!"

If you think it still bothers him 33 years later, you don't know Big Ko. "Do you know how much money I made on the speaking circuit from that?" He laughs.

The only real shame is that it's the only story Koharski gets asked about. He has a million more. Few bigger personalities have ever worn stripes, in any league. And after being unable to speak for months, he's ready to tell some tales.

"My favourite is about Ian Laperrière. He's playing for Colorado, and it's just a horrible game. They are losing 7–1 in the third. The opposing goalie stops the puck and freezes it, and we blow the whistle. Three solid steamboats afterward, Lappy runs the goalie. The goalie is down, the net is off the moorings. I give him a major penalty for goalie interference. Now, I have an option of calling a major or a major with a game misconduct. This one warrants the game misconduct. But I say to myself, 'If I gotta sit here and watch this horseshit hockey game for another 16 minutes, so does Lappy. He's not getting out of it. He's staying.'

"We go to a TV time out, and I'm having a drink of water. Lappy pokes his head out of the penalty box. He says, in this little French accent, 'Koho, Lappy would like to see you in his office.' Now, I love Lappy, but I'm not going into the penalty box to talk to him. He says it again. 'Koho, I would like to see you in my office.' So I skate over to humour him, and he sits back down in the box and says, "Come into my office to talk, Koho." I say, "Lappy, I am not going into your office. I'll talk to you from the door.' Finally he says, 'Koho, you make a mistake on dat call." I go, 'Lappy, the only mistake I'm making is keeping you in the game. But if I have to watch this horseshit game, so do you.' He says, 'No, no, Koho, you got da wrong guy on da goalie interference penalty.' I go, 'Lappy you came from downtown Denver to hit him! I'm supposed to throw you out. I'm saving you money.' He keeps saying, 'No, no, no, Koho.'

"So I steal a line from my old colleague Bryan Lewis. I say, 'Lappy, I'm gonna ask you a question. See that blue area around the net? If that was a pit of alligators, would you still have gone as hard as you did in there?' Lappy stares at me, thinks about it for a minute and says, 'You know, Koho, yes I would! I would go in and come out with two alligators. One for you, and one for me!' I crack up. Lappy sits back down and we finish the game."

A few years earlier, Koharski calls a game between the Avalanche and Kings. He's also doing the Kings game the next night. A massive snowstorm hits Denver, and he has no chance to make it flying commercial. The league scrambles and gets permission for him to fly on the Kings' charter right after the game.

Wayne Gretzky and the boys are relaxing up front. Koharski sits at the back, doubting the plane will ever take off.

"Then all of a sudden, the back door of the plane opens, and out go five autographed Gretzky hockey sticks," he says. "For the ground crew—probably one for the air traffic controller too. We're off the ground in eleven minutes. Pretty sure we're the last plane to leave Denver that night. That's the power of 99."

Big Ko gets to know the Great One and all the other great ones in his 32 years in the NHL. There is a photo you can find online with him and a young Sidney Crosby, smiling toward a camera at centre ice, just before an opening faceoff. It's odd, because right before a game, few players are as focused and serious as Sid.

"It's Sid's first trip to Canada," Koharski says. "He plays in Montreal and I have the game. A good friend of mine, Bob Fisher, is the Montreal Canadiens' photographer. I go to dinner with Fish the night before the game and ask if there is anything going on before the game. He tells me there is a ceremonial puck drop with

Saku Koivu. So I tell him, 'Okay, when that is over, I'm going to grab Crosby and I need you to get a picture of the two of us.' And he's like, 'How the heck are you going to do that when the game is about to start?' But I know there is always a commercial break right before puck drop on *Hockey Night in Canada*, so I have a few seconds. The two teams are lining up for the faceoff and I grab Sid by the shoulder, put my arm around him and say, 'Sid, see that guy over there with the camera? He wants to get a picture of the two future Hall of Famers from Nova Scotia. And Sid turns to me and says, 'Sure, Koho, but who is the other one?'"

Sid does stand-up! You can see the two of them smiling in the photo. "It's too bad there isn't a video, because Sid had a real belly laugh," Koharski says.

A ref might get suspended for trying that today. "I just didn't give a shit," he laughs. "Different times back then. I was a bit of a rebel. You have to communicate with the players. You need to have fun."

We eventually get around to Schoenfeld and the doughnut line. When Koharski gets to the referee's room after the incident, he's fuming. John McCauley, the NHL's director of officiating (and Wes's dad) tries to calm him down. "John was my mentor, and he just says, 'Don't worry about this. It'll go away.' But we are in there a long time before I calm down. It's after three a.m. before we leave the rink."

Schoenfeld is suspended, but the Devils are granted a temporary court injunction allowing him to be behind the bench for Game 4. The officials rally behind Koharski and stage a wildcat strike, refusing to come out of their room to work the game. It leads to the infamous Yellow Sunday, where three amateur officials do the game wearing yellow jerseys.

Koharski is back in the series for Game 7. "I would work eleven Stanley Cups, World Championships, the deciding game of the 1987 Canada Cup, but nothing has come close to the pressure I feel that night."

The game goes smoothly. The Bruins knock out Schoenfeld and the Devils. A couple of days later, Koharski receives a letter from Schoenfeld, handwritten on hotel letterhead. He still has it today.

"Schoenny apologizes, says he'd heard how upset my kids were, and how embarrassed his daughters were by what he did. It's a very nice letter."

Schoenfeld is fired by the Devils a year and a half later. He works for ESPN for a few years before being hired to coach the Washington Capitals in 1993. His first game back behind the bench, there is a familiar face in stripes.

"The papers are going crazy, with 'Schoenfeld vs. Koharski' headlines," Koharski says.

"When the anthem is over, we're just about to start the game and I hear that famous Schoenfeld whistle. I look over and he's calling me over. I shake my head, 'No, we're good Schoenny.' But he keeps calling. Ray Scapinello, who is doing the game with me, says, 'Just go over. Everyone wants to see you two on the same screen. Just give 'em what they want.' So I skate over and say, 'What's going on?' Schoenny leans over and says, 'Thanks for coming over. I bet the guys in the ESPN booth that I could get you over here. You just won me a steak dinner.' I laugh and go, 'You son of a bitch.'"

The two become buddies. When Koharski's son Jamie gets promoted to be an AHL referee in 2005, his second game is in Hartford, where Schoenfeld is now coaching. Big Ko comes on the road to watch his boy follow in his large skateprints. On the drive into Hartford, he orders Jamie to make a quick stop. "I have to grab something for Schoenny," father tells son. A few minutes later, he walks into Schoenfeld's office and drops a box of Dunkin' Donuts on his desk.

"Ko, only you would think of this," Schoenfeld laughs. He pulls a cigar out of his pocket and hands it to Big Ko. From cursing adversaries to gift exchangers. Such is hockey.

Though the two have long since put it behind them, the "Have another doughnut" line never goes away. Fans yell it at Koharski his entire career. But he prefers to dwell on the good things that came out of it (besides all the speaking gigs).

"I live on turning a negative into a positive," he says. "The security department the NHL now has started after that situation. They realized they needed security in all buildings. That's a good thing. And we got Officer Koharski, from Stan Mikita's doughnut shop in *Wayne's World!*"

The real Officer Koharski is still on the beat. He's the director of officiating for the National Lacrosse League. He kept working during his radiation. "I feel like Roger Neilson in the '70s, cutting videos, breaking down mechanics on my guys—and enjoying the hell out of it."

His cancer has a 70 percent curability rate. He's confident he will beat it. He has to. For his wife, Susan, his two sons, Kevin and Jamie, and his 10-year-old granddaughter, Lilly.

Big Ko and Little Lil go to Hockey Fights Cancer night in Tampa together in late 2024. Lilly proudly holds up her I FIGHT FOR POPPY sign.

Oh, and by the way, Big Ko never liked doughnuts. So he'll never "have another" one. No matter how often you ask.

THE SLEEP-IN SIX

A Group of Oilers Play Guilty for Glen Sather

The phone rings in Scott Thornton's room at the old Forum Hotel in Edmonton. It's the one right across from the Oilers' rink. The one the guys who get called up from the minors always stay in.

"It's a shithole," Scott says. "But you don't get a permanent place when you are up and down all the time."

The ring tone is your parents' annoying old-school rotary dial DLIIINNNGGG!!! It wakes Scott from a deep sleep. Or brief pass-out, if you want to get technical.

January 29, 1993, had been a very late night. The Oilers had a stag for soon-to-be-married teammate Brent Gilchrist at a downtown Edmonton bar. It lasted until, oh, a couple of hours ago. Scott makes sure to ask the guy at the front desk for a 6:30 a.m. wake-up call when he stumbles in. There are no handy cellphone alarms in '93. The Oilers have an 8:00 a.m. commercial flight to Buffalo for the start of a road trip. These are the pre-charter days of the NHL.

"You are completely reliant on some kid making minimum wage working the overnight shift to remember to get you up," Scott says. "It's wake-up call roulette."

Scott is groggy as he picks up the phone. He waits for that fake-friendly hotel-guy voice saying, "Good morning, Mr. Thornton. This is your wake-up call!" But the voice he hears isn't so friendly.

"Thorny, where the hell are you?!"

It's Oilers defenceman Luke Richardson. Scott and Luke had been traded to the Oilers together from the Toronto Maple Leafs and have become close friends. Luke is one of those guys who will do anything for you. He lends Scott his car to get around Edmonton when Scott gets called up from Cape Breton, the Oilers' AHL team in Nova Scotia. Unfortunately, Luke is also relying on Scott to give him a lift to the airport that morning. He was supposed to pick him up a half hour ago.

Turns out the guy at the front desk wasn't so reliable. It's 7:30. The Oilers' plane leaves in half an hour. Instant dread.

"I'm terrified," Scott says. "I'm twenty-two, and I don't want to get sent back down to the Cape. I can't miss this plane. And it can't be my fault other guys miss this plane."

Luke isn't the only Oiler who needs a ride from Scott. Louie DeBrusk, another recent Oilers call-up, is also staying at the hotel. Scott throws on clothes, grabs his bag and sprints down the hall to bang on Louie's door. Louie opens it in his underwear, bleary-eyed. Seems he didn't get the wake-up call either.

"We gotta go, Louie!" Scott says in a panic.

Luke Richardson's borrowed car screams out of the Forum parking lot at 7:35. They race to Luke's house to grab him and head to the airport. Which, if you know Edmonton, isn't close. To anything, really.

"Thorny is driving like Mario Andretti," Louie says. "My heart is pounding. I'm sweating buckets. I'm still on my entry-level deal. I can't miss this plane either. It's total panic mode."

The trio park and sprint through the airport toward their gate. Suddenly, out the terminal windows, they spot hope. It's their plane. "Holy shit, we made it!" Thornton yells out. And just as the words leave his mouth, the plane starts to taxi away.

Gate closed. Team gone. Hockey future questionable.

THE SLEEP-IN SIX

"I'm done," Scott says. "I'm going back to the minors. My career is over. The whole team out all night at a stag and the two freaking call-ups living in the hotel are the only idiots who don't wake up on time."

Well, actually...

About 20 minutes earlier, just as Scott, Louie and Luke are racing to the airport, Oilers forward Shayne Corson rolls over in bed and pries open his heavy eyes. It takes a second for the fog to clear so he can make out the numbers on his clock radio. 7:43. Wait. WTF?!

He leaps out of his bed like it's on fire.

"I did the old a.m./p.m. screw-up when I set the alarm," Shayne says. "May have been influenced by the night before." He wakes a buddy who is living with him in Edmonton. "You have to run me to the airport, right now!"

Apparently the streets of Edmonton are full of speeding, panic-stricken Oilers this morning.

"I keep yelling, 'Faster! Faster!'" Shayne says. "This is a disaster. I'm dead. Slats [Oilers general manager Glen Sather] is going to kill me."

Shayne rushes into the airport around 8:15, shirt still undone, tie thrown around his neck (the Brian Burke look, it would later come to be called). He feels like the loneliest man on the planet. Until he turns a corner and sees Scott, Luke and Louie.

"I've never been happier to see teammates," he says. "I'm saying, 'Yes, the flight is late and hasn't left yet!' And then Thorny goes, 'Not quite, dude, we missed it, and we need to get on another one.' Oh shit. This is bad. Still, I'm relieved I'm not the only idiot, and there are four of us in this mess together."

Four is also incorrect.

Moments later, in run Petr Klima and Zdeno Ciger. Suddenly, there are enough Oilers to start a game (albeit with the goalie pulled, since both Bill Ranford and Ron Tugnutt made the flight). "We're all just looking at each other, laughing, but still scared stiff about what Slats is going to do to us," Shayne says.

The Sleep-in Six are all able to get tickets on the next flight to Toronto, where they rent a van and drive the two hours to Buffalo. Sather is waiting for them at the team hotel. He calls them into a room and gives them a stern lecture.

"He calls us cowards," Scott says. "Because Gilly, the guy we had the stag for, was apparently a mess on the plane, throwing up the entire flight. And Slats says, 'That guy can make the plane, but you idiots can't?' Which is hard to argue with. So as he's saying this, I know I'm finished. I'm headed back to the Cape, and I'm never getting back up."

If he had been the only one, he might have been right. But there is strength in numbers. And though Sather is seething, he throws a bone to the boys in his doghouse. "If you play your asses off and win these next two games, I'll forget it ever happened," Sather tells them.

"We're all so relieved," Thornton says. "It's a stay of execution."

The next night, an extremely motivated Oilers team—well, at least one group of them—is trailing Buffalo late in the third when Ciger sets up Geoff Smith for a short-handed goal to tie it. They win 5–4 in overtime. The next night in Boston, Corson scores the opening goal and adds an assist as the Oilers beat the Bruins 4–3. "This is playing guilty on a whole different level," Corson laughs.

And true to Sather's word, no one is sent down. No one is suspended. No one is fined. Sather never mentions it again.

"He could have buried me," Thornton says. "Not only could he have sent me down, he could have called around the league and spread the word about what happened, and I would have been finished. But he didn't."

This isn't Hollywood. The Sleep-in Six do not go on to lead the Oilers back to Stanley Cup glory in 1993. (Though that would have really helped this chapter.) They finish second last in the Smythe Division and miss the playoffs. But they all go on to have long NHL careers. DeBrusk plays 11 seasons, Thornton 16, Richardson 22, Corson 19, Ciger 9. And Petr Klima plays 16 years. Sadly, he passed away in 2023.

The one stat all six share: None of them missed another flight.

19 TEAMS, 14 BROKEN NOSES, 2 BUNNIES

The Pro Hockey Journey of Zenon Konopka

Before he is Z, Zenon Konopka is Knopper.

That's the nickname they give him in junior with the Ottawa 67's, because they already have a Z: Jonathan Zion. So Knopper, with a silent *K*, it is. For now.

Knopper would later have a pet bunny named Hoppy. This is one of my favourite useless hockey facts. Hoppy has left us. [Moment of silence.] Replaced by another rabbit named Bun Bun. But I digress.

Knopper's nose, broken 14 times, is a twisted road map of a 16-year, 19-team odyssey through junior and pro hockey. We throw the word *journeyman* around a lot, without really pondering the journey. So let's take the entire wild ride with a beauty named Zenon...Z...Knopper.

TEAM 1: OTTAWA 67'S, OHL

Knopper is tough from the beginning. But he does much more than fight with the 67's. He's a star centre, with 73 points in 59 games his best year. He helps them win a Memorial Cup in 1999.

He adores Brian Kilrea, though the coach is relentlessly tough on him. Killer is always hardest on the ones he believes in. On one road trip through Northern Ontario, a flu bug runs through the 67's. By the time they get to Sault Ste. Marie for a Sunday afternoon game, they are down to two lines and four defencemen. Then a forward gets hurt. Five left.

"We are up 3–2 and just trying to survive," Knopper says. "I barely come off the ice. I end up playing sixteen minutes in the third period, and we hang on. So we get on the bus, and [assistant coach] Bert O'Brien says, 'That was unbelievable! I've never seen a forward play that much!' Finally, I get a compliment! Then Killer chimes in: 'That's nothing. Michael Peca played an entire third period. Never came off. So don't hurt your hand slapping your back, Knoppy.'"

So much for the compliment. Years later, Knopper ends up in Columbus, with Michael Peca. "Pecs, did you really play a whole period with the 67's?" Knopper asks.

"Yes," Peca answers, sheepishly. "I was taking long shifts. Killer was pissed. So he wouldn't let me change. Every time I came to the bench, he said, 'You want your long shifts? Stay the fuck out there!'"

Knopper shakes his head and laughs. "So when I play sixteen minutes, Killer brags about how Peca played twenty. Now I find out the only reason he played twenty is that Killer was mad and wouldn't let him come off!"

TEAM 2: WHEELING NAILERS

Knopper becomes Z when he joins his first pro team, the Wheeling Nailers in the East Coast Hockey League.

"My dad died when I was thirteen, and my mom raised me. She's a very conservative person. I finish junior and get my school financial package. I'm sure she is going to want me to go to school. But she says, 'I think you should go pro. If you don't, you'll always regret it.' So I sign with Wheeling."

Z's first pro game is in Reading, Pennsylvania, against the Nailers' rival, the Reading Royals.

"We're getting slaughtered, and I'm struggling. So I fight this lefty, and he catches me and breaks my nose for the first time," Z says. "I come back to win the fight, but we lose 7–1. I'm thinking, 'Why didn't I go to school?' I'm worried I might get cut. The trainer comes up and says, 'Broph wants to talk to you.' I'm like, 'Oh no.'"

Wheeling's coach is 70-year-old legend John Brophy. One of the toughest, occasionally craziest, coaches in hockey.

"I go see Broph, terrified, and he looks at me and says, 'You had one hell of a game, kid!' I'm like, 'I did?' And he starts showing me fighting techniques, standing up and pumping his fists, saying, 'When he does that, you come over the top like this! You're going to be great, kid!' That's the day I realize if we are losing, I have to fight."

Z racks up 230 penalty minutes in his rookie season. But it's a puck, not a punch, that takes him down. He's in front of the net on a power play, battling an opposing defenceman, when they both fall. At that exact moment, one of his teammates fires a one-timer that catches Z directly in the nose. This time it doesn't break. It shatters.

"I look down and there's this huge pool of blood," Z says. "I keep telling the trainer, 'I'm fine,' and he keeps saying, 'No, you're not.' I have a towel over my face to try to stop the bleeding. Broph comes over and I say, 'Broph, this guy says I can't finish the period.' And Broph yells at the trainer, 'Why can't he finish the period?' The trainer takes the towel off, Broph looks, and he says, 'You can't finish the period.'

"They take off the towel in the room and the doctor goes, 'Oh fuck.'"

Z goes to the hospital for surgery. The next morning, the doc says, "You can't play for a while. There's too much blood in there. You could get a clot." Z listens, but chooses not to hear. The Nailers are playing Reading again that night. He goes straight from the hospital to the morning skate. The trainer immediately asks, "What did the doctor say?"

"He says I can play as long as I wear a full mask," Z responds, lying.

He's getting fitted for a shield when the trainer grabs him. "Z, what the fuck? I just got off the phone with the doctor—he says you are out six to eight weeks!"

"No, no, he's mistaken. I'm fine if I wear the mask," Z replies, lying again.

Brophy comes over and gets in the middle of it. "He can't play, Broph. It's a liability!" the trainer keeps repeating.

"I'm fine, Broph!" Z keeps responding.

Brophy briefly ponders, then says, "Let him take warm-up and see how he feels."

Z has never worn a full bubble shield. In warm-up, it fogs up. His eyes are black and almost swollen shut. He can barely see. Still, he walks into Brophy's office after warm-up and says confidently, "I'm good to go!"

"Kid, you can't play," Brophy says. "I can't let something happen to you. You could die on the ice."

"I'll sign a waiver!" Z shoots back.

"Kid, I love you for trying, but you can't."

"Well, can I dress and sit on the bench?"

"Fine. Sit on the bench."

The game starts and the Nailers fall behind 1–0. Z is getting antsy. "Broph, put me in! I can play!" he keeps repeating.

"You're not playing," Broph barks back each time, sympathy now turning to anger.

But late in the second, with the game tied 1–1, Z turns and stares at Broph again, with black, swollen puppy dog eyes. And the coach gives in. "Fuck it, go!" Broph says. Z is over the boards in a heartbeat.

"I can't see anything, but the puck comes to me at the blue line and I throw it at the net," Z says. "It somehow goes through about forty-five guys and in, and we lead."

Alas, the Royals tie it late and win in overtime. "No way I should have played, but I love Broph for letting me," Z says. "I have a million Broph stories. He was nuts."

Case in point: The Nailers are playing a neutral-site game against Reading in Wilkesbury, Pennsylvania. They are trailing by a goal late when Brophy calls time out.

"He draws up a play, then says, 'If we don't tie it up, somebody better run their fucking goalie,'" Z says. "Well, the play doesn't work and they chip the puck out with a few seconds left. Everyone is skating out except our captain, this French defenceman, who is skating in. He slew-foots the goalie. All hell breaks loose."

The benches are next to each other, and as fights start all over the ice, the young Reading coach looks at Brophy and says, "What are you doing?"

"Fuck you!" Brophy replies and charges toward the Reading bench. He grabs a stick and starts swinging it at the coach.

"I've never seen, in my entire career, a coach as intimidating as Broph," Z says. "We get back to the room after and no one says a word. I'm a rookie. We're scared. Broph comes in and starts kicking things over and screaming, 'I hate that fucking coach! Let's get out of here!'"

Because it's a neutral-site game, there are two buses outside the rink. Broph is still fuming when he gets on the Nailers' bus. As they wait for the equipment to be loaded, he spots the opposing coach walking toward his bus.

"Broph takes off his jacket and runs off the bus," Z says. "So I follow right behind. This poor other coach is like thirty-five, forty years old, and here is this seventy-year-old guy who looks a hundred, hobbling at him, screaming, 'You said let's fight in the parking lot, so here I am!' The other coach is fed up and says, 'Okay, Broph, you really want to clear the buses and have a brawl in the arena parking lot?' And Broph says, 'No, this is between me and you. We're fucking going!' He starts throwing wild punches. It's surreal. The only other people there are parking lot attendants. Finally, it gets broken up and we all get back on the bus. And I'm thinking, 'What just happened?!'"

TEAM 3: WILKES-BARRE/ SCRANTON PENGUINS

Z gets called up to play four games in the AHL at the end of the season.

"I get one assist, but I don't fight anyone, don't really do anything," Z says. "All summer I keep thinking, 'If I get another shot, I have to make an impact.' I never want to say, 'I wish I would have' ever again. I want to say, 'Remember when.' That changes the course of my career."

TEAM 4: IDAHO STEELHEADS

After leading Wheeling in scoring, Z gets offered a deal with Utah, the farm team of the Dallas Stars. They guarantee he'll go to the Stars' camp and play at least 10 games in the AHL. But before he signs, he asks to speak to the Stars' ECHL coach in Boise, Idaho, John Olver.

"I know I'll probably end up playing in Boise a lot, so I call John and say, 'My name is Zenon Konopka. I played in Wheeling last year and missed the playoffs for the first time in my life. Winning is all that matters to me. So I have three questions: One, do we have a chance to win? Two, if I sign there, will I play a lot? Because I play better when I play. And three, I have some guys from junior I'd like to bring with me.'"

Olver has zero clue who Z is. But he promises to call him back after he does some research. An hour late, Z's phone rings. "I have your answers," Olver says. "One, we have a chance to win. Two, you are going to play a lot. And three, if you have guys that can help us win, I'll bring them in." Z signs.

That summer, he visits a horse farm near Niagara Falls.

"I grew up on a fruit farm in Niagara, and I've never been on a horse in my life. But we go over to the track, and they ask if I want to cool down one of the racehorses after it runs. I say, 'Sure, how do you do that?' They tell me you just get on it and walk it around slowly. Well, I do it. And I like it."

Z asks if he can come back and cool down the horses again the next day.

"This time I ask, 'How do you get the horse to go faster?' They say, 'No, no, these are racehorses. You don't want to do that.' But I keep pushing and they finally say, "Just squeeze your legs.'"

You've probably figured out the next scene. Z gets on this racehorse, in a T-shirt and shorts, and starts cooling it down. Soon he's bored. So he gives it a little squeeze. Nothing happens. He squeezes a little harder. Suddenly, the horse takes off at full speed, with Z holding on for dear life.

"I don't know what to do," he says. "I remember there is a safety mechanism on the stirrups, so if you fall off, you won't get dragged. But I guess I put too much pressure on the stirrup. It breaks and I go flying."

Everyone runs out to see if Z's alive. As he's on the ground, trying to figure out which body parts hurt the most, one of the track owners says, "You gotta get back on that horse."

"What the ... what?" Z says.

"If you don't get back on now, you'll never get on a horse again."

So Z staggers to his feet and climbs back on the horse. No squeezing this time. When he gets off, he's a mess. His ankle and thumb are in agony. They take him straight to the hospital. Nothing is broken, but he is far from okay.

Summer comes and goes, and Z's ankle refuses to get better. Soon it's September, time for the Stars' camp, and he can't skate. He gets called into the office of Brian Poile, the GM of Dallas's AHL team in Utah (and son of long-time Nashville GM David Poile).

"He tells me because it was a non-hockey injury, they are going to have to void my contract. Unless the Boise coach wants me."

That coach is John Olver, the same guy Z called before he signed. Olver wants him. Z is off to Idaho, in a walking boot. It's November before he's feeling better. Just before he's set to return, Olver calls him into his office. "We have a chance to get one of your buddies from Ottawa, Lance Galbraith," Olver says.

"Get him!" Z says. "He's awesome."

An hour later, Olver calls Z back in. "I've called ten people about Galbraith, and ten out of ten say, 'Do not touch this guy.'"

"Coach, trust me," Z fires back. "I won two championships with Lance in Ottawa. Get him."

He does. "Coach goes against everyone he talked to and trusts me," Z says. "I haven't played a single game for this guy, and he believes in me."

From the moment Z and Lance get on the ice together, they light it up. So much so that Z gets called up by the AHL team in Utah, where he stays for the rest of the regular season, racking up 198 penalty minutes in 43 games. Including five he'd rather have avoided.

TEAM 5: UTAH GRIZZLIES

The Grizzlies are playing in Houston one night, and Z gets in two separate fights with a guy named Erik Reitz. At the end of the second scrap, the two are down on the ice. Z claims Reitz scratches his face, leaving him leaking all over the place. Utah coach Don Hay tells Z he's going to get Reitz suspended, but Z wants no part of that. The two teams play again the next night. He'll take care of it himself.

On the first shift, Z goes right after Reitz, but a giant hand grabs him from behind.

He hadn't realized another Houston tough guy had been put out to protect Reitz.

"You're not fighting him. You're fighting me," says Derek Boogaard.

At this point in his career, Z has too much bravado to be scared. "Let's go, big boy," he says.

"I get a good grip on him, but he's six-foot-eight, so he can still hit me. And he keeps hitting me until he's tired. I go to the box, and it's the only time in my career that I am seeing stars. It feels like thirty seconds later the guy in the box tells me my five minutes are up. I have no concept of time."

When he goes into the room after the period, Z heads straight to the shower in his gear. Running his head under water is his only idea to clear the cobwebs. Grizzlies captain Jarrod Skalde comes in and says, "Z, what are you doing? You are showering with your equipment on. You're concussed—you can't play anymore."

Coach Don Hay agrees. But just like he did with Brophy, Z begs to sit on the bench, then begs to go back in. "If I don't finish the game, Boogaard wins," he tells Hay. Hay lets him finish the game.

"By the way, I don't recommend this to anyone," Z says. "Different time. Dumb move."

As the end of the season nears, it's clear Utah isn't going to make the playoffs. So Z does something few players ever do. He goes to Hay and asks to be sent down to Boise, so he can play with Lance in the playoffs. Hay's son is also on the Steelheads.

"Z, I'm not sending you down," Hay says. "If you want to be in the NHL someday, it looks better that you finish the season as an AHL player."

"But if I go down, I can help them win," Z says.

"Z, my kid is on the team. I wish you were right, but you aren't going to win."

But Z insists. So Hay sends him down. And Z, Lance, Hay's son, Coach Olver and the Idaho Steelheads proceed to upset four higher seeds in a row to win the 2004 ECHL championship.

"And that's what gets me out of that league for good," Z says.

TEAM 6: CINCINNATI MIGHTY DUCKS

The championship run in Idaho gets Z a deal with Anaheim, to play with their AHL farm team in Cincinnati. At the Ducks' camp, they give him number 66. "Never a good sign," Z says. "You know you are deep on the depth chart when they give you sixty-six. Guys are yelling, 'Hey, Mario!' I'm like, 'Why did they do me like this?'"

The timing isn't great for his first full-time shot in the American Hockey League. The 2004–05 lockout is on, and a bunch of NHL guys are playing in the minors.

"I'm not sure I'm going to make the team," Z says. "But I do, and then a bunch of centremen get hurt. They put me on a line with Joffrey Lupul, who is struggling. But our first game together, he scores. The next game, he scores again. When the other centremen get healthy, Lupul tells the coach, 'I want to keep playing with Z.' So we play the rest of the year together. It's the first time I show people I'm not just a fighter. I can play."

Near the end of January 2005, there are rumours the lockout is about to end. Michael Holmqvist, the third member of Z's line, comes up and says, "Get your suits cleaned, we're going to the NHL! I just talked to my agent, and when the lockout ends, they are calling our whole line up to Anaheim."

Z is in shock. His hockey dream never really got past the AHL. Now he's going to the Show. Except the lockout doesn't end. And he plays out the year in Cincinnati.

Ducks coach Mike Babcock sometimes comes down to watch Cincinnati play. One day, he says, "Z, I need to talk to you." The two go sit in the stands.

"I heard a couple of things about you and need to find out if they are true," Babcock says with a stern face.

"I'm shitting my pants," Z says. "What did I do? What does he know?"

"I hear you go to the children's hospital more than all the

other guys on the team combined. Is that true?" Babcock says. Instant relief. "Yeah, I guess so," Z tells him.

"That's awesome," Babcock replies. "Keep it up, and keep up what you're doing on the ice."

Z feels great. The Ducks' coach is a fan. Maybe the NHL really is just around the corner. But at the end of the season, Babcock leaves Anaheim for Detroit. Back to square one.

TEAM 7: PORTLAND PIRATES

The next year, the Ducks' AHL affiliate moves to Portland. But Z almost never gets there. He is close to making Anaheim's roster.

"I'm rooming with Chris Kunitz, and the last day we're brought separately into this big boardroom with Brian Burke and all the executives. I go first, and they say to me, 'Z, you played great. You just need to work on your skating, but you are going to get there.' And they cut me. Then Kunitz goes in and he gets cut too. When he gets back to our hotel room, he says, 'What did they say to you?' I tell him they told me to work on my skating. And he says, 'They told me I didn't want it enough.' He starts getting emotional. 'What am I supposed to tell my kids one day? That I didn't make the NHL because I didn't want it enough?' He's this close to giving up and going to play in Europe."

Kunitz gets picked up by Atlanta on waivers, plays two games there and is reclaimed by Anaheim. He plays five games in Portland before a Ducks winger gets hurt and he gets called up. The guy who didn't want it enough goes on to play 1,022 NHL games and wins . . . everything. "I still tell kids his story all the time," Z says. "From tears in our hotel room to four Stanley Cups and an Olympic gold medal. Never quit."

Z has a great half season with Portland, 44 points in 34 games. But it's cut short, when the call from California finally comes.

TEAM 8: ANAHEIM MIGHTY DUCKS

Corey Perry and Ryan Getzlaf are two of the greatest Anaheim Ducks ever. But in their rookie season, 2005–06, they both get sent down to Portland. The two forwards called up to replace them are Dustin Penner and a scrappy centre named Zenon Konopka.

In his first 23 NHL games, Z scores four goals and gets in a bunch of fights. But soon Getzlaf and Perry are back and he's in the press box. Ducks coach Randy Carlyle calls him into his office.

"Z, I'd love to keep you, but here are my four centres: Todd Marchant, Sammy Pahlsson, Andy McDonald and Ryan Getzlaf. You ever play wing?" This time, Z can't bring himself to lie. He has never played a shift on the wing in his life.

"I have to send you down," Carlyle says. "But I'm going to bring you up in two weeks for our game in Boston. The rookie party is the next night in Ottawa. You deserve to be there."

When Z gets to Boston two weeks later, he sees Teemu Selanne, one of his all-time favourite teammates, who is questionable for the game with a groin injury.

"Z! Are you in tonight?" Selanne says.

"I think it depends on you," Z replies.

"What? Well, I don't need to play. You play!" Selanne says, and then tells the trainer he's out.

In the Bruins game, one of the rarest plays in hockey history happens: a Scott Niedermayer mistake.

"Scott gets caught up ice for one of about three times in his career," Z says. "I'm back-checking, and Patrice Bergeron feathers a puck across. I dive to try to get it and crash into the boards. High ankle sprain. Back in a walking boot."

Near the end of the season, as he's almost set to return, Z is called into a meeting with Ducks GM Bob Murray. "This is how stupid I am," Z says. "I'm making thirty-eight grand or so, and I tell him, 'I can't help you in the NHL, but I can help them win a championship in Portland, so send me down.'"

Z has a Memorial Cup and an ECHL championship, and now he wants the trifecta. Murray obliges. True to his word, Z goes on a 23-game point streak in Portland, including the first 12 games of the playoffs. They get Getzlaf, Perry and Dustin Penner back for Game 7 of their conference final series against Hershey, but lose in double overtime.

Then Z takes another punch in the face, this time from Ducks management.

"I was leading the entire league in playoff scoring. My ankle is still a mess, I have a cracked shoulder, getting shot up every game, and then when the season is over, they qualify me for forty thousand dollars in the minors. All the top guys are getting ninety-five. That's all I want."

A Russian teammate in Portland tells Z he can make $500,000 if he goes to the KHL. When the official offer comes, he says no. "Then it's 550 . . . no, 600 . . . no, 650 . . . no, 700 . . . Hello, Russia!"

TEAM 9: TOLYATTI LADA

Z is in the middle of Tolyatti, "the hole of Russia," and has never felt so alone. "Literally no one speaks English in the entire city. I play four games, and I'm not getting paid, which apparently happens in Russia at the beginning. They want to make sure you don't go back. Sure enough, the day before the NHL season starts, the Ducks offer me my ninety-five K. I say, 'Fuck it. I'm going home.'"

TEAM 10: PORTLAND PIRATES (AGAIN)

It takes three connections from Russia to get to the Pirates' opener on time. Z picks up where he left off, leading the team in goals and points. Players start to get hurt in Anaheim. Four different forwards get called up, but not Z.

He hears Anaheim GM Brian Burke isn't happy he went to

Russia, so he's sending Z a message. This leads to a series of meetings with Burke.

"This is the single biggest regret of my career," Z says. "Burkie says teams want to trade for me, but he won't trade me to a team that will send me down. I should have told him right there that I don't want to be traded. I want to win a Cup in Anaheim. But I don't. A month later he trades me to Columbus. And they send me down to Syracuse. Of course, Anaheim wins the Cup that year.

"If we somehow won that double-overtime game in Portland, I could have won an AHL championship. Then I would have never gone to Russia, wouldn't have been traded and could have won the Stanley Cup with Anaheim. I'm pretty sure no one has a Memorial Cup, an ECHL championship, an AHL championship and a Stanley Cup. But, hey, not meant to be."

TEAM 11: SYRACUSE CRUNCH

When Z gets to Syracuse, they stink. But he looks around the room and sees the toughest team in the league with Jon Mirasty, Derek Dorsett, Tom Sestito and now . . . Zenon Konopka.

"I decide it's time to start showing how tough we are," he says. It starts in warm-up. No opposing player is allowed to come close to the red line. Z and Mirasty start playing games, skating in to touch the opponent's blue line, touch the top of their circles. They see who can go farther into enemy territory.

And the Crunch start winning. Fifteen in a row. In the middle of it, they travel to Manitoba to play back-to-back games against the Moose. "The first game, we're doing the same stuff, skating into their end during warm-up, yelling at whoever we think is tough on their team," Z says.

The morning of the second game, Z picks up the local newspaper and reads an article about a Moose player named Pierre-Cédric Labrie. It includes a quote that says, "He'll fight anybody." Z's eyebrows raise, roughly to his hairline.

During warm-up that night, Labrie skates by and Z starts beaking.

"Hey, Labrie, you're going to fight two of us," he says. "Don't worry, you don't have to fight four, just two. So pick two." Labrie isn't paying attention. So Z tells Mirasty to slash him the next time he skates by. Mirasty obliges.

"What the fuck?" Labrie says.

"You said you would fight anyone, so pick two of us," Z repeats. By this time, the teams are converging at centre ice, mayhem sensors buzzing.

"I never said that," Labrie tells Z.

"Yes, you did," Z replies. He takes off his glove, pulls out the newspaper clipping and places it at centre ice.

Moose captain Mike Keane is bewildered. "Z, you can't put a newspaper on the ice!"

Z, who has endless respect for Keane, repeats his demands. "Just showing you what he said, Keaner. So get him to pick the two of us he wants to fight."

The Crunch chase Labrie around all night, but he doesn't fight any of them. Guess he was misquoted.

TEAM 12: COLUMBUS BLUE JACKETS

After Z's two great years in Syracuse, team owner Howard Dolgon offers him a million dollars ($200,000 times five years) and a car to stay. Columbus assistant GM Chris MacFarland calls and says, "We're going to call you up for a few games just to say thank you for what you've done in Syracuse."

Z has a chance to finally settle in one place and be a pretty wealthy minor-league scrapper for the rest of his career. But Tampa Bay calls and offers a two-year deal, with the second year one-way. Meaning NHL money and a chance to be captain of their farm team in Norfolk. The journeyman moves on, again.

TEAM 13: NORFOLK ADMIRALS

Though Z will wear the C in Norfolk, he has a solid chance to make the Tampa Bay Lightning. But in a summer money tournament in Brampton (more on those later), he gets slashed and fractures his foot. He spends the last few weeks before camp training only with punching bags.

"So I fight about seventeen times in camp and exhibition games because I figure that's my only way to make the Lightning," Z says. "Coach Barry Melrose tells me, 'Just keep doing what you're doing.'"

Just before the Lightning leave to open their season in Europe, Melrose calls Z to his office. Everyone is there: Melrose, his assistant coaches and GM Brian Lawton.

"Barry says, 'Kid, you made my team.' But then he points at Lawton and says, 'But that guy won't let me keep you!' I'm like, 'Oh. Okay.' Melrose keeps going. 'You tell him whatever the fuck you want to tell him because you've earned that right. You want to call him a piece of shit? You do it! Because this is bullshit!' I keep saying, 'No, it's okay. I'm fine, Coach.' And Lawton says, 'Look, Z, we have fifteen forwards on one-way contracts. There's nothing I can do.'"

Down in Norfolk, Z makes peace with the fact he may never get back to the NHL. He's scoring, and fighting a ton with the Admirals. Still laser-focused on winning an AHL title.

But on December 10, 2008, he goes to take a nap on a game day and leaves his ringer on, which he never does. It rings.

TEAM 14: TAMPA BAY LIGHTNING

"Z, it's Julien BriseBois [Lightning assistant GM]. We're calling you up to play in Buffalo tonight."

"Whoa, that's awesome," Z replies. Buffalo is right next door to where he grew up. His family and friends can come watch him in the NHL.

Except... two problems. One, there are no direct flights from Norfolk to Buffalo. He'll need to connect through Detroit. Two, the game starts in five hours. The flight through Detroit arrives in Buffalo at 6:50. The game is at seven. "Just get to the rink as soon as you can," BriseBois says.

Z races to the airport, only to have his first flight delayed, meaning he'll have just a few minutes to make his connection. When he lands, he realizes the next flight is in a different terminal. Z sprints through the airport. Just as he arrives at the gate, exhausted, they shut the door.

"I say to the lady, 'Please, please, I have to get on this flight!' But she says, 'No chance.' Now I'm begging. 'Ma'am, this is my only shot to get back to the NHL.' She must see the desperation on my face, because she says, 'I'll call the pilot and ask him.' Somehow the pilot says yes. I get on the plane. I'm going to make it!"

But anyone who travels commercial knows making the plane is only half the battle. When Z gets to the baggage carousel in Buffalo, his equipment is nowhere to be found. He made the connector flight. His gear didn't.

Earlier in the day, when his Norfolk teammates found out Z was getting called up, they filled him in as to why. Seems the Sabres' Adam Mair beat up Tampa Bay's Steve Downie last time they played. Z is being brought up to settle the score. "I'm thinking, 'Okay, no problem, I've fought bigger guys than Mair.'"

But now he has no equipment. When he calls the Lightning's player operations guy to explain, the guy says, 'Don't worry about tonight. You're coming to Montreal with us anyway." But Z is worried about tonight. His mind goes into overdrive. He calls the Lightning guy back.

"Hey, when you say don't worry about tonight, do you mean you have someone replacing me? Or are you playing short?"

"No, we'll play short," the player op guy replies.

"Well, what if I could get a friend to bring me some gear?"

The Lightning official checks with GM Steve Yzerman, calls back and says, "Sure, go for it."

Z calls a buddy who is about his size and asks if he has his equipment in his trunk. The buddy responds, "I do. Wait, aren't you supposed to be playing in a half hour?"

"Yes," Z says. "Can you get to Buffalo right now? I need to fight Adam Mair. In your gear."

The Lightning do have some extra equipment: pants, socks, a helmet for Z. But they don't have shin pads, elbow pads, skates or a jock. So when his friend arrives, Z quickly throws together a mishmash of Lightning and beer-league-buddy gear and heads toward the bench.

The game has already started. He asked for a Mike Modano curve on the stick the Lightning are preparing for him. They hand it to him as he runs out of the room. "Wait, I'm left-handed!"

"Crap, we thought you were a righty!" They sprint off to get him a new one.

Finally, Z gets to the bench and sees head coach Rick Tocchet. "Coach, I know why I'm here. To fight Adam Mair. I'm ready."

"Don't you want a couple of shifts to warm up?" Tocchet responds. Z doesn't exactly feel comfortable in the equipment, especially his buddy's skates. So he passes. "Look, Coach, I'm more worried about being minus-two than having my nose broken for the twelfth time."

A few minutes later, Mair jumps on the ice, and Z leaps over the boards to chase him down.

"I'm not fighting you," Mair says.

"Oh yes you are. We are fucking going," Z replies. But as he reaches out, he stumbles a bit on the new skates and grabs Mair. Whistle blows. "Two minutes for interference."

"I'm an idiot," Z says to himself. The Lightning kill the penalty, and Z skates sheepishly to the bench. "Sorry, Coach, didn't mean to do that," he says.

Early in the second, the Sabres score, and Lindy Ruff puts Mair on right after the goal. Z looks at Tocchet, and the coach says, "Go."

He lines up against Mair at centre and pleads his case. "You don't know what I've been through today. We're fighting. And I hate to say this, but if you don't fight me, I have to sucker you."

Mair sighs and says, "Fine." As soon as the puck drops, they dance. Mair clocks Z right away, but he recovers and the tilt goes back and forth for a wild minute and 10 seconds.

"I think I get a misconduct and seventeen minutes," Z says. "When I finally come back to the bench, Tocchet says, 'That was awesome! You want a couple more shifts?' I say, 'No, I think I'm good!'"

Z plays a full season with the Lightning the next year (with a full set of his own gear), piling up 265 minutes in penalties. The NHL dream he thought was over a year before is now his life. He would never play another minor-league game.

TEAM 15: BRAMPTON SUMMER MONEY TOURNEY TEAM

Every summer, Z, Lance Galbraith and some of their junior buddies put a team in a summer money tournament in Brampton. A thousand dollars a team to get in. Winner gets about four grand. A few NHL players would put teams in, including Jason Spezza and brothers Chris and Anthony Stewart.

"We're playing the Stewarts in the semifinals the summer after my season in Tampa Bay," Z says. "It's getting chippy and Anthony slew foots me. I have a bad back, so I snap. Then Chris comes over and says, 'You fuck with my brother, you fuck with the whole family.' I'm about to fight him, but I realize we only have seven guys, so I can't get thrown out. So I say to Chris, 'I'll fight you at the end of the game.'"

Stewart's team scores an empty-net goal in the dying seconds, and Z and Chris meet at the faceoff circle.

"Okay, let's go!" Z says.

Stewart scoffs. "You've played one year in the NHL. I'm not going to fight you. But tell you what—if you are in the NHL this year, I'll fight you."

TEAM 16: NEW YORK ISLANDERS

Z signs with the Islanders that off-season, and six games in, they face Stewart and the Colorado Avalanche. During warm-up, Z spots Stewart and says, "Remember our deal!"

"I know, I know," Stewart says. Right off the opening faceoff, to the confusion of the play-by-play team, and likely everyone else in the building, the two drop the gloves and go for almost 90 seconds.

"I give Stewy a lot of credit for living up to the promise," Z says. "We'd play together in Buffalo later and become good buddies. I love that guy."

TEAM 17: OTTAWA SENATORS

Z's career comes full circle when he joins the Senators for the 2011–12 season, after a 307 penalty minute year on Long Island. As the Sens fight for a playoff spot down the stretch, Z keeps getting scratched.

"I'm at the point in my career where I'm embarrassed when I'm a healthy scratch," Z says. "I look back at it now and think that's crazy because you are in the NHL, but I'm miserable in the moment."

Late in the season, the Senators play New Jersey. Z catches up with his old assistant coach in Tampa, Adam Oates. He tells Oates about the shame he feels.

"Embarrassed?" Oates says. "Listen Z, you guys are going to sneak into the playoffs. You stay ready, because the playoffs will get rough and tough. They will put you in.' And he is bang on."

The Senators are the eighth seed, and play the President's

Trophy-winning New York Rangers in the first round. In the first game, the Rangers blow the Senators out and take some liberties with their star defenceman, Erik Karlsson. Z and fellow tough guy Matt Carkner are in suits in the press box. Needless to say, they both are in for Game 2.

In warm-up, Rangers defenceman Dan Boyle is doing an on-ice interview with NBC's Pierre McGuire. Z skates by and says (essentially), "Retribution game, Boyle. You are fucking dead!" The mic picks it up and Z ends up getting fined $2,500 by the NHL. (His teammates pay it.)

Boyle, for the record, lives. But Z sends a message and ends up staying in the series, playing a major role. "I get my playoff mojo back from the old days in the minors and play sixteen minutes in Game 6, and seventeen in Game 7," he says. "We lose in seven, but it feels great to be a meaningful player again in the NHL."

TEAM 18: MINNESOTA WILD

"Here's the only thing I'll say about my seventy-three games in Minnesota," Z says. "I arrive there thinking Dany Heatley is a selfish dick who only cares about scoring goals. He's the total opposite. He's the best team guy I've ever played with. He loves the game. We would just get a case of beer and watch games in my room. Just talk hockey all night. He's a great person. People need to know that if they've heard different, it's bullshit."

TEAM 19: BUFFALO SABRES

Z's back is wrecked by the time he gets to the end of what would be his final season, in Buffalo. He misses eight games in a row but doesn't want to go out on injured reserve. So he returns for the Sabres' final game, against the Islanders. When he arrives at the rink, fellow Sabres scrapper John Scott tells him the Isles have called up two fighters from the minors, Justin Johnson and Brett Gallant.

"John says, 'Z, we don't have to fight these guys.' And I say, 'John, we kinda do.'"

Sabres coach Ted Nolan walks up to the pair and says, "This kid Justin Johnson they called up is a killer, the toughest pound-for-pound man in hockey. So you guys be careful."

John Scott is fearless and will fight anyone. But Johnson is a leftie. Scott is better against righties. Z used to study how Tie Domi fought as a lefty. He figured out he could beat lefties by spinning them around continuously. So they make a plan. Z will fight Johnson. Scott will fight Gallant.

Two minutes in, a winger comes off and Scott jumps on. Z is yelling for the centre to change so he can get on, but it's too late. Johnson is on for the Isles and goes right for Scott. They square off. Plan foiled.

Scott is a mountain, but Ted Nolan was right. Johnson catches him and knocks him out. Scott stumbles back to his feet and gets to the penalty box, but he's clearly dazed. Five minutes later, Scott gets back to the bench and sits next to Z. "John, what happened to the plan?" Z says.

Scott turns to Z. "We probably should have stuck to the plan."

Z would fight Gallant later in the game. It would be the last fight and the last game of his career. Seventeen seasons (counting junior), 19 teams (if we throw in the summer money league), 14 broken noses.

He's Zenon again now. He lives in his hometown of Niagara-on-the-Lake with his wife, Brittney; his children, Christian, Zenon, Hunter and Shyloh; Nopper the Chihuahua, Chisel the rescue dog from Turks and Caicos, Puffs the hamster, Samantha the bird and, of course, Bun Bun the bunny. The journeyman is finally home.

For now, anyway. He's still grinding in the game. His new dream is to coach in the NHL. And start the journey all over again.

WINNING IS INFECTIOUS

Blake Coleman Wins Two Cups, and Almost Loses an Arm

A lot of guys say, "I'd give my left arm to win a Stanley Cup." Blake Coleman almost did.

Technically he almost gives up the arm and risks death *after* he wins the Cup. But close enough.

Both of Blake's Cup wins with the Tampa Bay Lightning are a little strange. The first comes in the COVID bubble in Alberta, when the Lightning beat the Dallas Stars and hoist the Cup in front of... no one.

"It's bizarre skating around with the Cup above your head staring at a bunch of tarps," he says.

The good part is that the team gets a full night to celebrate, all by themselves.

"That part never happens when you win the Cup so it's really cool, but after a while we kind of look around and say, what do we do now? Somehow it turns into a thirty guys in the shower slip-and-slide with the Stanley Cup. Thirty naked dudes jumping up and down, singing songs. And every couple of minutes somebody comes ripping down the middle on their bare back and ass, flying into the Cup. Every time I go to Edmonton and get in that shower, I flash back to that. I hope they cleaned that thing well."

Well, this got weird fast. And we haven't even gotten to the near limb sacrifice yet.

The second Lightning Cup win a year later is a little more normal. Despite another COVID-impacted season, there are actual fans there to see the Lightning battle the Montreal Canadiens.

Every player hurts somewhere on their body during a Cup Final. Blake is no exception. He falls on his left arm early in the series. His elbow pad had slid off slightly, so it leaves a mark and the elbow swells up. He cuts his wrist on a separate play. Neither bothers him much. Being this close to back-to-back titles is like natural Toradol.

Tampa Bay leads the series 3-1, and Game 5 1-0, as the final seconds tick down. Blake gets his stick in the way of a puck headed for the front of the Lightning net. Yanni Gourde clears it down the ice and out of danger.

Buzzer. Screams. Madness. The Lightning are repeat champions.

"I am in my gear until three or four in the morning, just pouring beer and champagne and everything else down my sweaty pads," Blake says.

It's the beginning of a four-day celebration ... okay, bender ... for Blake and his Lightning teammates. On night three, there is a team party at captain Steven Stamkos's house in Davis Islands in Tampa. There's food and live music. All the players and their wives are there. It should be one of the best nights of Blake's life. But he's woozy. And it's not from the ... boozy.

"I just start to not feel good," he says. "I notice my arm is really hot and swollen. So I go upstairs and lie down for a while. When I come back down, Sergy [Mikhail Sergachev] looks at me and my arm, and his eyes get big as saucers. He says, 'What's wrong with you? You need to get to the hospital ... now!' I'm like, 'Why?' And he goes, 'Your arm is fucked!'"

Blake and his wife, Jordan, head straight to the hospital. It turns out Dr. Sergy was right. Blake has a severe staph infection and is put on an IV and antibiotics immediately.

"We're going to need to keep you in here for a minimum of a few days to get this infection under control," the doctors tell Blake.

"Uhhh, yeah, that's not gonna work," Blake replies. "We just won the Stanley Cup, and we have our boat parade tomorrow. I've waited my whole life for this. So I'm going."

Jordan isn't so sure.

"She is definitely choosing life over Cup parade," Blake says. "But she's also like me. She doesn't want to miss a moment of something we've dreamt about for so long. So she is the one asking the doctors, 'Ummm . . . is this a live-or-die kinda thing here?'"

Doctors are trained to always consider worst-case scenarios. The next morning, they try one last time to convince Blake to stay in his hospital bed. "We don't feel good about this at all," they tell him. "But if you insist, go for a couple of hours, then get right back here. But just so you know, it could get worse. You could lose your arm. Or . . . yes . . . die."

"Worth the risk," Blake says, chuckling . . . kind of.

His arm is burning hot, swollen and beyond tender. Touching it feels like a slapshot to the nuts. But it's a Stanley Cup parade, and Blake is going to be on that boat float.

"We do the parade and it ends up at this venue with a stage and music," Blake says. "But it starts raining and turns into a giant slip-and-slide, with everyone ripping their shirts off. At one point, someone snaps a shot of Blake holding the Cup over his head. Adrenaline and beverages can make a man temporarily forget an infected elbow. A fan who sees the photo notices it and tweets at him.

"Dude, get to a hospital."

So Twitter apparently still does have a value. At least in 2021.

Because the message reminds Blake it's time to get back. When he checks in, the elbow has gotten much worse. They take him into surgery. And it's a little like the chestburster scene from Alien.

"I have this pretty gruesome video of them cutting it open, and all the crap that pours out of my arm," Blake says.

Once the alien is out, he gets stitched up and they run a PICC line to his heart. The risk is the infection will get in his blood. That's when you could lose the limb. Or . . . worse.

"The *die* word does get mentioned again," Blake says. "I don't know what the actual percentage chances are. But fortunately they test and it's not in my blood. I spend a couple of days in there, and then they send me home with three different antibiotics. I'm in bed and my wife has to come down and inject me. Meanwhile, we have a three-week-old baby at home. So, good times for Jordan."

On top of it all, he finds out he's had COVID the entire time.

But slowly, Blake gets better. He signs with Calgary that summer as a free agent. His two years in Tampa have given him two rings—and one heckuva story to tell baby Carson someday about the first few weeks of her life.

Years later the elbow is fine, though a scar remains. A lot of guys get a tattoo to commemorate a Stanley Cup win. Blake's is just a little more . . . unique.

"Kind of looks like a vagina on my elbow, but other than it, it's fairly normal."

THE MANY AWKWARD INTRODUCTIONS OF EMMA MALTAIS

A Budding Star Leaves Some Strange First Impressions

Meet Emma Maltais. I'm introducing you formally, to ensure it goes well. (Explanation forthcoming.)

So . . . this is Emma. Forward for Team Canada and the Toronto Sceptres of the Professional Women's Hockey League. She's hilarious. She overflows with energy and positivity, and lights up every room she bounces into. With the exception of the opponents she drives nuts, everyone who meets Emma loves her.

Just maybe not . . . right away.

You see Emma has this weird history of first impressions going *Saturday Night Live* skit–level wrong.

It starts at Ohio State. Emma might be the youngest player ever to commit to an NCAA program. She's 14 when she makes her unofficial visit to OSU. She stands next to LeBron James on the sidelines of the Buckeyes' football home opener. One hundred thousand fans screaming in the stands around her.

"I'm going here!" she tells her parents instantly.

She picks the Buckeyes even though their women's hockey program is a mess. "They are so bad," Emma says. "While I am there, they lose an exhibition game to a high school team that

THE MANY AWKWARD INTRODUCTIONS OF EMMA MALTAIS

I had been playing against back home in Toronto. But there is something inside me that says, 'I need to go here.'"

This is where the awkward introductions kick in. In one of her first conversations with the Buckeyes' head coach on that visit, she asks, "Do you let the players drink?"

"My mom is horrified," Emma says. "I'm in Grade 8."

The coach laughs, fortunately. Or maybe nervously. Or probably uncomfortably.

"Hey, Ohio State has this reputation of being one of the biggest party schools," Emma says. "I just want to know I can have some fun when I get there in a few years."

That coach is gone by the time Emma makes her official recruiting visit in Grade 12. The new leader of the Buckeyes is Nadine Muzerall, whom Emma has already had an awkward first encounter with. On cut-down day of Emma's first Hockey Canada camp two years earlier, Nadine is the one who knocks on her door.

"We had been talking throughout camp how she is the scariest coach there," Emma says. "When they make the last cuts, a coach comes to your room and takes you down to this big room with a long table where the GM sits and tells you if you made it or not. Nadine, who is pregnant at the time, is the one who walks me down. She doesn't crack a smile or say a word to me. I'm petrified of her." (Emma made the team, by the way.)

But now Emma is one of Ohio State's prize recruits. And when she finally makes that official visit, coach Muzerall pulls out all the stops. "She makes the whole team come to a birthday dinner for me," Emma says. "Can you imagine the veterans having to come to a dinner on a Friday night for some kid they don't even know? Oh my God, I would have killed that recruit."

It gets worse. Waaay worse. Turns out it's Emma who leaves the Buckeyes with an unexpected birthday party loot bag.

"My head is itchy during the trip and I keep scratching," Emma says. "When people ask if anything is wrong, I just say it's psoriasis. Which it isn't. But I have to come up with something, so I just make that up because I'm embarrassed."

She leaves Ohio State and flies to Saskatchewan the next day with Team Ontario for the U18 Nationals. The head scratching is getting worse. Emma keeps making jokes about it, because . . . that's what Emma does. Until the girl sitting next to her on the plane, Jessica DiGirolamo, says, "Ummm, Emmm, I think I see little black bugs jumping around your head."

"I'm freaking out," Emma says. "You are supposed to get lice when you are, like, seven! I just went to a birthday party with the entire Ohio State hockey team and flew across the country with the entire Team Ontario. How many girls have I given this to?!"

Many, apparently. On both teams. The Buckeyes need to call an emergency meeting to get all the players tested. "Worst recruit visit in the history of recruit visits," Emma says. "I'm horrified."

She figures she must have gotten the lice from a helmet she wore on a high school trip to one of those wilderness adventure camps. Doesn't matter. She still has to show up at Ohio State the next fall as "the lice girl."

Oh, and remember the drinking question she asked that other coach on her first visit in Grade 8? When Emma arrives for her freshman season, Coach Muzerall announces it will be a dry season.

"I am a goody two-shoes that year because I'm still terrified of Nadine," Emma says. "But a couple of my teammates break the rule one night while I'm out with them. Eventually Nadine finds out and we have the toughest week ever. Six a.m. skates every day. We pay a price."

So yeah. The first impressions haven't been great for Emma so far. And I'm not even going to get into the time she steals the bike from the lacrosse team party while dressed as a banana.

But the hockey side is looking up. Coach Muzerall has started to turn the program around. The Buckeyes go on an early-season run, and by the time they face the best team in the nation, Wisconsin, they are ranked fourth in the country. "And we get killed 8–0," Emma says. "It's my birthday [no lice party this time], and I'm sobbing on the bench as the Wisconsin crowd chants, "We want more!" My linemate is saying, 'Stop crying!' I have so much PTSD from that game."

But when Wisconsin returns to visit Ohio State later in the season, Emma and the Buckeyes are ready. She scores the lone goal in a 1–0 Buckeyes win in the first game. They sweep the weekend series, shocking the number one team in the nation. "Just the craziest scene," she says. "The building is erupting, and all of our parents pour into the room like we won the national championship. It's a monumental upset and it puts us on the map."

Emma won't say it herself, but she is a Buckeyes star now. Those embarrassing first impressions are all behind her. Or . . .

She starts dating Archer Brookman, a catcher on the Ohio State baseball team. His three sisters come to town for a game. Emma is going to meet them for the first time and wants to look her best.

"I'm so blond, I never really had eyebrows you could notice as a kid," Emma says. "I had someone in Toronto who would give me brows, but I didn't have anyone at Ohio State. So I go into this salon to get them laminated. I ask for light brown but I must have gotten the employee in training, because she gives me these crazy-dark black eyebrows. She also misses my brows and dyes all the skin around my eyes. I can't tell you how devastating it is. I look totally insane. I meet Archer's sisters, and the first thing I say is, 'This is not how I really look!' They are laughing their heads off."

Emma's entire life, it seems, is a rom com. The lice fiasco wasn't really her fault. Nor the horror movie eyebrows. But sometimes, these awkward first meetings are her own doing.

At 20, she makes the Canadian national team for the first time. She joins them for a Rivalry Series game against Team USA in Pittsburgh. And she's starstruck.

"My best friend and I from high school are totally obsessed with Natalie Spooner," Emma says. "She's our favourite player and we watched her on *The Amazing Race*. So I get off the bus in Pittsburgh and they are passing out key cards, and Natalie is so nice and bubbly, and she says, 'Emma, you are with me!' I freak out and text my friend, 'I'M ROOMING WITH SPOONER!!!'"

Emma tries to contain her fangirling, but it's fruitless. "In the room, I keep taking selfies with her in the background and sneaking pictures of her when she isn't looking," Emma says. "I Snapchat them to my friend for days."

When Spooner becomes a good friend, Emma confesses her creepiness. "Yeah, I knew," Spooner tells her. "But I didn't know how to tell you to stop." (Emma tells this story with multiple horrified self-aware laughs.)

It's much the same with Canadian legend Marie-Philip Poulin, whom Emma sits next to in the Team Canada room. "I don't speak to Pou the entire tournament because I'm so scared," Emma says. "But when we get to Calgary for centralization, I notice she is laughing at some of my jokes, and that makes me a little more comfortable. She ends up being one of the people who really egg me on."

One of Emma's first games with Team Canada comes at the 2021 World Championship against Russia.

"I'm on a three-on-one and I whiff on it really bad," Emma says. "I come back to the bench and I'm devastated. Pou just looks me dead in the eye and says, 'Emma, be a goldfish. You got this.' We are both big fans of *Ted Lasso*, so I know exactly what she means. She makes a lot of effort to help me early on. It's crazy—just a few years ago I was scared to say a word to her, and now we are really close."

Poulin, Spooner and all her Team Canada and Ohio State teammates say the same thing: Awkward Emma becomes Irresistible Emma quickly. Because of her quirky personality, yes, but also because she's a terrific hockey player and teammate.

In 2022, Emma plays in her first Olympics in Beijing. She's still new, playing on the fourth line with Laura Stacey and Jill Saulnier. Before the tournament, goalie coach Brad Kirkwood makes a declaration to the trio, who aren't expected to get much ice time. "If your line scores two goals, we are going to win the gold medal."

Emma and her linemates take it one step further. If they get two goals in the tournament, they will get matching 4 tattoos to honour their line.

They get those two goals in the opening game against Switzerland. "We just look at each other and say, 'Okay, I guess we are winning this thing and getting tattoos!'"

The Canadians win their first six games and lead their archrivals, the United States, 3–1, in the final minute of the gold medal game. "We are up by two and I am already celebrating on the bench," she says. "And then they score, and two of our veteran defenders, Jocelyne Larocque and Renata Fast, are staring down the bench at me. Oops!"

Canada holds on. Emma is off the bench and leaping in the pile in record time. "Just the most incredible feeling," she says.

Besides the gold medal, each player receives a cheque from the Canadian Olympic Committee. Emma's fourth line played only a couple of shifts in the gold medal game, so she can't resist doing some math for head coach Troy Ryan at the after-party. "Hey, Troy, do you know I'm the highest-paid player per shift on Team Canada?"

Ryan laughs and rolls his eyes. "I think you played one shift too many."

At least it wasn't the first time she met him. Emma Maltais has already made her first impression on Ryan, and on Canadian hockey fans. One of a star in the making. And they can't wait to get to know her better.

99 FOR A NIGHT

Sam Gagner's Unlikely Eight

"Dad, what was it like playing against Wayne Gretzky?"

Dave Gagner's young son, Sam, has always been a curious kid. He lives and breathes hockey. So as they drive to the rink together on a winter morning in the late '90s, the former NHLer is happy to feed his boy's obsession.

"Sam, one of the things that made Gretzky special is that he never stopped. He would have five points in a game and just keep pushing for more. The night he broke the record for most goals in a season, they stopped the game for a ceremony, and then he went out and scored two more."

The boy nods and stares out the window, the story stored in his young hockey mind. *Never stop. Keep pushing.*

The veteran takes a seat in his stall in the Edmonton Oilers' dressing room. He sighs and shakes his head. Another frustrating 20 minutes, in a season full of them.

"I played awful," Sam Gagner says to himself.

It's February 2, 2012. At 22, Sam is already in his fifth NHL season. It's been a tough one. He suffers a high ankle sprain in a pre-season game against Calgary and misses a month. When he returns, he struggles—just six points in his first 18 games. Now his Oilers are in a free fall, winning just seven of their last 28. A .250 win clip doesn't cut it in the National Hockey League. And tonight, they're behind again, trailing the juggernaut Chicago Blackhawks 1–0 after one.

Coach Tom Renney comes into the room right before the start of the second and shuffles the lines. Renney has to try something to get his boys going. Sam skated with Jordan Eberle and Philippe Cornet in the first. If you just muttered, "Who?" You aren't alone. This would be the second, and last, game of Cornet's NHL career. Spoiler alert: He picked a remarkable one to go out on.

"Hallsy, Ebs, Gags," Renney says as he announces the new lines. Sam isn't sure if it's pity or desperation, but somehow his miserable first period has led to a spot on a remodelled top line, with the Oilers' two best forwards, Taylor Hall and Eberle.

But before they even get a shift together, Patrick Kane feeds Patrick Sharp and it's 2–0 Chicago, 40 seconds in. "We're like, 'Oh no, here we go again,'" says Ryan Whitney, who has already suffered through two and a half long seasons as an Oiler. "We're a team going through a brutal time. And you feel like it's going to be another one of those nights."

A couple of minutes later, Gagner's new line gets pinned in its own end. A Chicago goal here and this one is probably over early. But Sam eventually finds the puck, and looks up to see Hall flying up the left side.

"I think Hallsy is just impatient because of how the game is going, so he just takes off out of the zone," Sam says.

We're broadcasting the game on TSN. Gord Miller is on the call.

"Sixteen to nine now the shots for Chicago... Long lead pass for Taylor Hall. Shoots! Scores!"

Sam's stretch pass is perfection. Hall has a step on Brent Seabrook and beats Corey Crawford. It's 2–1. The Oilers have awoken. Five minutes later, the new combo strikes again.

"*Eberle... Gagner... tries to feed it across... Leddy broke that up... back in front... Gagner scores!*"

Sam tries to feed Eberle on a two-on-one, but Nick Leddy goes down and blocks the pass, sending it right back to Sam. Crawford commits to Sam's side, but Sam holds the puck and goes wraparound. Crawford can't recover. Sam stuffs it in the open net. 2-2. That horrible first period is forgotten. A few minutes after tying it, the Oilers are at the tail end of a power play.

"*Sam Gagner comes dancing in across the line. Sam Gagner... a nifty move... a bouncing puck comes back to the line for Whitney. Ryan Whitney tees it up... scores!*"

"I think maybe if it was on the road, they may not have given an assist to me," Sam says. "Or today, the way they review everything with betting. Because as I'm making the move, Niklas Hjalmarsson gets a stick on it, then [David] Bolland tries to clear it and it goes to Whit. So two of them touched the puck. But I'm sitting on the bench and hear them announce my name as first assist. I think, 'Hey, maybe this is my night.'"

Sam, this is definitely your night. Two minutes into the third:

"*Back in front... Whitney with a shot... deflected high and wide... rebound back in front... Score! Sam Gagner's got two!*"

Crawford complains that Hall interfered with him. Today, he might have a case. Goalie interference reviews are dice rolls. But in 2012, there is no such thing as a coach's challenge. It's 4-3 Edmonton. Sam has four points. It's officially a heater. And on his next shift, he wins a faceoff in the Hawks' end to Andy Sutton.

"*Sutton busts in off the faceoff win... save made... now Barker shoots... scores! Cam Barker!... And Sam Gagner has his fifth point!*"

A career night already. But Sam is still the sidebar story to a wild game, very much in doubt. Because every time the Oilers seem in control, Chicago answers. Bolland makes it 5-4 six minutes into the third. Renney immediately sends Sam's line back on the ice.

"*Now Taylor Hall streaking in, behind Hjalmarsson. Hall...*

centres it . . . Gagner . . . scores! Hat trick, Sam Gagner! Six-point night!"

We've all wondered what it would be like to be Wayne Gretzky or Connor McDavid. To be able to score almost at will. To see the game in slow motion, while you are thinking and moving faster than everyone else. And fans like us aren't the only ones who have that fantasy. NHL players do too. They are all elite to have made it to the league, but they still dream of being that once-in-a-generation player, even for a moment. For Sam, this is that moment.

"Everyone talks about flow state or being in the zone—that third goal is it for me," Sam says. "Taylor does all the work hunting down the puck. It's on my stick, I look and see high blocker is open, and I put it there. It happens in an instant. But to me it happens so slowly. It's a feeling I've rarely had in my career. You wish you could bottle it. I wish everyone could feel what that is like."

It's 6–4 Edmonton. Sam has been in on every goal. On the bench, it starts to hit him. He hasn't had a six-point game since junior with the London Knights. He never thought he would have one in the NHL.

"At this point, we're all starting to talk about it on the bench," says Eberle.

Back in the studio, I'm on a panel with Bob McKenzie, Darren Pang and Aaron Ward. We're starting to freak out. We look up the Oilers' record for points in a game. It's Gretzky, of course, with eight. Turns out Paul Coffey shares it. But these were the high-flying '80s when it seemed every Oilers game ended 9–4. And Gretzky and Coffey are two of the best offensive players of all time. Sam has never had more than 49 points in a season. He came into this game with 18. Now he's two from the record.

As he sits on the bench, Sam remembers what Dad told him about Gretzky when he was a kid. "I'm sitting there thinking, 'What would Wayne do in this situation?'" *Never stop. Keep pushing.*

There are six minutes left when Sam gets back on the ice.

"Andy Sutton, nifty pass there . . . cross-ice pass to Eberle . . . back in front . . . Gagner scores! Four goals for Sam Gagner! He's one away from the Oiler record for points in a game!"

"The bench is going nuts, just hootin' and hollerin'," Whitney says. "This is insane! None of us have ever seen anything like it."

At a certain point history starts to feel inevitable. It's 7–4, and the lead finally feels safe. Hall and Eberle start asking teammates about the Oilers' record. Someone yells, "One more!"

The entire building roars when Sam steps back on the ice for his next shift.

Eberle back for Taylor Hall . . . a rolling puck . . . he's got Gagner with him! For the record! Back in front . . . scores! Wow! Sam Gagner has just tied a record with eight points in a game!"

Sam could have scored. He has Emery one on one, but at the last second, he spots Eberle alone with a wide-open net and slides it across to him. And into history.

He has no idea he just cost someone a million dollars. TSN is running a contest called *Safeway Score and Win*, where a viewer wins a million if someone scores five goals during a game we broadcast. "Greatest moment of my career and I cost someone a million," Sam laughs. "Sorry, whoever you are."

There is still 3:45 left, and for a brief moment back in the studio, we collectively ponder the possibility of Sam matching Darryl Sittler's all-time, and seemingly untouchable, record of 10 points in a game. On the Oilers' bench, Whitney is doing the same thing. "You start thinking, could he actually get two more?"

Alas, no. It ends 8–4. Sam Gagner's final line: four goals, four assists, instant legend. "We still all start calling him Sittler for a while after," Whitney says.

Sam is named the first, second and third star of the game. The media scrum is massive, and by the time he has answered every question, most of his teammates have already gone home. But one of his closest friends is waiting for him. It's Joey Moss, the

Oilers' long-time dressing room attendant, who was born with Down syndrome.

"Joey and I had a really special relationship," Sam says. "He just never had a bad day, always bringing positive energy to our room. We would go to movies together, and he would come sleep over at the house I shared with Andrew Cogliano and Tom Gilbert."

Sam walks in the room and he sees Joey wearing a huge grin. "I'm proud of you, buddy; you want to have a beer?" Joey says. And the two sit in the dressing room, sipping a cold one, talking about the greatest night of Sam's hockey life.

"That's the memory I'll cherish more than any other," Sam says.

When he checks his phone after, there are a thousand texts. But the first one he clicks on is from the guy whose record he just equalled.

Congratulations on your big night. —99

"So cool," Sam says. He keeps it saved on his phone for years after. Paul Coffey calls and says the same thing. Sam is still in disbelief, trying to figure out how he belongs in this club.

The last eight-point game was Mario Lemieux in 1989. And there hasn't been another since Gagner's. Just Sam, for 35 years and counting.

"I got lucky because it was a close game," he says. "I've watched Connor have five points halfway through a game a couple of times, but it's usually a blowout and he barely plays the rest. Our game was tight until the last couple of goals."

And the once-in-a-lifetime zone Sam was in isn't over. In the Oilers' next game against Detroit two nights later, he gets two goals and an assist . . . in the first period. When he skates out for the second, Detroit star Henrik Zetterberg, one of Sam's idols, skates by and says, "Hey, kid, slow down."

"It was pretty funny," Sam says. "Unfortunately, I listened to him." The three points would be it for the night. Sam returns to his "normal" production for the rest of the season. And career. He averages about a point every two games over 16 years in the NHL.

After spending his first five years in Edmonton, Sam becomes a journeyman, playing for eight different franchises over the next decade. In 2023, he returns to the Oilers and has one more magical night, scoring two goals in his return from double hip surgery. "I kind of have that same weird feeling as the Chicago game," he says. "Where everything just . . . slows down. It's a special night."

He still gets asked about the eight-point game often. If you run into him, feel free to bring it up. He doesn't mind.

And though Sam fell short of Sittler's all-time record of 10 points in a game, I realize while writing this that he may have set a record no one talks about. He was pointless in the first period against Chicago, then had three in the first against the Red Wings the next game. So Sam recorded 11 points in three consecutive periods of hockey. I email stats wizard Randy Robles from the Elias Sports Bureau, to see if this has ever been done before. He responds a few hours later.

"I can't believe I've never seen this anywhere else before. Sam Gagner is the only player in NHL history to record 11 points over three consecutive periods. There have been 23 instances of a player getting 11 points over a two-game span. I checked each of those spans to see if a player ever had 11 points over three periods . . . and Gagner is the only one."

Sam had no idea. "Oh wow, that's pretty cool," he texts when I tell him.

The stick from the Chicago game sits in his cottage north of Toronto. He's waiting for a forever home to hang it up in. Sam and his wife, Rachel, have three kids: Cooper, Beckham and Cali. They are still too young to understand what Dad did that night in Edmonton. But someday, he'll have a helluva story to tell them. The time Dad was 99 for a night.

THE WOUNDED WIZARD OF WACO

Brad Treliving's Adventures Before Running the Leafs and Flames

---

Long before he becomes the general manager of the most valuable franchise in the NHL, Brad Treliving is a big, tough defenceman who lumbers through the BCHL, WHL, ECHL, IHL and AHL.

But the most forgotten and fascinating acronym of Treliving's hockey life is the WPHL. (Which, to be clear, is not me trying to type PWHL while drunk.)

"I am nearing the end of my playing career, but thinking about playing one more season, when guys approach me about buying a team in the East Coast League," Treliving says. "But then one thing leads to another, and we put a group together to start a new league."

The Western Professional Hockey League was born in 1996 to serve the hockey hotbeds of . . . Texas and New Mexico?

Rick Kozuback, Treliving's former junior coach, believes there is untapped potential in minor-league hockey in the American southwest. He convinces Brad to partner with him, and they go all in. The original six WPHL franchises are the Central Texas Stampede, El Paso Buzzards, New Mexico Scorpions, Austin Ice Bats, Amarillo Rattlers and Waco Wizards.

The last of the six to open their inaugural season are the

Wizards. They are playing in an old six-thousand-seat rodeo barn called the Heart O' Texas Coliseum.

"All of the teams have owners, but Rick and I are running around, going to each city, helping them get started," Treliving says. "I wake up in Waco on the day of their opener and go for a run. It's really, really hot. This is October, but it's Texas. I turn on the news and they says it's going to be ninety-eight degrees with ninety-nine percent humidity. Uh oh."

When they get to the rink, you can't see the ice. Pure fog. There is no air conditioning in the Heart O' Texas. Cowboys apparently like to sweat when they rope them dogies. Brad and Rick scramble to find a refrigeration guy in Dallas to bring in several giant dehumidifiers. But they can only help so much. It's a sauna.

"I walk in for the game wearing this light blue dress shirt," Treliving says. "And in ten minutes, you could have wrung it out. It's soaked. We're like, 'Oh crap, this isn't good.'"

The crowd is equally drenched. The ice is mush. But it's opening night. The show must go on.

The Wizards' mascot is, shockingly, a wizard. Google the team logo and that's pretty much what he looks like. Superhero-sized costume, large cartoonish head. Typical mascot gear. It's night one on the job for the guy inside the wizard outfit, so he is eager to put on a show. Leaping around the stands, pointing his wand at sweat-soaked children, who are likely begging his spell to be an eternal cold shower.

The lights go out for opening night introductions. Dramatic music plays. High above the rink, the wizard is hooked up to a wire and descends dramatically toward the ice. He's waving his wand, pumping up the crowd. And then, 20 feet above centre ice, he passes out.

"He just goes totally limp," Treliving says. "I'm like, 'Oh fuck.' They lower him to the ice, and he's still not moving. Just completely out. It must have been a hundred and twenty degrees inside that costume. But the rest of the opening ceremony keeps going. There are fireworks going off, pump-up music playing and this poor wizard, lying limp at centre ice."

After a minute or so, everyone realizes this is not weird Waco performance art. The wizard is not going to suddenly rise from the dead to intimidate the visiting team.

Medics run out to help. They pop off the wizard's giant fake head, a humiliating last-resort move in mascot culture, and try to revive him. An ambulance arrives and drives onto the ice through the Zamboni entrance. The wizard is rolled onto a gurney, lifted into the ambulance and driven away.

He's fine. Just overheated, dehydrated and temporarily unable to cast spells, make potions or shoot fireballs from his wrist (mandatory wizard requirements).

As soon as the wounded wizard of Waco exits, the puck is dropped. It splashes when it lands. But somehow, they get the game in.

Despite the sweaty start, the WPHL actually . . . works. Six teams grow to 18. It eventually merges with the Central Hockey League. But there are other limp-wizard-on-a-wire-type moments.

At one point, the team in Fort Worth has to be taken over by the league. Treliving, still in his twenties, goes in to clean up the mess. One of his first tasks is payroll.

"The players get paid weekly, so I have to go to the bank to get out cash to pay them," he says. "And it's not round numbers. Some guys are making $310.75. So I have all these bills and a shitload of change. I've never really done this before, so I just line them up by number and call them in, one by one. I should be using exact change with each one of them, but I'm not. I'm just rounding up to the dollar. So eventually I get to the last guy and I've given away almost all the bills."

That last player is number 35, goalie Rob Laurie.

"I don't know what to do," Treliving says. "So I find a hockey sock, pour all the change in it, tie it up, and call him in. I say, 'Rob, thank you for your contributions to the team this week. Here is your four hundred and seventy-two dollars and forty-eight cents,' or whatever the amount was. That's when you know for sure you are in the minors. When you got paid in change. In a sock."

Twenty-five years later, Brad's highest-paid Toronto Maple Leaf, Auston Matthews, makes $13.25 million, or $509,615.39 for each week of the six-month season.

"I would need a really big sock," Treliving laughs.

THE HANGOVER

Kevin Bieksa Gets His Big Break at the Worst Possible Time

Kevin Bieksa steps on the ice and almost falls over. He's beyond wobbly. Teammates try to protect him by hiding him at the back of drill lines. They cut in front of him over and over, hoping the coaches won't notice what everyone else already has: Bieksa is hungover. Bad. Or maybe still drunk. Either way, it's about to be a really lousy day to get the break he's been waiting for his entire hockey life.

It's fall 2006. A few games into Bieksa's first full NHL season with the Vancouver Canucks. The previous year had been a nightmare. He was expected to make the Canucks roster after an outstanding year with the American Hockey League's Manitoba Moose.

"And the first day of camp, I get a high ankle sprain," Bieksa says. "Just battling with a guy in the corner, tweaked it, and it never gets better. Worst injury of my career. They send me back to Manitoba to rehab, and I am just miserable. The most depressed I've ever been in my life."

It takes months to be healthy enough to play again, but he's finally recalled by the Canucks and plays his first 39 NHL games, before rejoining the Moose for the AHL playoffs.

Bieksa starts the 2006–07 season in Vancouver as a third-pair defenceman. He's used sparingly in the first few games of the year. It's eating at him. He knows he can do much more. He just needs a chance to prove it.

Markus Naslund, whom Bieksa still calls one of the best captains he's ever played with, decides to host an early-season team party at his house. The Canucks have just returned from a season-opening four-game road trip and have two days before their home opener against San Jose. Naslund invites the entire team over, plus all the wives and girlfriends. Prime team building.

Bieksa is still one of the new guys on the Canucks and is a little nervous about the party.

"My wife, Katie, and I are still living at a hotel downtown, as I'm still not sure how solid my spot is on the roster," Bieksa says. "When we show up at the party, we don't feel like we can stand in the middle of the room and mingle with all the vets. I mean this is a team with Jovo [Ed Jovanoski], Brendan Morrison, Matt Cooke, Bert [Todd Bertuzzi]... super vets. So we say our quick hellos and go outside and find a quiet corner—my wife and I, Ryan Kesler and his wife, Josh Green and his wife. The six of us just sit outside and drink nervously."

The party is catered, and they are serving J. Lohr red wine. Lots of it. So Bieksa and his group sit quietly on the patio—chatting, sipping wine, trying to stay out of the way. At some point during the night, Naslund comes out and joins the group.

"I remember thinking, 'Wow, this is cool, the captain coming out and hanging out with the rookie guys.'" Bieksa says. "And Markus stays a while. We're having a great conversation, laughing. And the servers just constantly keep refilling the wine. At one point I start to think, 'Man, Markus has been out here a while. I wonder if he should go back in with the rest of the crowd?' And then his wife, Lotta, comes out. She's wonderful, but they have young kids and it's a school night. So Lotta says, 'Markus, it's time to go to bed. Everyone has left.'"

Wait, what? In Bieksa's wine-flooded head, he's been there for about an hour. It's actually been *five*. Five hours without once leaving his seat. Getting fed J. Lohr like it's on intravenous.

He gets up . . . and can barely walk. If he had to say his own name, it would likely come out like the Don Cherry version: "Bee-ess-ka." His captain isn't much better. Naslund walks his guests to the front door, hugs Bieksa's wife, Katie, says, "Thanks for having me," and walks out. "Markus, where are you going! You live here!" Lotta says. "They are the ones leaving!"

"That's the state we are in," Bieksa laughs.

This is foreign territory for the rookie. He doesn't drink much and takes great pride in acting like a seasoned veteran when he does. "My family can handle our booze," he says. "We aren't pukers."

Well, maybe most of the Bieksas aren't. A couple of hours later, Kevin, the black sheep Bieksa, is standing in his bathtub (not sure why he chose this over the toilet, but we make no judgments here), puking violently all over his hotel bathroom floor. Katie is left to clean up the mess after he passes out.

"Sweetest girl ever. I'll always owe her for that one," he says.

When his alarm goes off a couple of hours later, it sounds like an arena buzzer has been implanted in both ears. It slaps him upside the head with a terrifying realization: the Canucks have morning practice.

"This is the only moment of my entire career where I am a complete mess," Bieksa says. "It would never happen again. I would be a total pro for the next twelve years. But the nerves from the party led me to drink way too much. And now, I'm beyond worried. How the hell am I going to get through this practice?"

His teammates quickly realize the shape Bieksa is in (it's bad) and hide him in those drill lines. But you can't escape for an entire practice. And, it turns out, this is not going to be an ordinary skate for the young defenceman.

Coach Alain Vigneault blows his whistle. "We're going to flood the ice and then do power play and penalty kill," he yells. "And Bieksa, you're taking Sami Salo's spot on the power play."

Pardon? Here? Now? In this . . . condition?

It's the opportunity Bieksa has been waiting for since he joined the Canucks. A chance to show he can play a critical role on this team. And he's wrecked.

"I'm thinking, 'Oh my God, what am I going to do?'" Bieksa says. "I had played a ton on the power play in the minors and was waiting for this chance. Now it comes at the single worst moment. I'm screwed."

He goes into survival mode, deciding not to hold the puck for more than a second. "It's on my stick and off instantly," he says. "I'm seeing double and triple, just trying to stay upright and not make a glaring mistake."

(Naslund, by the way, somehow looks fine. Rapid detoxification is another critical captain quality, apparently.)

When it's mercifully over, Vigneault skates up and says, "You know you can hold the puck and walk the line a bit. You are supposed to be the quarterback of the power play."

But that's his only criticism. Bieksa doesn't fall down. Or barf, again. Somehow, he kind of pulls it off. And the next night, with Salo out injured, he's on the first-unit power play against San Jose.

Six minutes into the second period, Sharks forward Ryan Clowe takes a double minor. Ninety seconds into the power play, Brendan Morrison finds Jan Bulis behind the Sharks' net. Bieksa, now stone sober and ready to seize the day, jumps into the slot, takes a Bulis pass and fires it cross-body past Vesa Toskala for his first NHL goal.

"Just the most amazing feeling," Bieksa says.

Note: After the game, he does not celebrate with champagne, beer or J. Lohr.

"And that game solidifies my spot on the power play," he says.

"I go on to score forty-two points that season and have my best year ever."

As a former college free agent, Bieksa is on a two-year entry-level contract. So it's up at the end of that season. He's in a Shoppers Drug Mart in Grimsby, Ontario, in June when his agent, Kurt Overhardt, calls. "Great news! Vancouver wants to extend you for three years," Overhardt says.

"That's awesome!" Bieksa says, giddy that he's going to be an NHL player for three more seasons.

"3.75 million," Overhardt adds.

"That's great! So 1.25 a year?" Bieksa responds, ready to sign on the spot.

"No, 3.75 *per year*."

Bieksa starts laughing in the middle of the drug store. "I'm like, 'Shut up! There's no way they want to pay me that much.' Then I call my dad and say, 'Dad, the Canucks want to extend me for 3.75 million over three seasons.' And my dad says, 'That's great! So 1.25 million a year?'"

Bieksa goes on to have a stellar 13-year NHL career, captaining the Canucks power play for much of it. He still wonders if it would have happened if he hadn't survived that overlubricated practice.

"Sometimes you only get one chance in the NHL," he says. "Maybe if that doesn't happen, I get labelled a defensive defenceman, a fighter, and never get a shot on the power play. But because I get through that practice and score the next night, it happens. It could have been a disaster. Imagine if I had fallen over and disrupted practice because I had been overserved the night before? I could have been kicked off the team."

Bieksa now spends his Saturday nights on TV, as one of the best studio analysts in the sport. He still drinks red wine, by the way. Just not by the gallon. Katie has made it clear: She's not cleaning up again.

BURN THE BOATS

The University of New Brunswick Reds' Historic 43-0 Season

Make today your masterpiece.
—JOHN WOODEN

It's John Wooden who first gets Gardiner MacDougall to ponder perfection.

Gardiner—half hockey coach, half philosopher—studies the legendary UCLA basketball icon religiously. He uses Wooden's quotes, among many others, constantly. And when his University of New Brunswick Reds go undefeated though the first four months of the 2009–10 hockey season, Gardiner starts to dream of accomplishing what Wooden did four times at UCLA: an undefeated season. Sport's Holy Grail. A masterpiece.

It's a ludicrous idea, even for a powerhouse like UNB. Hockey isn't college basketball. There is no Lew Alcindor (soon to be Kareem Abdul-Jabbar) to play 42 minutes and score seven goals a game. The greatest teams in hockey history lose 25 percent of the time. Bad bounces . . . bad calls . . . getting goalied . . . there are just too many games and too much that can go wrong on any given night to be perfect.

And yet Gardiner finds himself thinking about it more and more as the wins pile up in the winter of 2010. He's already built a juggernaut in his decade at UNB, with two national championships and multiple near misses. But the possibility of perfection tantalizes.

"It creeps into your head that this is something that hasn't been done, and maybe . . . we can be the ones," he says.

By the time the Reds get to 26-0 late in the season, the road to undefeated winds its way through Gardiner's head constantly. *Two more regular-season games left. Win those, sweep the two playoff series, roll through the nationals and . . . history.*

Then, in game 27, the Reds blow a 4–2 lead to St F.X. and lose 5–4. Two weeks later, the X-Men sweep them three straight in the first round of the playoffs.

"And I tell myself, 'To heck with the perfect season!'" Gardiner says. "I make a promise I'm never going to think about it again. Ever."

He laughs as he tells this story. The 65-year-old legend with the Ned Flanders moustache and Ted Lasso positivity (he greets everyone he meets each day with "Top of the morning to you!") doesn't lament the heartbreaks. In 2011, the season after their flirtation with perfection, the Reds bounce back to win the school's third national championship. They also win in 2013, go back to back in 2016 and 2017, win again in 2019, have the dynasty briefly interrupted by COVID, then win Gardiner's eighth title in 2023.

So when the team arrives for training camp for the 2023–24 season, UNB is firmly established as the most successful university hockey program on the planet. It is the new Big Red Machine.

And despite the promise Gardiner made to himself in 2010, he's about to do dance with perfection again.

"I'm going to tell you our most important word this season."

The room is silent as Gardiner addresses his Reds for the first time. It's August 30, 2023. Day one of camp.

"It's a four-letter word," he says. "It starts with *L*. And ends with *E*. It's *love*. Because repeating as national champions is not easy. You need to love who you are and your role on this team. You need to really love the game of hockey, because I'm going to have to push you harder than you've ever been pushed. And you have to love your teammates."

All this love talk might sound a little too mushy for a rough, tough sport like hockey. Until every single Reds player you talk to uses the same word. Over and over.

"It's how much we love each other that sets UNB apart," says 2023–24 assistant captain Kade Landry. "We have the best players, yes, but we also have the best culture. The commitment of every player to getting better every single day. To love coming to the rink. To love the grind. To be selfless and play only for each other."

> *The strength of the team is the team.*
> —PHIL JACKSON

Before love comes talent. The story of the Reds' 2023–24 season is remarkable. But this is no Miracle on Ice—no group of underdog misfits out to shock the world.

When Landry says the Reds have "the best players," he isn't flexing. The team is beyond stacked. Three former Ontario Hockey League captains, who all scored 80-plus points in the O, make up their *fourth* line. St. Francis Xavier's best defenceman transfers to UNB and becomes the Reds' *eighth* defenceman. The best players in the country want to come to Fredericton.

So how exactly did the man players call GMac build a two-decade-long dynasty and a team about to chase history?

It starts with letters. Sent to recruits by this old-fashioned thing your parents used to use call "mail." And these aren't photo-copied form letters signed in bulk. They are personal, and hand-written by Gardiner. Reds goalie Sam Richard gets his first while playing for Rouyn-Noranda in the Quebec Maritimes Junior Hockey League.

"My English isn't great at the time, and Coach's handwriting isn't the best either, so it takes me a half hour to figure out what he has written," Sam says. "He just tells me they really like me and are keeping a close eye on me. I have this friend who had played there for two years, and he tells me, 'If you get a letter from UNB, you go. It's a no-brainer. If you want to play pro hockey someday, you go play for Gardiner MacDougall.'"

Besides winning, this is UNB's allure. In 2019, 20 Reds (87 percent of the team) signed AHL contracts. A ludicrous number for any school, anywhere.

"One of GMac's big selling points when I decide to come to UNB is that half of his players will play games in the AHL," says 2023–24 captain Jason Willms. "To have a shot at a championship every year, while getting an education and increasing your chance to play pro hockey . . . that's impossible to beat."

The letters Gardiner writes don't stop when you join the Reds. They come every summer. He lets each player know, in careful cursive, what they achieved the previous season and what their goals should be for the next one.

"My last one is still sitting in my room at home," says Willms. "It shows how much he cares about every one of us."

The letters are followed by phone calls. Many lasting hours.

"Other schools might take you because you are a great hockey player, and that's all that matters to them," Landry says. "GMac and I had a dozen calls that lasted an hour long when he recruited me. Four years later, I find out he had a twenty-page booklet on me. He had written down every single thing I had told him. He invests in you as a person. He got to know my parents. He knew my sister was on the women's team at Brock. He would check her scores and talk to me about her games the next day at practice. He asks constantly about my brother-in-law in school in Australia.

It's like that for every single individual on the team. That's why we want to do so much for him."

> *Consistency is the Mother of Excellence.*
> *Incremental Improvement is the Father.*
> —ROBIN SHARMA

After the letters and summer calls comes the binder. Every player gets handed one when they arrive for camp. It's full of inspirational quotes from Sharma, Wooden and countless other sports and literary figures. There are stats and history from UNB's teams from the past—a reminder of what is expected—and a manifesto for the upcoming season. "Protect. Build. Believe."

"Protect what's already been done here," Gardiner tells his team. "Build on those accomplishments. Do something new. And you can't do any of that if you don't believe."

"There are probably fifty pages of motivational stuff in that binder," Willms says. "Whenever you need a little push, you pick it up, choose a page and off you go."

Before they start beating up opponents, the Reds must first take on each other. Creating a culture of competition is another of Gardiner's principles. The fitness testing at UNB is legendary. Gardiner doesn't just want the most talented team; he demands the fittest. Results are posted everywhere around the room and gym. You can't hide from a bad beep test.

There's also the second most important trophy of the season, next to the national championship: Gardiner's University Challenge Cup (UCC). He divides the team into four groups in training camp, and for 10 days, they compete at everything. On-ice skills games during practice, football, dodgeball, kayaking . . . you name it. The grand finale is a trivia contest at a dinner at Gardiner's house in Fredericton that decides the champion.

"He's just a master at getting our competitive juices going

and bonding us before we've played a single game," Willms says. "He somehow has this way of making us work incredibly hard, but always making it fun."

> *Hard work without joy leads to drudgery or apathy.*
> *Hard work with joy leads to high performance.*
> —GARDINER MACDOUGALL

When they start playing real games in the fall of 2023, the Reds' performance is high. They blow teams away . . . 5–0, 7–1, 9–2. In one game, they score more goals (eight) than the opponent has shots (seven).

"I knew they were good, but I start saying to myself, this team is special and is at a different level than we've seen in the past," says Rob Hennigar, Gardiner's long-time assistant coach.

But there are scares too. St. F.X. and Moncton both take them to overtime in the first month of the season.

"This guy Matthew Struthers on St. F.X. gets a breakaway on us in OT but doesn't score, and we end up winning," says Landry. "I run into him the following summer, and he's still thinking about it. 'I had your streak on my stick!' he tells me."

Because of what happened in 2010, the idea of a perfect season is never mentioned by Gardiner or the players. Even as the wins start to pile up into the new year.

"As a coach, you almost start looking for a loss," says Hennigar. "Once a week I'd say to our trainer, Chris Becker, 'Becks, we're going to lose one soon.' And he would always look at me and say, "But what if we don't?'"

The media isn't exactly in a frenzy over the Reds' run. University hockey doesn't get the national attention it deserves in Canada. And in Fredericton, there just isn't much local media anymore.

"When I arrive in 2000, the *Daily Gleaner* [Fredericton's newspaper] has four sports reporters," Gardiner says. "There are feature articles on the team every weekend, and in-depth analysis of every game. There are nine pages in the sports section. Now there are no sports reporters, and the entire paper is nine pages, just three times a week. It's sad. But I suppose a small blessing in some ways that there isn't much outside pressure."

Social media is a different story. When the Reds' winning streak gets into the 20s, several accounts start to track it. Word is out around rival schools. The Reds start packing every rink they go into. When they get to 26-0 in February, there is no avoiding the parallels from 2010. It's the exact point the streak ended. And in game 27, they are facing the same rival who ended it: St. F.X.

A snowstorm is burying the East Coast, but the Keating Centre in Antigonish is still rocking. Especially when the X-Men take a 3–2 lead into the final minutes. UNB is dominating but can't buy a goal. It feels like 2010 all over again.

Except on the Reds' bench. "There are no nerves, no pressure, no griping at one another," Willms says. "Just the same message. Keep pressing. Keep pressing."

With just under three minutes left, the Reds tie it. Thirty seconds later, they take the lead. An empty-netter seals it. 27-0. "In the dressing room after, that's the moment we look at each other and say, 'We can do this. We can go undefeated,'" Willms says.

They win their final regular-season game and the first two games of their best-of-five playoff series with St. Mary's. The Reds are 30-0 as they head to Halifax for Game 3. If they lose, not only will the streak be over, they'll have to stay there for Game 4. When the players get on the bus for the drive down, Gardiner hands them each a piece of paper with a story on it. Here is a condensed version. The all caps are his.

BURN THE BOATS

In February 1519, Hernando Cortez set sail on the final leg of a voyage that was to take him from Cuba, a stopover, to the shores of the Yucatan. He commanded 11 ships, with more than 500 soldiers, 100 sailors and 16 horses, bound for Mexico to take the world's richest treasure. The precious jewels, gold, silver and sculptures sheltered on this limestone peninsula had been hoarded by the same army for 600 years.

But there was ONE MORE LEVEL OF COMMITMENT that Cortez wanted to get from his men when they arrived at that place on that last, historic day, as they lined up to march inland. Before they would be allowed to seize the treasure that no army had taken for 600 years, Cortez would speak to them.

As they listened, Cortez leaned in and said three simple words that changed everything: "BURN THE BOATS."

"Excuse me?" they must have said.

"BURN THE BOATS," he repeated. "Because if we are going home, we are going home in their boats. And he torched them. He burned his own boats, and by doing so, he raised their commitment level to new and astounding heights! And an amazing thing took place: Cortez's band took that treasure. And why did they win? The answer is very simple. They had no choice! It was "Take it or die"—no options. Their boats were burned.

This is the attitude WE must embrace in OUR hearts and minds. TONIGHT we must burn the boats.

WE ARE GOING HOME TONIGHT!

EVERY DAY in EVERY WAY, I AM . . . GETTING BETTER AND BETTER!

INVOLVED. COMMITTED. POSSESSED.

BURN THE BOATS!

Please rip this up and destroy it as you leave the bus.

"We read it and are looking at each other like, 'Holy shit,'" Landry says. "We walk off that bus ready for war. They don't have a chance. It's our best game all year." The Reds score five goals in the first 28 minutes and win 5-1. Boats burned. Treasure seized.

Of course the real bounty would have to be taken in Toronto, at the nationals. During that first team meeting back in August, when Gardiner talks about love, he also shows his team a video. He knows he has 15 players from Ontario. The video shows the old Maple Leaf Gardens, where the national final will be played, and the date: Sunday, March 17.

"We have players who had graduated early and could have left," Gardiner says. "But to win a championship at home in Ontario, that's sacred. That's something they'll remember forever. And so we remind them from day one: That is our destination."

The Reds sweep Moncton in the Atlantic final to get to Toronto. They shut out Brock (4–0) and host Toronto Metropolitan (7–0) in the quarters and semis. Counting pre-season games, UNB is now 42-0.

Toronto is 1,366 kilometres from Fredericton, but the nationals are home games for the Reds. The stands are packed with their fans and alumni, wanting to be part of perfection. The day before the final, Gardiner texts Hunter Tremblay, the best player in UNB's history, to see if he can make it. Hunter's last season was in 2010–11, when undefeated turned to eliminated in a crushing heartbeat. He lives up north in Timmins, Ontario, so Gardiner figures it's a long shot.

"You should be here," Gardiner texts. "I've got your game ticket." Early Sunday morning, Gardiner is on his daily run through the still-quiet streets of downtown Toronto when his phone buzzes. Tremblay has texted a pic of his plane ticket. He's on the 6 a.m. flight.

"When we get on the ice for warm-up, it's a sea of red, like the entire UNB family is there," Landry says. "One of our themes is that we are the pride of New Brunswick. Some people think New Brunswick is the armpit of Canada. We don't have the economy or some of the things other provinces have. But New Brunswick residents are very proud of this hockey team being the best in the country. So to have all these fans, all these alumni in the building, reminds you ... this is bigger than us. We want it for all of them."

In the first few minutes, the Reds look nervous. Behind the bench, assistant coach Hennigar definitely is. The 2007 New England Patriots—a team that won 18 straight before losing the Super Bowl—keep flashing through his mind.

"All I could think about the last couple of months of the season was, what if we go 42-0 and lose the national final? It would just be so catastrophic to everything we had done. That's why I was looking for a loss earlier. When it wouldn't have really mattered. When we would have been able to get up the next day and still be playing. But please, not the last game."

Seven minutes in, Hennigar briefly exhales. Austen Keating sets up Brady Gilmour to give the Reds a 1-0 lead over UQTR (Université du Québec à Trois-Rivieres). Eight minutes later, Keating feeds Cody Morgan to make it 2-0. That lead holds through two periods.

Before the third, Gardiner, the master motivator, enters the dressing room, contemplating the right thing to say 20 minutes before history. But what he sees leaves him temporarily speechless.

Two players have dislocated shoulders. Sam Richard, his starting goalie, who has eight straight shutout periods at the nationals, is lying in the middle of the room, bleeding. He has suffered a deep cut to his lower leg, courtesy of his own skate blade right at the end of the period.

"I'm trying to give my pep talk, and Sam is sprawled out face down on the floor as our team doctor, Denny Johnston, is trying to stitch him up," Gardiner says.

"The scene is pure chaos," Hennigar says. "We had no clue Sam was even hurt, it happened so late. The other team's room is close by, so Denny doesn't want them to see him stitching up our starting goalie. We're trying to find a room to do our video, and guys are just getting treated everywhere. Craziest between-periods scene of my career."

Gardiner tells the backup goalie, Griffen Outhouse, to be ready just in case Sam can't go. Besides that, there is no "Burn the Boats" rallying cry this time. No Herb Brooks's "Tonight, we are the greatest hockey team in the world." Just the same routine the team has done before the third period of every single game this season.

"You could be down three, down two, down one, even, or ahead. What would it be?" Gardiner asks. The players respond in unison.

"Money in the bank."

"What would it be?"

"Money in the bank!"

"What would it be?!"

"Money in the bank!!"

And like every other game, it is.

There is no doubt or drama in the final 20. The 2023–24 University of New Brunswick Reds are too good for that. Sam's stitched leg is fine. The other wounded play through the pain. Keating scores 4:34 in, and Isaac Nurse (brother of Sarah, cousin of Darnell and Kia) adds one more with 37 seconds left. Gardiner sends his captain, Willms, and the other senior players out for the final shift.

"It's me and Austen Keating and Brady Gilmour," Willms says. "We all played against each other growing up, and became brothers at UNB. We just look at each other before the faceoff, thinking, 'Holy smokes, we actually did it!'"

4-0, final. 43-0, forever.

"I had never won a championship before UNB, at any level," Willms says. "I'd always wondered what it would be like to throw your gloves up in the air and hug your teammates. When we won last year, hoisting that trophy meant everything. But this time, the trophy doesn't really matter to me. It's just the feeling of making history... with your best friends."

"No matter how many years I play hockey, no matter what level, I'll never be able to replicate this," Landry says. "This is the peak. Twenty-four brothers who would do anything for each other. Practice every day was at three o'clock, and three-quarters of our team would get there at eleven. We would spend eight hours together at the rink because there was just such joy and fun. No one wanted to leave. You talk to players from other schools and they laugh at us. They think we're in a cult. And it is. A cult of guys who love each other. And win."

Fourteen years after vowing to never ponder perfection again, Gardiner MacDougall has his masterpiece. It's also his ninth national championship in 24 years at UNB. He brings Hunter Tremblay, the star who never got his perfect season, and all the other alumni into the dressing room to celebrate with the team.

"It's so neat, seeing some guys from recent teams, some guys seventy-five years old," Gardiner says. "I just sit back and cherish the moment. Watching them all celebrate together, just so proud of our program."

> *If you always do what you've always done, you'll always get what you've always got.*
> —GARDINER MACDOUGALL

There's only one problem with perfection. Where do you go from there?

Gardiner had offers to coach elsewhere in the past but always felt like there was nothing better than making a difference at UNB. A few weeks after the win, he's named head coach of Canada's U18 team for the World Championship in Finland. Just before he leaves to head overseas, his phone rings.

It's Robert Irving, billionaire owner of the QMJHL Moncton Wildcats. He's just fired his coach, and he offers Gardiner the job on the spot. Gardiner drives down to meet Irving and tour the arena and facilities. He instantly has a good feeling. But he doesn't give Irving an answer. He needs time. So he heads to Finland and leads the best young players in the country to gold. (Going 7-0, obviously.)

When he returns, he tells Irving, "If I'm going to do this, I need to be in charge of everything hockey." No problem. Irving wants that too. On the drive home, Gardiner calls his son, Taylor, an up-and-coming NHL player agent.

"If I take this, I have to find a GM."

"Well, I'd be interested in that," Taylor replies. That seals it for Gardiner. How often do you get a chance to build a team with your son?

He retires from UNB and is introduced with Taylor in Moncton the next day. "Seventeen hours, twenty-two minutes . . . shortest retirement ever," he jokes at the news conference.

Hennigar, his trusted assistant, takes over the Reds. With the impossible task of trying to follow perfection and the greatest coaching run in Canadian university hockey history.

The Reds finally lose, in their ninth game of the 2024–25 season, after 63 straight wins. "It's a little bit of a relief," Hennigar says. "Obviously you want to win every night, but I started to feel it was more about the streak than playing the right way. So it's over. You get up, and you move on."

There may never be another team like the undefeated Reds. New rules mean Canadian Hockey League players can now go play in the NCAA. It could have a massive impact on university hockey in Canada. The players are fully aware this was a once-in-a-lifetime.

At the time of writing, captain Jason Willms is playing pro hockey in Vienna. Kade Landry plays for the Florida Everblades in the ECHL. I asked him what Gardiner and the Reds mean to him.

"Next to my dad, he's the number one mentor in my life," Kade says. "Not just hockey-wise, but just as a person. He taught me so much. I'm so grateful for my four years at UNB. I'm an Ontario kid, but when I'm done hockey I'll probably live in Fredericton for the rest of my life. It's in my blood now."

POSTSCRIPT: *UNB went on to have a terrific 28-2 season in 2024–25 but were upset by the University of Ottawa Gee Gees in the national quarter-finals.*

In his first season in Moncton, Gardiner MacDougall led the Wildcats to the Quebec Maritimes Junior Hockey League championship. They would lose to the eventual champion London Knights in the Memorial Cup semi-final. MacDougall was named Canadian Hockey League Coach of the Year.

SEVEN SHORT STORIES BY KEITH YANDLE

And a Couple More from His Sidekick, Kevin Hayes

Two of the first people I text when I start this book are Ryan Whitney and Paul Bissonnette.

I got to know both when they were guest analysts, separately, on the NHL on TSN during their playing days. Years before *Spittin' Chiclets* becomes the biggest hockey podcast on the planet. They are both key characters in the first *Beauties*. Whit tells the story of having to sit in the bathroom of Mario Lemieux's private plane en route to an All-Star Game because there aren't enough seats. Biz's chapter recounts his last fight, on two torn spaghetti-legged ACLs.

Whit and Biz have interviewed countless characters from the game on their pod. So I ask them if there is anyone obvious I missed in the first book. They respond with the same answer.

"Keith Yandle is incredible." (Eight months after their recommendation, Keith would join the *Chiclets* cast.)

It takes a few months for Keith and I to get together. Mainly because his phone breaks during his summer in Nantucket, Massachusetts, and he doesn't bother to get a new one for two months. A decision I admire greatly.

Usually if a player tells multiple stories, I'll try to weave to-

THE SNAPPING (STICKS) OF CLAUDE GIROUX
Claude Giroux has forgiven friend and teammate Brady Tkachuk for a prank that almost went horribly wrong.

BRUCE, THERE IT IS! Getting caught streaking hurt Bruce Boudreau in the NHL draft and led him to sign with the WHA's Minnesota Fighting Saints. They folded just months later.

THE BEER-LEAGUE MIRACLE Summer beer-leaguer Luke Strickland (#26 in yellow) faces off against Leon Draisaitl, with Connor McDavid on his wing. *Courtesy of Gracie Duthie*

LOST BOY Mike Johnson with his sister, Jennifer, and parents, Wendy and Ron, after his first home game with the Toronto Maple Leafs. An hour later, he would get lost en route to his first charter flight with the Leafs.

TERRY RYAN: THE MOVIE Terry Ryan (with daughter Penny-Laine) found happiness and stardom as an actor, years after being labelled a first-round NHL bust.

SHARKNADO Rick Celebrini's unique training methods helped Steve Nash get to the Basketball Hall of Fame and helped Rick's son Macklin become a budding NHL superstar.

TOUCHING RANDY Brad May (with daughter Samantha) learned how to play Touching Randy, and how to win a Stanley Cup, in Anaheim in 2007. *Courtesy of Jim Ruymen/UPI/Alamy*

THE MASKED MARVEL Fate (or a COVID test error) gave Sarah Nurse a chance to shine, and to make history, with Canada at the 2022 Olympics. *Courtesy of Dave Holland*

THE ELEPHANT AND THE MOUSE
Brendan Morrison's agent gifted him a permanent reminder of his bizarre salary arbitration hearing.

WALRUS AND WAFFLE MAN
George Parros turned Corey Perry's questionable walrus drawing into a T-shirt that would sell out in Anaheim.

BIRON'S BIZARRE BUFFALO BOOKENDS In his Buffalo home, Martin Biron proudly displays the photo of the night he got pummelled by Ray Emery. It turned out to be his final home game as a Sabre.

THE RIGA REDEMPTION Late arrival Andrew Mangiapane (left), captain Adam Henrique (middle) and Connor Brown (right) went from an 0-3 disaster to world champions in 2021.

BIG KO Don Koharski and his granddaughter, Lilly, at Hockey Fights Cancer night in Tampa.

19 TEAMS, 14 BROKEN NOSES, 2 BUNNIES After a wild hockey journey that saw him play (and fight) for 19 different teams, Zenon Konopka (with his family) is finally home.

WINNING IS INFECTIOUS Celebrating a Stanley Cup win could have cost Blake Coleman (with daughters Charlie and baby Carson) his arm . . . or worse.

THE MANY AWKWARD INTRODUCTIONS OF EMMA MALTAIS After an awkward introduction (her trademark), Emma Maltais and Natalie Spooner have become close friends.

99 FOR A NIGHT Sam Gagner's favourite memory from his historic eight-point game was celebrating with close friend Joey Moss.

THE HANGOVER Kevin Bieksa, with teammate Ryan Kesler, wisely choosing water instead of wine.

BURN THE BOATS Captain Jason Willms and the UNB Reds cap off their historic 43-0 season.

SEVEN SHORT STORIES BY KEITH YANDLE Keith Yandle and Kevin Hayes became best buddies, despite their rocky "white Wrangler" beginning.

THE HUSTLER Darcy Hordichuk captures an alligator that he would leave on Roberto Luongo's front porch.

WHEN A KILLER CALLS Goalie Kevin Weekes grows to love being an Ottawa 67 despite an intimidating first phone call from legendary coach Brian Kilrea. *Courtesy of the Ottawa 67s*

THE SHINER Frankie Corrado's "welcome to the NHL" moment was getting a black eye breaking up a fight between teammates in an elevator. *Courtesy of Jeff Vinnick*

THE CAPTAIN AND THE SWEDE Lanny McDonald, Borje Salming, Tiger Williams and Darryl Sittler, during Borje's final visit to Toronto, just two weeks before his death in 2022.

FREE MEGAN Megan Keller and teammate Amanda Kessel made it to the 2022 Olympics (barely) after a stressful few weeks in COVID hell.

BEFORE HE WAS A STAR Marty Turco had a career's worth of adventures before he played a single game with the Dallas Stars. *Courtesy of the Dallas Stars*

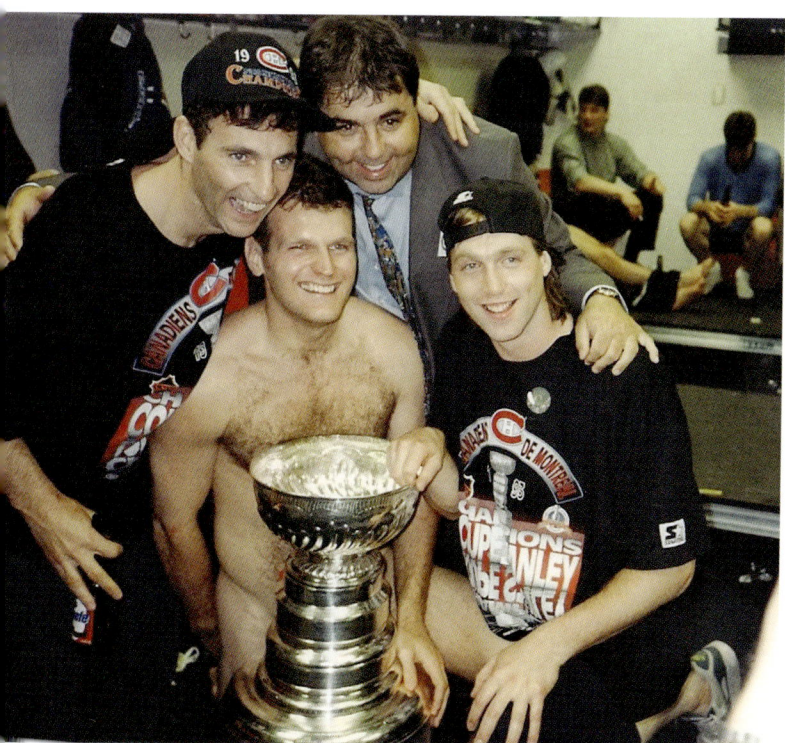

VINNIE'S PRIVATE PLANE
Vinnie Damphousse (with a well-placed Stanley Cup) lived his dream in Montreal before being traded in the sky.

HOCKEY NIGHT IN KENYA Kenya's Ice Lions dream of taking on the world.

"THE BIGGEST BUNCH OF BEAUTIES EVER ASSEMBLED" Matthew Tkachuk celebrates his first Stanley Cup win with sister Taryn and brother Brady.

gether the ones with a similar theme. But Keith's are all over the map. Thus, *Certified Beauties* proudly presents a novella within a book:

Seven Short Stories by Keith Yandle

THE OLD TOILET PAPER PRANK

I'm playing with the Coyotes, and we have a game on Halloween night. I live in the same neighbourhood as Shane Doan, Michal Rozsival, Derek Morris and [Coyotes coach] Dave Tippett. I think Don Maloney [Coyotes GM] and Brad Treliving [assistant GM] live around there as well. Doaner drives me home from the game, and as we go by Tippett's house, we see all the coaches' and management guys' cars there. Which is just an invitation to do something stupid. For whatever reason, this rental house I'm in has hundreds of rolls of toilet paper in a storeroom. So I look at Doaner and say, "Should we toilet paper Tippett's house and all their cars?" Doaner is our very responsible, mature captain. So he looks at me and says, "Absolutely."

For the next two hours, we absolutely unload toilet paper all over Tippett's house and yard. They left their cars unlocked so we demolish them too. Toilet paper everywhere. Michal Rozsival comes over and helps. A couple of other neighbours come out and help. It turns into a real community project. Doaner gets the bright idea to grab the hose to wet the paper so it sticks better. True captain leadership.

It's a gated community, so when we're done, we call the gatehouse and say, "We think we just saw some teenagers toilet papering a house!" Then we hide in the bushes and watch security pull up. All the coaches and management guys come out, looking around like, "What just happened here?"

Next day at practice, Treliving comes up and says, "So what did you do after the game last night?" I go, "Nothing really, just went to bed. I left everything I had on the ice last night, so I was exhausted." Treliving smiles and says, "Did you run out of toilet paper at your place?" I act dumb. But we break into smiles. He knows. But we don't get in any trouble. Brad and Dave and all the coaches are all good sports about it. I think they truly appreciated the effort we put in. It was a lot of toilet paper. Terrible one-ply stuff we never used anyway. We play in the National Hockey League. You have to use three-ply.

FANBOY

My rookie year with the Coyotes, Pittsburgh is playing Detroit in the Stanley Cup Final. My degenerate buddies and I rent an RV from Boston to go up for Game 6 in Pittsburgh. Most of them are still in college, so we just go to have a good time. I still love going to games. Inside the rink, there are these guys who draw caricatures of fans in Penguins jerseys. My buddy says, "Let's do that!" So between periods, the two of us sit down and the artist draws these funny pictures of us. All of a sudden Eddie Mio, the Coyotes' director of player development, walks by and sees me doing this. He looks at me like, "What the fuck are you doing? YOU ARE IN THE NHL, dude. You can't be getting a drawing of yourself in a Penguins jersey at the Stanley Cup Final!" So yeah. That's a moment I wish I had back.

NICK'S STICK

It's tough when you make the league but you are still a huge fan of guys you are now playing against. I have always loved Nick Lidstrom. So early in my career, we are playing Detroit at home. This is a time before players asked other players for autographs. Happens more often today. But back then, maybe you would ask your trainer to ask their trainer to quietly get something signed. That would be it. But I'm such a massive fan that I see Nick in the hallway before the game and I'm starstruck. I say, "Nick, would you please sign a stick for me and get it to me after the game?" Nick's the best. So he says, "For sure, no problem."

In the second period, the Wings get a penalty. I'm on the Coyotes' power play. Nick is lined up behind their centre. Their centre wins the faceoff and snaps it back. Nick goes to clear it, but he fans on it a bit, for probably the only time in his career. The puck goes right to me. Now it's just me, alone with Chris Osgood. It happens so fast, Chris doesn't really expect it, and I score. We're celebrating, going through the line, and Nick skates by me and says, "Last fucking stick I sign for you." The way he says it, I know he's just kidding. But I'm still starstruck, thinking, "I can't believe Nick Lidstrom remembers that I asked him for a stick!"

And he still gives me the stick after. Pretty freaking cool.

BJUGSTAD'S BAR TAB

I go to Nick Bjugstad's wedding in Middle of Nowhere, Wisconsin. Alex Petrovic flies in with me and my wife, Kristyn. We're all teammates on the Panthers. It's like *Planes, Trains and Automobiles* to get there. Oh, and boats too. We take this little pontoon boat out to where we are staying in the middle of a lake. It's beautiful. But it takes forever to get there. All-day trek. By the time we arrive, all we want is a beer or a glass of wine. So we dump our stuff, get changed and go to the pre-wedding party. And . . . it's not open bar. I'm pissed. This guy is making like four million dollars a year!

The place we are staying on this island is almost like camp. All the players on the team are in one house, but in different rooms. Now it's the night before the wedding. The boys are getting after it pretty good. I'm still pissed about the no open bar. So I tell my wife I'm going to steal Nick's soon-to-be-wife Jackie's wedding dress. I'm going to take the keys to the pontoon boat and hang the wedding dress on it. And then drive the boat out and leave it the middle of the lake. Well, Kristyn shuts that plan down pretty quickly. She's like, "You *cannot* steal the bride's wedding dress the night before the wedding." Which is fair.

So instead I steal Nick's suit.

You can't make me pay for drinks at your wedding, no matter how good a teammate and friend you are. I sneak in and grab his suit and take the keys to the boat. But by this point, I've had more than a few. So I'll wait until morning to take it out on the lake.

The walls are thin in this place. You can hear everything. My wife wakes up the next morning to Nick on the phone in a panic. "Hey, Uncle John! Have you left Minnesota yet? I forgot my suit and need you to go to my house and get it!"

I haven't told my wife I took the suit yet. So she shakes me awake and says, "Did you steal Nick's suit?" I say, "No, why?" But she knows my antics, so she repeats it. "Did you steal Nick's suit?" I give in. "Fine. Yes. Why?" She goes to our door, opens it and yells, "Nick! Keith has your suit! You don't need Uncle John to go get it!"

Nick comes down to get the suit. Now he's pissed at me. But I tell him, "This is what happens when you don't have an open bar at your wedding." It's a teaching moment.

THE WHITE WRANGLER

When I get traded to the Rangers in 2015, Kevin Hayes is the only guy on the team whose phone number I have. I don't really know him well, but I call him. He says right away, "I'll pick you up and drive you to the game tomorrow." An early indication of how great a guy he is.

But he shows up in this white Jeep Wrangler. I feel like a teenage girl getting picked up for prom. I say, "Dude, I appreciate the ride, but we can't be driving around in a white Jeep Wrangler. We're in the NHL."

The potholes we're hitting are going to give me a concussion.

I'm just giving it to him the whole way to the game. And in the locker room. I have the whole team calling it the Barbiemobile.

Literally the very next day, he picks me up in this brand new silver Audi A8. And he says, "Is this good enough for you?"

I have no idea how he changed it so quickly, but that's just the type of guy Hayesy is. He's always trying to please others.

He quickly becomes one of my best friends. When his brother, Jimmy, passes away, I sign in Philly and I live with Hayesy, which is a blessing. We're together every day. He's been through so much, but he's just the best person you'll ever meet. I just needed to set him straight on the white Wrangler.

LIVING WITH BIZ

When the Coyotes claim Biz on waivers in 2009, I call Whit and say, "How is this Bissonnette guy?" And Whit says, "He's going to come in so hot, the guys are going to hate him. And then you are going to end up absolutely loving him."

So Shane Doan is the biggest warrior I ever played with. Never in the training room. You have to beg him to put an ice pack on. He breaks his ribs one time and he won't even go get an ultrasound. Just a complete farm animal.

Well, Doaner breaks his finger just a couple of days after Biz joins the team. Our trainer, who we call Broadway, has to beg Doaner to come into the training room for treatment. This is back in the ice-and-stim days. So he is stimming his finger, and I'm in there talking to Doaner. Biz walks in and says, "Holy fuck, Doaner, back on the table again."

I've never seen Doaner's face go so red. I'm thinking, "Oh my God, he is going to kill this guy."

Fortunately for the future of *Spittin' Chiclets*, he doesn't. But Broadway is screaming at Biz, telling him he has no idea what he's talking about and that he had to beg Doaner to come in.

We go out for practice, and Biz and I are battling. He drops the gloves. I'm thinking, "First he gives Doaner a hard time, and now I have to fight this clown in practice?" I'm about to drop them, then I'm like, "I'm not fighting this kid. He has nothing to lose." So I hold my stick up like I'm going to hit him in the head with it. I say, "Hey, Biz, do you like it here, or do you want to go to San Antonio [the Coyotes' American Hockey League team]?"

He's like, "What the fuck?"

Doaner comes in and grabs him from behind, so nothing ends up happening. After practice, Biz gives me a ride home. Typical hockey players—almost fight and then drive home together.

I'm living in Derek Morris's house. I've just gotten married, my wife is pregnant, and Biz, who is always asking how much everything is, asks me how much rent I'm paying. So I say, "Mo just lets me stay here for free because he's the best." And Biz says, "Can I just move in with you? We can hang out. I'll drive you to the rink."

I'm like, "Biz, do you think my pregnant wife wants to live with another animal?"

You would have thought I told him his dog had died. He's so upset that I won't let him live with me. He ends up getting his own place. Best decision I ever made. Living with Biz would have been an absolute disaster.

Whit was right, though. Before long, we absolutely love him.

THE CALIPER CAPER

When I'm with the Panthers, we have this new trainer who has never been in the NHL before. He keeps doing body fat testing. Ask any hockey player and they'll tell you body fat testing is the worst. It's usually after a holiday or a long road trip when we eat like shit. And this guy would always do it on the worst possible days. So finally I say, "Fuck it, I'm going to steal the body fat caliper."

There is one at the game rink. I steal it. There is one at the practice rink. I steal that one too. And I know the trainer is too embarrassed to ask the team to buy new ones. So we don't do body fat testing for the rest of the year. The guys are so happy. Should have really won MVP for that.

Kevin Hayes, after reading this novella: "Wait, I got a couple more."

Title edit: *Seven Short Stories by Keith Yandle: And a Couple More by Kevin Hayes.*

First of all, the Wrangler story is true. I call my buddy on Long Island and say, "Dude, I need a new car ASAP. This new guy is all over me." And he gets me it the next morning. I can't be driving a Barbiemobile.

Yands is ruthless. He would always make me drive to every game, whether it's in my (new Yands-approved) car or his. We always stop at the same coffee shop. So there's a bad snowstorm in New York City one day. He goes to get our coffees, and on the way out, there are these two old guys carrying a couch. And they are really struggling with it. So Yands says, "Hey, excuse me, guys. Do you know what time it is?" These guys have both hands full, they're slipping all over the ice, and he asks them for the time! They lose their minds and say, "You should be helping us!" Yands says, "Oops, sorry, I gotta go to work." He gets in the car with our coffees and we drive off. Such a smartass.

In 2015, we are with the Rangers and lose in Game 7 of the Eastern Conference final. We have exit meetings a couple of days later. Yands and I go together. He's an older guy, I'm a younger guy, and he knows we're going to be there a long time because the older guys always get to go first and the young guys go at the end.

We pull up to the Rangers' parking lot and J.T. Miller's car is right outside the door, running. We go inside and Yands says to one of the equipment guys, "Why is Millsy's car running?" And the guy says, "He's trying to get his meeting done quickly so he can get back to Pittsburgh."

Well, this team has Henrik Lundqvist, Rick Nash, Marc Staal, Dan Girardi, Yands, Ryan McDonagh . . . and a bunch more guys way older than Millsy. So Yands decides this is not acceptable.

He says, "Hayesy, follow me in your car." He gets in Millsy's car, drives it to the highway, parks it in the breakdown lane, gets back in my car, and we go back to the rink.

Millsy gets out of his exit meeting and has no idea where his car is. Yands tells the trainers where they can find it. One of them eventually drives him out to get it. But it takes him an extra two hours. He is so rattled.

Yands is nuts. But I love him.

THE HUSTLER

Darcy Hordichuk Wheels, Deals and Wrestles Alligators

David Ross, the best player agent you've never heard of, is working the phones. Hard.

"I need a McLaren for Roberto Luongo," Ross tells the Vancouver car dealer on the other end of the line. "The guy is one of the best goalies ever, and the biggest star in this city. You give him a car, and he'll make a handful of appearances at the dealership, and you can bring a few of your guys in for a VIP tour of the dressing room after a game. Win-win!"

It's 2010. Ross is trying to work car deals for the Vancouver Canucks. He gets that McLaren for Luongo. Secures new Volvos for the Sedin twins. He dials up a BMW dealership next. "I need vehicles for Alex Burrows and Darcy Hordichuk." There's a few seconds of awkward silence on the other end of the line.

"I'm not sure about Hordichuk," the dealer finally replies. "He's just a fourth-line fighter. He's not a big enough star."

Ross pushes back. "Listen here, Darcy Hordichuk is a huge fan favourite! He won't just do a bunch of appearances at the dealership. He will stay after for hours! He's great with the kids. He'll sign all the autographs you want. Trust me, it'll be worth your while."

Hordichuk and Burrows are soon driving new BMWs. By the

time David Ross's work is done, half the Canucks are riding around Vancouver in free cars. Oh, and he gets them a yacht trip too.

I had never heard of David Ross before writing this book. Unlike many agents who crave a high profile, Ross is a ghost. You can't find a trace of him anywhere. It's Darcy Hordichuk who introduces me to Ross. Darcy admires hustlers, because he is one.

Raised in the tiny town of Kamsack, Saskatchewan, Darcy was constantly trying to come up with his ticket out. "I'm driving the tractor or shovelling grain in the bin for ten hours a day, and I'm just trying to find a light at the end of the tunnel as far as 'What am I going to do for the rest of my life?'" he says.

Hockey feels like his best shot. But when he doesn't get drafted by the Saskatoon Blades, the dream seems dashed. He gets a call from Blades coach Brad McCrimmon, who lays it out for him.

"Darcy, you're eighteen years old. This is your last chance. There is one spot left on this team, and you are up against three tough guys for it. You have to be better than them at what they do."

In other words, Darcy needs to fight for his hockey career. The most imposing of his tryout rivals is 6-foot-5 giant Steve MacIntyre. So Darcy goes to camp and fights MacIntyre three times. The Blades end up keeping both of them. (MacIntyre gets traded to Prince Albert later in the season, and ends up being a frequent combatant for Darcy.)

He has found his ticket out: his fists. Darcy decides he will fight anyone, anywhere, if it will get him to the NHL. "I start studying tapes of Tie Domi and Brad May and a bunch of guys," he says. "I realize it's almost like an art. And I want to be an artist."

Darcy's hustle is not reserved for hockey. He is constantly trying to make a buck or find a bargain. On a road trip to Portland with the Blades, he talks a teammate into going halfsies on a set of speakers, bought from a guy out of the back of a van. They sneak them back over the border underneath the team bus.

"They were ten-thousand-dollar speakers for five hundred," he says. "Or so the guy said. Of course we figure out when we get home that it's a scam. They aren't real. But I'm still able to sell them in a pawn shop and break even."

Darcy's fists are not fake. He racks up more than five hundred penalty minutes in two seasons in Saskatoon. Atlanta takes him in the sixth round of the 2000 NHL Draft. He is assigned to the Orlando Solar Bears of the International Hockey League. In his first pro game, he fights Mel Angelstad, one of the toughest guys in the minors for nearly a decade. (Mel would eventually land a role in the movie *Goon*.) You can still find the fight on YouTube. It's one of the wildest scraps in hockey history and goes viral before *going viral* is an actual thing.

"This guy Mel's nose is on the other side of his face, and I know I'm in trouble," Darcy says. "I'm throwing rights, lefts, lefts, rights, and in junior most guys just go down. But this guy is eating every punch, and throwing just as many back. After the fight, my hands are mangled. I can't even tie my skates."

But the Hustler's business is about to boom. He has started a website, HordyFights.com, and it blows up after the Angelstad scrap. The two battle again two weeks later, and the rookie's reputation as a legit enforcer is cemented. Darcy ends up leading the IHL in penalty minutes with an eye-popping 369 in 69 games.

"Chris Neil has me by thirty PIMs going into the last game of the season, but there is no way I'm finishing second," Darcy says. "So I undo my tie-down, jump in the other team's bench and start a line brawl. I think I end up with fifty-five minutes. Neil is so angry that I beat him."

For the record, Darcy also scores three critical playoff goals as the Solar Bears win the Turner Cup. He's an Atlanta Thrasher the next fall, the first stop on a 12-year, six-team, countless-punch NHL journey.

Darcy fights anyone. And apparently, any*thing*.

He's with the Florida Panthers in 2003 when he breaks his foot, knocking him out of the lineup for a month. Which is far too much free time for the Hustler. His house backs on an inland waterway, and an alligator has been hanging around on the bank. So Darcy does the typical Florida Man thing and starts feeding it chicken. His next-door neighbour has a little shih tzu. And soon the two realize the gator is edging closer, staring at the tiny dog like it's an appy at Chili's.

"So I say, 'Let's catch this thing,' because I've watched *Crocodile Hunter* and he makes it look so easy," Darcy says.

The plan is simple. Also, completely bonkers. His friend puts chicken on the end of a broomstick with a rope attached and lures the alligator up the bank. The NHL enforcer sneaks behind and pounces on the gator's back, all while wearing a walking boot on his broken foot.

"This thing is eight or nine feet long and I jump on it, and the tail is swinging like mad and I'm just holding on for dear life," Darcy says. "I pin it down and my friend grabs the face and tapes the jaw shut with electrical tape, and puts a potato sack over its head. We figure we'll just put it in my trunk and go release it in the Everglades."

I mean, what could go wrong with a foolproof plan like that?

"I have a Grand Prix, and as we're driving the gator pokes its head through the part that separates the back seat and the trunk, and we're just shitting our pants screaming in the car," Darcy says.

Obviously, the logical move at this point is to call the Florida Fish and Wildlife Conservation Commission, right? Or, alternatively, take the gator to some teammates' house to terrify them.

Kristian Huselius and Andreas Lilja are enjoying a day off when Darcy calls and tells them he's outside their place and wants to show them the new car he just bought. "They come outside and I'm hiding around the corner with the gator, and I slap it on its tail and it goes shooting across the lawn and they just lose it, skipping and jumping and freaking out."

Darcy enjoys this so much, he makes another stop down the road at Roberto Luongo's house, and puts the gator (jaw still taped shut, in case you're wondering) on his patio.

"I'm taking a nap and the doorbell rings," Luongo says. "I'm half asleep, but I have these two windows by my door and I look out, and I'm like, 'Holy shit . . . is that an alligator tail?' It's pretty freaking scary for a few seconds. Then I see Hordy's car parked, and he's hiding behind it, smiling. I'm like, 'Dude, what the hell are you doing?!' How and why would someone catch an alligator, put it in their car, drive it to my house, carry it to my door. This is not normal!"

Darcy and his neighbour eventually take the tape off the gator's mouth and release it in the Everglades, near the Panthers' arena. I guess it isn't too scarred by the ordeal because within a few weeks, it's right back on the bank behind Darcy's house, hoping free chicken, or shih tzu, is back on the menu.

Thankfully, for both alligators and his Panthers teammates, Darcy is soon back on the ice. Enforcers are still highly valued in the early 2000s, but not necessarily highly paid. Darcy is a minimum salary guy most of his NHL career. So he keeps wheeling and dealing, in every city he plays in.

He is reunited with his old pal Luongo in Vancouver in 2009. Lui is driving a Mercedes Benz G-500, and Darcy tries to convince him to sell it to him for a bargain. "The guy offers me Lululemon and Best Buy gift cards for my G-Wagon," Luongo says. "That's not a joke. I eventually give him an unbelievable deal, but he does have to pay actual money. Then after a few weeks I start getting these letters for parking tickets because he hasn't changed the registration. So one home game, I tell our trainer, Red, to go take off the plates during the game. And he does. And then Hordy drives around with no plates for a few more weeks."

CERTIFIED BEAUTIES

Soon Darcy realizes the G-Wagon, even used, is out of his league. "It's $2,200 to fix a broken windshield," he says. "I'm just a fourth-line plug. I can't even afford a used Mercedes."

Which brings us back to that mysterious agent, David Ross. He got into the business years earlier in Phoenix, when he noticed none of the Coyotes had car deals. So he starts cold-calling dealerships.

"I would call and tell them I represent all Coyotes players, and that it would be beneficial for their marketing to have them driving around in their vehicles," Ross says. "And the dealer would say, 'Okay, the cost of the lease for a year is twenty K,' and I would say, it's five K an appearance for this player and six K for that player, and we'd get a deal done."

In Arizona, a Cadillac dealership signs up. Later in Vancouver, McLaren, Volvo, BMW... they are all lining up to get Canucks players into their cars. Soon Ross branches out. He pits Bauer against Warrior to get a lucrative stick deal for Alex Burrows. It's all incredibly impressive.

Especially when you find out that David Ross doesn't exist.

"I had a good buddy named David when I was a kid, and Ross was my billet family's name in Saskatoon," Darcy says. "So that's what I came up with for my pseudonym."

Yes, for much of his NHL career, Darcy Hordichuk does deals for himself and his teammates by posing as a fictional agent.

"Sometimes they'd say, 'We only want Luongo for this appearance,' and I [David] would say, 'No, he's thirty grand for an hour but we can get you Darcy Hordichuk and Alex Burrows for way cheaper.'"

Darcy... David... whoever... gets so good at this, he lands a contract to handle the grand openings for Steve Nash's chain of gyms in British Columbia. "They'd give me, say, seventy grand, and I'd get Mason Raymond for two grand, and Milan Lucic for maybe six, and Brent Seabrook for a few more. And I'd just tell the guys, 'You are just going to show up, and we are going to cut some ribbons, take some pictures and kiss some babies!"

Appearances aren't the only thing guys on the other ends of these deals want. Thus "the Exclusive Canucks Dressing Room Tour" becomes Darcy's go-to closer.

"I remember touring the Swift Current Broncos' dressing room when I was a kid, and it really influenced me and made me want to be a hockey player," he says. "So wherever I play, I would always give tours to kids and families, and sure, car dealers too. One time I say to this guy, 'What would it take to get us all on your yacht?' And he says, 'Take my grandson on a tour of your locker room.' Done. But I wear out my welcome in Vancouver to the point Mike Gillis bans locker room tours because of me. I still sneak a few more in later."

He would also barter with game sticks. If you scored a hat trick, Darcy would likely have your stick signed and given to some connection's son or daughter before he left the rink. "Pretty sure every Sedin stick ended up in the back of Hordy's car," Luongo laughs.

Twelve years after retiring, the Hustler is still hustling.

"To this day, if you are an NHL player and need anything—you want to go on a private jet, you want to go on a yacht in Croatia—I'm your guy, because I have the connections," he says, proudly.

He lives in Scottsdale, Arizona, and has a company called Canada to USA, helping Canadian hockey players and others settle in American cities. He's also a member of the exclusive Thunderbirds organization. If you want to get a spot on the 16th hole at the Waste Management Phoenix Open, Darcy is your guy.

Or call David. He'll make you a deal you can't refuse.

WHEN A KILLER CALLS

Kevin Weekes Gets Tough Love from a Legendary Coach

───

"Weekesy, you have a call!"

"What?"

Kevin Weekes is puzzled. You don't get calls while you are in the middle of a practice. He's not even sure who knows he is skating with the Saint Mike's Buzzers, staying in shape while he tries to figure out his future.

It's the fall of 1994. For the past two seasons, Weekes has played goal for the Owen Sound Platers in the Ontario Hockey League. But the net's been crowded. He's been sharing time with another top goaltending prospect, Jamie Storr, a first-round pick of the Los Angeles Kings. Weekes is a Florida Panthers second-rounder. The two are good buddies, but both realize they need to play in order to get ready for pro hockey. So Weekes doesn't report to the Platers' training camp, looking for a fresh start.

Now he's watching one of the trainers waving frantically at him from the Zamboni entrance. A coach relays the message that's he's wanted on the phone.

"So I get off the ice, sweating in all my gear, and go to the trainer's room where the phone is," Weekes says. "And the trainer whispers . . . 'It's Mr. Kilrea from Ottawa!'"

Weekes's hand starts shaking as he grabs the phone. "Hello... this is Kevin."

"KEVIN... BRIAN KILREA HERE... FROM THE OTTAWA 67's. HOW... ARE YOU?"

(Note: All caps and ellipses are the only ways to truly represent the way Kilrea speaks. He bellows, and there are little pauses between every few words. Weekes does a bang-on impression.)

"Oh, I'm great, Mr. Kilrea, thank you."

"WE MADE... A TRADE. YOU'RE COMING HERE... TO OTTAWA... TO BE... A 67!"

"Wow, Mr. Kilrea, thank you for the opportunity. I'm very grateful."

Weekes is more than grateful—he's pumped. He starts thinking about Ottawa's barber pole jerseys. He always loved them when playing against the 67's. And his mind wanders to all the great NHL players who have come out of Ottawa...

"KEVIN. ARE YOU... STILL... THERE?"

"Sorry, yes, Mr. Kilrea."

"DO YOU HAVE... ANY... QUESTIONS... FOR ME?"

"Yes, Mr. Kilrea. Can I wear my number, double zero?"

"KEVIN... I DON'T CARE... WHAT NUMBER YOU WEAR... AS LONG AS YOU STOP... THE FUCKING... PUCK!"

Weekes is briefly stunned, as if he took a slapshot to the noggin.

"Okay... Mr. Kilrea, one more question. Can I still wear my Vaughn goalie equipment?"

"I DON'T CARE... WHAT PADS YOU WEAR... AS LONG AS YOU STOP... THE FUCKING PUCK!"

The 19-year-old goalie is now fully rattled. "I'm like a hot stick of butter, melting into the chair in my gear," he says. "I'm terrified. I just say meekly, 'Okay, Mr. Kilrea.'"

"THE TEAM'S GONNA BE... IN BELLEVILLE... TOMORROW. HAVE YOUR PARENTS... BRING YOU... TO

BELLEVILLE. YOU CAN COME BACK . . . WITH US . . . ON THE BUS . . . TO OTTAWA. AND I HOPE YOU CAN STOP . . . THE FUCKING PUCK!"

Weekes hangs up the phone and tries to sort through a full lineup of emotions. "I'm sad to leave Owen Sound, I'm euphoric to get a fresh start for this legendary coach, and I'm in shock because it sounded like I was just getting recruited to join the Royal Marines or the Navy Seals."

When he joins the team, he quickly learns Killer's tough f-bomb-filled delivery is a regular part of his routine.

"One night we are in North Bay, and just getting hammered," Weekes says. "Mr. Kilrea comes into the dressing room, with his usual suit and turtleneck, and an unlit cigar dangling from his mouth. And he starts ripping us. One of my teammates is Rich Bronilla, a solid, smooth-skating defenceman. But he's having a rough night. And Mr. Kilrea turns to him and says, 'BRONILLA . . . YOU HAVE THREE OPTIONS! YOU CAN GET . . . THE PUCK . . . OFF THE GLASS . . . OR . . . YOU CAN FUCK OFF . . . OR . . . YOU CAN FUCK OFF!' And then he kicks the table with the Gatorade on it and he walks out of the room. We're all trying not to laugh because Mr. Kilrea is a legend. We have so much respect for him. So it's dead quiet. We're all making eye contact with each other, trying to keep it together. But then we all just burst out laughing."

Weekes already has a good friend on the 67's in Dave Nemirovsky (who would become a teammate on the Florida Panthers a few years later). They grew up together in Toronto. Dave's billet mom, Steph Desmarais, had lived in Barbados for seven years.

"She's very fluent in the Caribbean culture, and with my parents being from Barbados, it's a match made in heaven," Weekes says. "So I ask if I can live there, and they take me in."

He had missed all of training camp with Owen Sound and several weeks of the season, and he's nervous about stopping . . . THE

EFFING ... PUCK! But somehow, he starts hot. One solid performance after another. So he has no trouble with Killer at the rink. Weekes's issue is getting there.

"Our billets lived off Woodroffe Avenue, which is a bit of a drive from the rink in downtown Ottawa, and from Canterbury, the high school I go to," Weekes says. "I had this 1985 Honda I bought for twelve hundred dollars. And I'm just chewing through gas."

So a few weeks in, he works up the nerve to have another call with his new coach. "Mr. Kilrea, it's Kevin Weekes. As you know, our billets live out here in Nepean. Would it be possible for me to get a little extra gas money?"

Silence at the other end of the line for a few seconds.

"I'll GIVE YOU ... TEN DOLLARS A WEEK ... AS LONG ... AS YOU KEEP ... STOPPING ... THE FUCKING PUCK!"

This time Weekes is smiling at the other end of the line. He's learned quickly that Killer's gruff act masks a coach who cares deeply for all his players. The two quickly form a bond.

"Killer loves Anne Murray," Weekes says. "Whenever we're on a long bus trip, Anne Murray plays constantly. And even though we're worlds apart—this old-school cigar-chomping Canadian and this kid from the Caribbean—my culture loves all types of music, and my family listened to a lot of Anne Murray when I was growing up. So before long, we're cruising down the 401 on the team bus, Killer puts on Anne Murray, and I sing along with him word for word."

He remembers another tough road game, when he didn't stop the effing puck, and the 67's are beaten badly. The bus is silent as it rolls through northern Ontario. Weekes feels he's let the team down. Then Killer puts on Anne Murray's "A Little Good News." And the coach and the kid break into song.

At this point in our interview, Weekes is belting out the tune. (He has a great voice by the way. If the goalie thing hadn't worked out, a one-man Anne Murray cover band with a Bajan flair would have been a solid career option.)

Alas, the goalie thing would work out. Weekes would go on to play 11 years in the NHL and become one of hockey's best-known analysts and news breakers in his second career as a broadcaster.

"I don't think I would have ever gotten there without Killer," he says. "He was tough, for sure, but he gave me so much guidance. And underneath that bellowing voice and all the f-bombs, he is just a super person. All class."

POSTSCRIPT: *The first book I ever wrote is about Brian Kilrea (They Call Me Killer). I didn't interview Kevin Weekes for the book. That was a mistake. But every player I did interview told similar hilarious stories. Most left Ottawa loving the man like a father. Killer turned 90 in 2024. At a birthday roast in Ottawa in his honour, multiple players told versions of the "You have three options" story. He used it a lot. The last two options never changed.*

THE SHINER

Rookie Frank Corrado Catches Friendly Fire in a Brawl Between Teammates

Mike Gillis stares at his rookie defenceman, with a poker face the kid just can't read. Frankie Corrado sits across the desk from him, his swollen left eye a nasty black and purple mix. He knows Gillis watched him the entire playoff series. No fights. No pucks in the face. No errant high sticks. Nothing.

Gillis takes a long look at the eye and gives Frankie a wry smile.

"Crap," Frankie thinks. "Does he know?"

Frankie's page on HockeyFights.com isn't exactly a deep rabbit hole to go down. There are four junior fights with Sudbury and Kitchener, with no video evidence available. Ditto for Frankie's first pro fight in the American Hockey League in 2014 against Cody Beach. Nothing. But the only scrap with video attached is worth your while. Binghamton Senator Darren Cramer goes after Frankie on April 15, 2015, while he's with the Utica Comets. That triggers Comets goalie Jacob Markstrom, leading to minor-league mayhem.

"It's Cramer and Corrado. Those two were all over one another on Saturday!" the play-by-play announcer says. "Corrado wanted nothing to do with Darren Cramer on Saturday night. Apparently wants nothing to do with him here. And now it's going to be Markstrom going after Peter Mannino! Markstrom skating all the way down, Mannino perhaps goading him on, and we're going to have a goalie fight down to my left in the Binghamton zone!"

Markstrom gets a couple of blows in, but it ends quickly, with smiles and friendly hair tousles from both tenders. Frankie somehow emerges unscathed from the Cramer fight. "Fortunate for me, because he's legit tough and I'm built like a wet noodle," Frankie says. He's also unharmed by the handful of other scraps in his four years of junior and 11-year pro career. Nary a blemish.

And yet he walks into that first NHL exit meeting in 2013, a critical moment in a rookie's career, looking like Edward Norton back at his day job in *Fight Club*. Gillis hasn't asked him about it yet. Good thing, because he has no idea what he'll say.

Long story, Mr. Gillis. And if you don't already know the details, you probably don't want to. (Unless maybe it's in a book a dozen years later.) You see, Frankie's eye is the remnant of a wild scrap from the night before, far away from the ice. The punchline (sorry) of the craziest few weeks of his life.

Frankie comes out flying in his last season of junior hockey with the Sudbury Wolves. The fast start earns him an invitation to Canada's World Junior camp. He scores two goals in the training camp games and feels he's on the cusp of one of his childhood dreams.

"Bob McKenzie is on *SportsCentre* saying, 'I'm pretty sure Frank Corrado is going to be on the team,'" Frankie says. "I'm pumped. And then the last day, I get cut. I'm crushed."

Steve Spott coaches Canada's World Junior team that year. And though Frankie is the last defenceman he lets go, he likes him. A lot. So when the tournament is over and Spott goes back to coaching the Kitchener Rangers, he immediately trades for Frankie. The Rangers go on a run but get knocked out of the playoffs by the eventual OHL champion London Knights in the second round.

"It sucks when your OHL career ends," Frankie says. "Best time of my life. But I get a call right away that I'm going to the Chicago Wolves. Immediately you have these new feelings of excitement."

The Wolves are the farm team of the Vancouver Canucks, who drafted Frankie 150th overall in 2011. They are winding down their regular season and are right on the playoff bubble. Frankie leaps headfirst into an intense race for a final spot. He moves into a room at the Residence Inn, right next to the Wolves' arena in Rosemont, Illinois. He plays four games and has barely settled in when his hotel room phone rings.

"Weird," Frankie says to himself. It's 2013. Everyone has cellphones. Who would be calling him?

"Frankie, it's Scott Arniel," the voice on the other end of the line says. Arniel is the Wolves' head coach. Frankie's mind is instantly racing. *I've only been here a week. What have I done wrong?*

"They are calling you up to Vancouver. They need you to play Monday against Chicago."

Sorry . . . what?

"Are you freaking kidding me?" Frankie says (to himself, not Arniel). "I just got here from Kitchener. Now I'm going to the NHL?!"

The Canucks have a bunch of injuries on their D. And after watching Frankie play those few games with the Wolves, they want him to fill in. "I call my parents and no one can believe it," Frankie says. "We are all completely shocked. "I was a fifth-round pick. There was no red carpet for me. My mindset was that I would play a couple of years in the minors, and if I worked really hard, maybe I'd get a chance to play in the NHL. Not a few days after junior."

He jumps on a plane to Vancouver and gets set to make his NHL debut.

"The whole thing is unreal," Frankie says. "When you are drafted, you get a prospect number. Mine is fifty-eight. It shows where you are in the pecking order. But I get to the rink and all my gear has a real number on it. Twenty-six. I'm thinking, 'Wow, this is actually happening. This isn't a prospects camp anymore.'"

After the morning skate, assistant coach Rick Bowness comes up to Frankie and says, "Just go play. Have fun and don't be afraid to make mistakes. It's the time of your life. Enjoy it."

As he's leaving the rink, Canucks goalie coach Rollie Melanson grabs him and delivers a similar message.

"You have one of the best goalies in the world behind you [Corey Schneider]. Just go play."

Frankie gets the typical rookie treatment, leading the team out onto the ice for warm-up and doing a couple of laps by himself, while his teammates hang back. It's a veteran Canucks group, with the Sedin twins, Ryan Kesler, Kevin Bieksa and Alex Edler, who will be Frankie's D partner for his first game.

"I look across the ice and there's Toews, Kane, Hossa, Seabrook, Keith," Frankie says. "And I'm like, 'Okay. This is big boy stuff now.'" Frankie handles it like a big boy, playing 17 solid minutes against the Blackhawks. He stays up for the Canucks' final two regular-season games with Anaheim and Edmonton, playing over 20 minutes against the Ducks.

The Canucks make the playoffs and are set to face San Jose in the first round. The injuries to their other defencemen have healed, and Frankie expects to be a black ace—one of those guys who skate with the team but don't play. But coach Alain Vigneault likes what he sees from the kid. So he keeps him in the lineup. Frankie plays all four games of a San Jose sweep. It's a disappointing end for the Canucks, but a dreamlike start to Frankie's career.

"To go from being cut from the World Junior team to playing in the Stanley Cup playoffs just a few months later is beyond surreal," he says.

The final act of this whirlwind rookie run is the Canucks' season-ending party. The team has dinner at a Vancouver restaurant, the first stop on what is going to be a long night. A chance for players to let loose after a gruelling eight months.

Frankie is still learning the inner dynamics of the Canucks' room. He notices as the night goes on that there is friction between star defenceman Kevin Bieksa and forward Zack Kassian. "They have been going at each other all night, just firing little snips and shots," Frankie says. "They are just getting in each other's face a bit, jokingly . . . or maybe not. As the night goes on, it seems to be getting a little more personal and heated."

The party ends up at the Roxy (note: Every NHL Vancouver party in the 21st century ends up at the Roxy) and then moves to an after-party in someone's high-rise condo.

The players arrive in different groups. Frankie ends up walking in with Bieksa, Kassian and fellow rookie Andrew Ebbett. As they walk into the building, a brawl breaks out that you won't find on HockeyFights.com.

"Kass has just been beaking all night and I have had enough," Bieksa says. "So I shove him in the lobby as we walk in, and we start going at it."

By the time the quartet pours onto the elevator, it's a full-fledged fight, with Bieksa's patented leaping Superman punches included.

"We're in that six feet by six feet box going all the way to the rooftop, and these two big, tough veterans are throwing bombs," Frankie says. "I'm the youngest kid on the team. I was in junior three weeks ago. I have no idea what the hell to do!"

He tries to get in the middle and break it up. The elevator is now shaking and stops between floors. And right about then, Frankie gets popped. "To this day, I still don't know who hit me," Frankie says. "They weren't trying to, but I get absolutely clocked."

"It's like a *Simpsons* episode," says Bieksa. "Like Bart and his sister Lisa punching and kicking each other. We aren't really connecting . . . except with Frankie's eye."

Maybe it's Frankie getting drilled, maybe it's the elevator getting stuck, but the fight fades quickly. Kassian leaves. Bieksa goes home shortly after.

"Funny thing is when I get in bed a couple hours later, my phone keeps buzzing," Bieksa says. "I finally look and it's Kass. He's outside walking the streets somewhere, and he says, 'Where are you, let's finish this!' I go, 'Get lost, I'll see you at the rink in three hours.' We get to the rink that morning and pass each other in the hallway and just start laughing. We hug and say, 'Man, that was a fun night!'"

Hockey players: different breed.

Meanwhile Frankie walks into the rink looking like he went three rounds with Tyson in his prime. And it's exit meeting day. Because he's the youngest and newest, he's the last player to sit down with Gillis.

"I just got called up to the NHL, and now I'm going to my meeting needing to explain how the hell I got a black eye when I didn't have one when I left after the last game. What kind of first impression is that? It's been four weeks of being nervous every single day. Going from the OHL playoffs to the AHL playoffs to the NHL and the Stanley Cup playoffs, to breaking up an elevator fight between teammates at three in the morning." And it culminates in this 20-year-old doing an exit meeting with his GM with a black eye.

Word has clearly gotten around. When Frankie goes to clean out his stall, there is a referee jersey sitting on top of his gear.

Shockingly, the exit meeting goes okay. Gillis gives the black eye a couple of quizzical looks but keeps the chat to hockey and the list of things he wants Frankie to work on.

But as Frankie is walking out, Gillis says, slyly, "Have a great summer. And be careful of those elevators."

ONE-TIMERS

Stories That Can Be Read
During a Single Shift

═══

MIKE GARTNER
(AND THE SMOKING LOBSTER)

I'm with the Capitals in the mid-1980s, and we have a guy on our team named Glen Currie.

His nickname is Kid Currie, after the western outlaw Kid Curry, who ran with Butch Cassidy and the Sundance Kid back in the late 1800s. Our Kid Currie is a real easygoing guy, bit of a surfer dude. He always gets jokes played on him because he's the first guy to fall asleep on the plane. So he gets his tie cut or gets shaving cream in his shoes. All the dumb stuff we do on road trips to amuse ourselves.

This is the age where NHL teams still fly commercial. The sweet life of charter flights is still a few years away. It's hard to fathom today, but there are smoking sections and non-smoking sections on the planes. Usually the last five or six rows are the smoking section, as if there is some mystical barrier in the middle of the air that is going to keep the smoke from moving to the rest of the plane.

We go through Logan Airport in Boston on our way home from this trip. At Logan, you can buy a live lobster. They box it up and you carry it on the plane. Kid Currie thinks this will make a great dinner, so he buys a lobster. He tucks the box under his seat like you are supposed to. And just like every flight, he falls asleep as soon as we take off.

It's been a long trip and guys are getting punchy. We're sitting in the smoking section, and Dennis Maruk gets an idea. He slides the box out from under Kid's seat, takes the lobster out, lights a cigarette, and places it in the lobster's claw. There's an elastic band around the claw, so the cigarette fits right in. So this live lobster starts meandering down the aisle of the plane with a cigarette in its claw. Everyone is in hysterics. It's truly one of the funniest things I've ever seen. The commotion wakes Kid up and he asks, "What's going on?"

"Well, Kid, your lobster's having a dart at the back." Kid laughs, but the flight attendant is not happy. Understandably. So the lobster's freedom is short-lived. He's soon back in his box under Kid's seat. I don't think things ended well for him that night, so we're glad he escaped for one last smoke.

You can't change nicknames. But Kid Currie should really have become Lobster Curry from that day forward.

KEVIN HAYES (AND THE KING'S SUIT)

When I make the Rangers out of Boston College, I get to play with the King, Henrik Lundqvist. You know how stylish he is. He would wear a new suit to every game.

One day we practise before heading out for a road trip. I get off the ice and decide to go for a steam. I go in the steam room, and there's a suit hanging there. I'm young and didn't know people hang their suits up in hot temperatures to get the wrinkles out. But I just assume if I turned on the steam room, I would make it even better.

I'm only in the steam room for 15 minutes, but the steam runs for an hour. So Lundqvist goes in later to get his suit, and it's soaking wet. Like, drenched. Like, almost ruined soaked.

No one knows I was in the steam room, so Henrik is going around asking everyone who was in there. He's not happy. I don't have the balls to tell Henrik freaking Lundqvist I ruined his new suit. So I never say anything. He still doesn't know. I hope he doesn't read this.

KARL ALZNER
(AND THE TRAPPED TEAMMATE)

I'm playing for the Capitals and we're in Dallas, staying at one of the biggest hotels I've ever been in. It's connected to the convention centre, and you can get lost easily in there. It's a game day, and I eat with John Carlson, my regular breakfast buddy. Joel Ward joins us. As we're finishing, Joel says he has to go to the bathroom and he'll meet us at the bus. But when we get there, Wardo is nowhere to be seen. It's been 10 or 15 minutes. The bus is leaving. And Wardo is missing. So Carly and I, trying to be good young teammates, go look for him.

We head to the bathroom, worried he might be sick. "Wardo, you in here? You okay?"

This little voice replies from the stall. "Guys, help me." We walk over and see Wardo's eyes peeking over the top.

"What's going on, buddy?"

"I can't get out," he says. "It won't open. I've tried everything." We just start dying laughing.

It's one of those stalls where there is no hole at the bottom, for extra privacy. Just a few open inches at the top. Wardo is peeking over, looking desperate. The bus is leaving for the pregame skate, so we need to think of something. Fast. We figure our only option is to try to squeeze him through the top. So Wardo gets back up on top of the toilet and sticks his arms out. Carly grabs him and tries to slide his body and shoulder press him out the slot. I'm helping, but also taking videos so I can document it for the boys. This is one for the ages.

Now Wardo is basically horizontal. Picture a pairs figure skater lifted over her partner's head. Except Wardo is about 6-foot-2, 215, and we're trying to slide him through this tiny gap between the top of the stall door and the ceiling. Somehow we pull him out and drop him down on his feet. He's so relieved. We race to the bus and have one great story for the guys on the way to the rink.

We never let Wardo forget it. I just sent him the pic recently of his eyes peeking out over the top of that stall. We were both laughing our heads off. He says he has no idea what he would have done if we hadn't come. Would have been the strangest healthy scratch ever.

Joel Ward—OUT, still locked in shitter.

MACKENZIE WEEGAR
(AND THE JUMBO VEGAS NIGHT)

I'm starstruck when Joe Thornton walks into our dressing room in Florida in 2021. You see that beard and this huge smile. You've heard so many stories about him. I just can't believe Joe Thornton is on our team. I have loved him since I was a kid. My cousin Craig Rivet played with him in San Jose, and I was always trying to get stories about Joe. For the Olympics they used to have these pins you could get at the gas station. The two I always wanted were Joe and Jarome Iginla.

We head to Vegas for our annual game there, and when we land, Joe says to me, Ecky [Aaron Ekblad], Huby [Jonathan Huberdeau] and a couple of other guys, 'You want to go hit the tables for a bit?' There is no way we are saying no to a night in Vegas with Jumbo. We're so fired up.

When the team gets to the hotel, there are two Rolls-Royces

waiting for us. I'm like, "Oh my God, I don't have the money to be a high roller and go spend a hundred K or something at the tables." But Jumbo says not to worry. We can bet as little as we want.

The cars drop us at Caesar's Palace. We go in this underground tunnel I didn't even know existed. Only a select few people know about it. We go through the tunnel and get to this line of lockers. There's one for Tiger Woods, one for A-Rod [Alex Rodriguez], one for Michael Jordan . . . and of course, one for Jumbo. Joe doesn't make a big deal out of it. We're all trying to act like we've been there before, but this is insane! I never experienced anything like this growing up. I'm looking around like a wide-eyed kid. Fish out of water. We go to the tables. Joe had markers, of course. I lose a little money, but he wins a bunch. Mostly we just want to watch him all night. This is the first time I feel like, "Wow, this is NHL life for a superstar." It's so cool that he brings us with him.

Florida ends up being the final stop of Jumbo's 25-year Hall of Fame career. It's amazing being part of it. He doesn't play all the games, but he's so good in the room with all the guys. He brings his kid on the plane sometimes. Just the greatest guy. And he gives me a night I'll never forget.

CHERYL POUNDER
(AND THE LOCKED-OUT RIVAL)

Everyone knows how we felt about our American rivals. On the ice, we hated them. And they felt the same. That's what makes it such a great rivalry.

I'm still playing, in the heat of that rivalry, when I get an uncomfortable request. I'm running a hockey school in Mississauga, Ontario, in the summer. One of the guest instructors is my teammate, Colleen Sostorics. She's staying at my house. Colleen is known for her, let's just say, extra heavy disdain for the Americans.

I have another friend and club teammate named Heather Logan who is also coming to the hockey school. Heather happens to be good friends with Angela Ruggiero, one of the best players on Team USA and a future Hockey Hall of Famer. So Heather asks if she can stay at my house for a night. And . . . if Angela can stay there too.

I'm torn. Angela plays for the archenemy. We've had some run-ins on the ice. She hit me really hard a couple of times. But how do you not open your home to someone? And if I do, how am I going to tell Colleen, who is sleeping on my basement couch. She can't stand being on the ice with American players, let alone stay in the same room with one! But it's the right thing to do.

Colleen understands. We figure we can manage to let the enemy in for one night. Besides, Heather and Angela are going out and say they'll be home late. We'll barely see her! They ask me to leave a key out for them. So I stick one outside the side entrance to our garage.

The next morning I wake up and go downstairs, but they aren't there. Weird. I just go about my routine, getting ready for hockey school. Then I open the door to the garage and . . . there are these two women, sleeping on the concrete floor! They'd pulled together some junk from the garage . . . a few towels and things to use as pillows, but it's a rough sight. They wake up as I walk in.

"What are you guys doing out here?!"

"You only left us the key to the garage, not the house key," a groggy Heather Logan answers. "We knocked but no one came."

I'm mortified. Angela doesn't say much. She just kind of looks at me and says, "Don't worry, Cheryl, I'll offer you the same hospitality if you ever come to my town."

It's an honest mistake. *Sure, Cheryl.* No, really! I can't even make it up to them by making them breakfast. I just put my tail between my legs and head to the rink. Colleen, meanwhile, thinks it's the greatest thing ever.

I don't really know Angela, so I've never had a chance to talk about it since. I would apologize. Not about the two times we beat her in the Olympic gold medal game. Or the five times in the World Championship gold medal game. But for having to sleep on my garage floor, yes, I am sorry.

(A little.)

COLE CAUFIELD (AND THE WARM-UP NO-NO)

In 2021, I finish my season at Wisconsin and sign my first contract with the Montreal Canadiens. I play 10 games and jump right into the playoffs. It's the bubble year with the North Division. We beat Toronto in seven and play Winnipeg in the second round.

I still can't believe I'm in the Stanley Cup playoffs a month out of college. The morning skate before Game 2, we're just doing the normal warm-up drill. I'm so excited. Too excited.

I rip a wrist shot right off Carey Price's head. You could hear the noise echo around the rink. I can't believe it. I just drilled one of the best goalies ever, and the key to our chances, right in the melon. I feel awful. I don't know what to do. It's the first time I ever feel like I need to get off the ice. Right now. And hide.

Thankfully for the team, and probably for my future as a Montreal Canadien, Carey's okay. Corey Perry comes up to me and says, "That can never happen again." I know! For the rest of the skate, I'm so scared. I don't even want to hit the net.

I go up to Carey right after we get off the ice and apologize. He says, "It's all good kid. It was a muffin."

Of course, he gets a 30-save shutout that night. And we win four straight. Thankfully. That helps everyone forget the rookie who doesn't know the most important rule of warm up.

From that day forward, every one of my warm-up shots is on the ice, half-speed. Even today, I'm not going anywhere near waist-high on our starter in warm-up. Muffins galore.

THOMAS HICKEY
(AND THE WHITE-KNUCKLE RIDE)

I'm playing in the AHL in New Hampshire with the Manchester Monarchs early in my career, and a couple of teammates and I decide to drive home to Alberta after the season. We're too cheap to ship our cars home. Bud Holloway and Dwight King both have pickup trucks, and I have this little Audi 4. I don't have winter tires. But it's May, so I figure I'm fine.

It's a long trip, several days driving 13 hours a day. We have walkie-talkies to talk to each other because we're kids. And it's fun. Day three we're coming through South Dakota to North Dakota, and one of the guys gets on the walkie-talkie and says, "A big storm is coming."

He's right. It's a total blizzard. I'm driving behind the other two and can't see a thing. The fields on either side are flooded, and the snow is blowing sideways. It's like driving on a bridge without guardrails . . . in a whiteout. I'm terrified.

We finally get to the Canadian border in Manitoba and the border guards are shocked. "Why are you guys still on the road?" We're like, "We know—we're pulling over as soon as we find a hotel." But we can't find one. There's no vacancy anywhere because everyone has pulled off the roads. So we keep driving, and it's getting worse and worse. The most stressed I've been in my entire life. We've been on the road eighteen hours when we get into Winkler, Manitoba. As I'm driving in I see two cops have pulled over Bud and Dwight. So I pull into the parking lot, and one of the cops knocks on my window. He's really serious, and he says, "Have you been drinking?"

"No, I've been driving for eighteen hours in a blizzard."

"I definitely smell alcohol," he says.

I'm exhausted and now I'm rattled. And it's about to get worse.

"Sir, we have reason to believe there is a dead body in the trunk of your car," the cop says.

"What?!" I feel like I'm in some movie. I have no idea what's going on, and I'm freaking out.

Finally, he breaks into a smile. "Thomas, we used to be linesmen in the WHL when you played," the cop says. "We recognized your teammates and figured we'd have a little fun with you. Just follow us and we'll get you into a nice B and B up the road."

I've never been so relieved. I get into bed at the B and B and close my eyes. All I can see is snow. Most stressful day of my life.

Fortunately, I was able to get rid of the body the next day without the cops suspecting anything. Joke!

JAMIE MCLENNAN (AND THE ROCK STAR NIGHT)

In 2003, when I'm with the Flames, I have a mask with KISS on it. But I really like Nickelback, so I add them to the mask. Chad Kroeger [Nickelback's lead singer] sees me on *Hockey Night in Canada*, and they reach out to our PR guy, Peter Hanlon, to set up a meeting. We just hit it off and are still great friends today.

One night during the lockout in 2005, I fly down to LA to visit Tyler Connolly from Theory of a Dead Man, whom I met through Chad. They are recording, so I come down to watch and hang out. It's such a cool experience watching these guys work and hearing songs no one else has heard.

We're at Nobu for dinner when Chad calls and says, "I hear you are in LA. I'm at a concert with a buddy. Meet me at the W Hotel at midnight." Tyler needs to sing the next day, so he isn't going out. I head there by myself. It's chaos at the W. You can't even get close to the lobby. Chad sends out hotel security to bring me in. Full rock star treatment for a backup goalie, which is hilarious.

I get to the table, and it's Chad, Dave Grohl from the Foo Fighters, Scott Weiland from Stone Temple Pilots and Cindy Crawford—whose husband owns the hotel. I'm thinking, "Where do I fit in here . . . ?" And there's one other guy, the buddy Chad was at the concert with. He's impossible to miss, but Chad is introducing me to everyone, and he says, "And this is Bob."

As in Bob Ritchie. Also known as Kid Rock. The concert Chad was at was Kid Rock's concert. So I'm hanging out with all these rock stars and a supermodel, and then Chad says, "We're going to Bob's house." We jump in this big entertainment van and head off to Malibu. Kid Rock is dating Pamela Anderson at the time, but she isn't there. Sadly.

The house is exactly what you'd expect. There's a real Batmobile, a grand piano Elton John gave him, and a stripper pole in the living room. The whole scene is surreal. Kid Rock is still in his concert outfit, this white suit with a hat, and he's making us all fried bologna sandwiches. Then he starts playing these new tracks he's been messing around with. "What do you think of this one?" he asks. I'm like, "Sounds great!" Turns out it's an early version of what would become "All Summer Long" (his biggest hit).

Pretty soon, everyone has left or gone to bed, and Chad and Kid Rock go into the recording studio and start playing. It's just the three of us. I'm just sitting there listening to these two guys play guitar. I end up sleeping on a couch in the recording studio. Backup goalies don't exactly live rock stars lives. But for a night, I got to.

THE CAPTAIN AND THE SWEDE

Darryl Sittler and Borje Salming

Darryl Sittler is running.

Down the stairs in his pyjamas to the Christmas tree in his home in St. Jacobs, Ontario. It's Christmas, 1956. Darryl starts shaking boxes, searching for that one gift he wants more than any other. He's six years old, and hockey crazy. When he finally unwraps the Montreal Canadiens Jean Béliveau number 4 sweater, it's over his head and on him in a heartbeat. It rarely comes off for months after. Béliveau is Darryl's idol.

Leap forward 14 years. Darryl is a rookie centre for the Toronto Maple Leafs, playing at the Montreal Forum. He looks up, and there is Jean Béliveau, now 39, taking the faceoff against him.

"Just a dream," Darryl says. "Surreal. He was always the kind of player and person I hoped to someday be. The classiest of captains."

Jump ahead again, 31 years to 2001—a Hall of Fame career and half a lifetime later. It's the worst day of Darryl's life. He's just lost his wife, Wendy, to cancer. He's at his home in Buffalo the morning of the funeral when the phone rings.

"Darryl, it's Jean Béliveau. I want you to know I am thinking about you on the most difficult day of your life," the legend tells . . . the legend.

"I'll never forget that call," Darryl says. "For him to somehow get my number and take the time to do that. It shows me that if you have a chance to touch someone, to make an impact, it can mean everything."

———

Darryl Sittler is running.

He moves with strong, powerful strides around the track at the University of Toronto. It's September 1973. The first day of the Maple Leafs' training camp.

This is a different era in hockey. Most players don't train much in the summer. That's cottage time. They use camp to get back in shape. But not Darryl. He has always taken care of himself, even in the off-season. Something in him has always wanted . . . needed . . . to be ready. So while many of the Leafs are labouring as they do their annual six-mile run, Darryl feels great.

Until the two new Swedish players go sprinting past him.

"They are just flying," Darryl says. "They are in unbelievable shape. We realize quickly they are on a different level than the rest of us."

It's Darryl's first introduction to Borje Salming and fellow Swedish rookie Inge Hammarstrom.

Hammarstrom is the player the Leafs wanted. Their scout, Gerry McNamara, went to Sweden to see Inge play but was distracted by a quick, agile defenceman on the same team. The Leafs sign both of them. Hammarstrom would struggle to adapt to the intimidating North American game. But not Salming.

"He's a warrior from day one," Darryl says. "He has a target on his back, because he's one of the first Europeans in the league. Everyone is after him. But when they try to intimidate him, he just plays harder. He comes into the shower after games and has welts and bruises all over his body from spears and slashes. But he never complains. Never says a word."

That toughness makes Salming beloved by Leafs fans. When

he's introduced on Team Sweden at the 1976 Canada Cup at Maple Leaf Gardens, he gets a standing ovation longer than any of the Canadian players.

"I'm on the other team and I get goosebumps," Darryl says. "You need courage to play in that time. The fans could feel it in Borje. They love him for it. And so do we. No disrespect to Denis Potvin and Larry Robinson and the guys winning Norris Trophies back then, but Borje is as good as any of them."

When Salming first comes to Toronto, he lives in Mississauga in the same subdivision as Darryl. The two have dinners and drive to the games together. But Borje wants to be closer to the city and soon moves to High Park, hanging out with fun-loving teammate Jim McKenny.

The Captain and the Swede share a friendship and mutual respect throughout their time in Toronto. But they don't become really close until Salming moves back home to Sweden after his 17-year Hall of Fame career.

"The NHL has its hundredth anniversary, where Borje and I are both named to the top one hundred players list, and we have four or five days to spend together in Los Angeles," Darryl says. "We have both remarried and my wife, Luba, and his wife, Pia, become really great friends as well. So every time they would come back to Toronto for Hall of Fame weekends or whatever, we would always get together. Crazy after all those years as teammates that we get much tighter afterward, living on opposite sides of the ocean."

Darryl, Borje and their wives chat often on Zoom. Especially during the pandemic. But when Pia's and Borje's faces pop up on his computer screen one day in July of 2022, Darryl knows instantly something is wrong.

"I can see the emotion in their faces right away," Darryl says.

"We have something we need to share with you," Pia says, choking back tears. "Borje has ALS."

"I know exactly what that means the second I hear it," Darryl says. "We are devastated. All I say is, 'We're going to help you, Borje. We are going to fight this with you.'"

———

Darryl Sittler is running.

A large crowd lines the street, cheering. For Darryl, yes. But more for the man he is running beside: Terry Fox.

It's July 1980. Terry's cross-Canada run has captivated the country. When he arrives at the Ontario–Quebec border, he is asked if there is anything special he'd like while he crosses the province. Terry says he would love to meet his idols: Bobby Orr and Darryl Sittler. When Sittler is told this, he agrees in a heartbeat. He's been following Terry's run closely. Inspired, like every Canadian.

Terry has already run 13 miles on this summer day in Toronto. He's in his Yorkville hotel room, about to head back out, when Darryl walks in to surprise him.

"Hey, would anybody like to go for a run?"

Terry is bent over, tying his shoe. He looks up at his favourite player and breaks into a huge grin.

"There are moments in life you never forget, and that is one of them for me," Darryl says.

A few minutes later, the two are running down University Avenue together, with crowds lined 10 deep on both sides. Before Darryl left home that morning, he tucked his All-Star sweater from the previous season in a brown paper bag. Their run ends at a stage in Nathan Phillips Square, where Terry is being honoured. Darryl pulls out the sweater and gives it to Terry. The image of Terry Fox addressing the crowd in Darryl Sittler's number 27 is one of the iconic moments of Terry's run. A Ken Danby painting of the scene still hangs in Darryl's office.

That day changes his life.

"Terry's courage and caring stick with me forever," Darryl

says. "We talk a lot and get to know each other. The Leafs happen to be in Vancouver after he had to end his run. I bring him into our dressing room to meet the guys. He is doing chemo and is feeble, gaunt and pale. It just hits me what he has given. He didn't do it for himself. He has no ego at all. Just humility and humbleness. He just wanted to make a difference. He's still my hero. The greatest Canadian ever. I am so blessed to have known him. And I know it happened for a reason."

When the Zoom call with the Salmings ends, Darryl and Luba cry. Then he gets to work. His first call is to another former teammate, Mark Kirton, who is also battling ALS.

"When Mark joined the Leafs, I was the star and he was the third- or fourth-line centre trying to break in," Darryl says. "But he was super competitive, very tough to take faceoffs against. I had so much respect for him. When he is diagnosed, I realize he is a lot like Terry Fox. He's going through the same devastating adversity and being so mentally tough. And he has the same humanity and humility in him, wanting to help others more than himself."

Mark's ALS started in his fingers. The first time he noticed it, his hand slipped off a golf club. Borje has a much more aggressive form of the disease called bulbar-onset ALS, which started in his throat. It causes significant speech impairment and difficulty swallowing. He likely has just months to live.

"One of the things Mark tells us right away is that Canada is more advanced than Sweden as far as treatment and the availability of drugs," Darryl says. "We need to get him help here."

Over the next few weeks, there are countless calls between Mark, Darryl, Canadian doctors and Borje's daughter Theresa, who becomes her dad's conduit, while Pia takes care of him.

Borje is having trouble getting the drugs that could help prolong and improve his life. At one point, Mark puts Darryl and Theresa in touch with another ALS patient in Ontario who has just switched medications. She has a supply of her previous drug left over. Darryl and Luba drive to her home outside of Toronto.

"Here's this young lady in her late forties in a wheelchair, and she just gives us thirty thousand dollars' worth of this drug to give to Borje," Darryl says. "I take it straight to the FedEx office to ship it. But I suddenly realize it's probably illegal to ship prescription drugs to someone in another country who they aren't prescribed to. So I take the drugs back. But we want so badly to get them to Borje. Jimmy McKenny offers to put them in his suitcase and take them over. Which is also illegal. So we just can't make it happen. But it just shows our desperation to help our friend. To give him some more time."

Mark is able to set Borje up for an appointment with an ALS specialist in Montreal. Darryl and McKenny drive down to be there. By this time, Borje is having trouble swallowing and talking. He's extremely emotional, another ALS symptom. He's told he'll likely have a feeding tube put in.

"The one thing Borje keeps saying in Montreal, over and over, is that he's coming to the Hall of Fame weekend in November," Darryl says. "Though I won't say it to him, I'm thinking the percentage chance of that happening is really small."

Darryl makes more calls. The first is to one of the Leafs' owners, Larry Tanenbaum, who promises he will cover the cost of all of Borje's medications and treatment. Then Darryl calls Leafs president Brendan Shanahan. Shanahan says the Leafs will take care of everything for Borje and his family if they can make it to Hall of Fame weekend.

"We get to November, and we don't know right up until the last two days if Borje is going to make it here," Darryl says. "It's not an easy trip in his condition. You need oxygen tanks, you need wheelchairs, you need medical assistance. But somehow, everything falls into place. Borje makes it to Toronto with nine members of his family."

The Captain and the Swede are reunited by the Directors Lounge in Scotiabank Arena, just before Friday night's Hall of Fame game.

"He's in a wheelchair, and he has really deteriorated since I had seen him in Montreal," Darryl says. "And yet the first thing he says to me is that he wants to walk out onto the ice. That's Borje. He doesn't want to go in front of those fans in a wheelchair. So I help him up and we go out. As we walk past the players on the Leafs' bench, I'm thinking, 'That was Borje and me, forty, fifty years ago.' Then I see Willy Nylander, who has tears in his eyes. Borje and Willy's dad, Michael, had been buddies. Borje had known Willy as a little kid, and here he is now—a star with the Leafs. It's all overwhelming. I can't contain my emotions. I can't believe Borje is here. We get to centre ice, and I just grab his arm and raise his hand above his head. The ovation is something that will stay with me forever."

Shanahan gives Salming and his family the team's suite for the game, and the one the following night. Throughout the two games, there is a steady procession of Leafs alumni coming through to see Borje. The actors starring in the movie they are making about his life also drop by.

And then Mark Kirton is wheeled in. Darryl's wife, Luba, captures the moment on her phone. The two men embrace. Both wipe away tears. They hug again. And cry some more. Few words are spoken. None are needed.

"There is a bond between Borje and me that is difficult to describe," Mark says. "It's a bond all ALS warriors share. But when it's a former teammate, it's over the top. The love in that suite you could see in everyone's eyes. I'll never forget it."

On Monday night, the Leafs arrange for a private room at elleven restaurant to watch the Hall of Fame induction ceremony. Borje, his family, Darryl, McKenny and Tiger Williams sit together and watch three Swedes get inducted into the Hall: Daniel Alfredsson and Daniel and Henrik Sedin. Three players Borje paved the way for.

"That entire weekend . . . it's perfect," Darryl says. "For all of those things to come together . . . Borje to even make it to Toronto, that ovation he got . . . his three countrymen to be going in that year . . . it was just meant to be."

———

Darryl Sittler is running.

This time in a panic. It's the Tuesday afternoon after Hall of Fame weekend. Darryl, Luba, Tiger and his wife, Brenda, had been driving downtown to say goodbye to Borje. He's leaving for the airport shortly. But Toronto traffic, always a problem, is a disaster today. Darryl pulls over and drops the three others off, several blocks away, hoping they can get there and keep Borje around for a few more minutes.

Darryl stares at the little clock on his dashboard. Minutes tick by, and he's still not moving. He's not going to make it. So the Captain pulls over and abandons his car on Lakeshore Drive, right underneath the Gardiner Expressway. He knows this will likely be the last time he ever sees his friend. He has to be there. He sprints through the downtown Toronto streets in the rain. And makes it to Borje's hotel just in time.

There are long hugs. Smiles. More tears. The group takes one last photo together with Borje and his family. And then the van door closes.

"You look in that window at him as they drive away, and I just feel the weight of everything that weekend meant," Darryl says.

He's in Florida 12 days later when he gets the call from Theresa in Sweden. Borje is gone.

Darryl spends the day doing interviews with every TV and radio station that asks. Because it's therapeutic to talk about his friend. And because it will spread the word about ALS, and maybe help Mark, or someone else down the road.

"Borje died a good death," Mark says. "I'm so glad he was able to attend the tributes and have his loving family around him. He didn't allow the ALS monster to rip him apart piece by piece over time. King outsmarted the fucking disease. He knew what kind of a burden this would become on his family. You think he was a smart hockey player, but he was an even smarter man. I'm glad our friend can rest now."

Before Borje passed, Darryl had six special sticks made to commemorate his NHL-record 10-point game. He signs them, and gets Borje, Lanny McDonald and Tiger Williams to sign them too. He gives one to each of them, one to Mark and puts the other in an auction for ALS.

It's become his cause. In September 2024, Darryl goes to Ottawa with Mark, Wayne Gretzky and others to lobby the government for more help. He goes on Mark's weekly Zoom calls with other ALS patients so he can hear their stories.

"My emotional attachment is personal, so I won't stop pushing," Darryl says. "For Borje, for Mark . . . for anyone. It's what Terry Fox and Jean Béliveau showed me. Do whatever you can."

The Captain is 75 now. This is what keeps him running.

POSTSCRIPT: *Borje's final visit to Toronto ends up being the catalyst for a huge fundraising drive for ALS research, led by Mark Kirton. Canadian NHL teams contribute over $1.3 million in the year after Borje's death. Today, all 32 NHL teams are contributing.* Kirton says, "I truly believe one day we may look back at Borje's passing, and the support from Darryl, the NHL and the ALS awareness that was created, as the turning point in the search for a cure." *Sadly, Mark Kirton passed away in August 2025, just months after speaking with me for this story.*

BEFORE HE WAS A STAR

Marty Turco's Wild Ride to Dallas and a Stanley Cup

Dallas Stars' rookie camp. July 1998.

UNNAMED STARS ROOKIE: *"Hey, who is that guy playing wing?"*

OTHER UNNAMED STARS ROOKIE: *"That's Turco, our new goalie."*

UNNAMED STARS ROOKIE: *"Then . . . why is he playing forward?"*

OTHER UNNAMED STARS ROOKIE: *"Because he wanted to."*

UNNAMED STARS ROOKIE: *"Umm, this is an NHL camp. Is he going to play goalie . . . at some point?"*

OTHER UNNAMED STARS ROOKIE: *"Nope, he doesn't even have his gear."*

UNNAMED STARS ROOKIE: *"This is weird."*

Oh, and it's going to get weirder, kid. Marty Turco's road to becoming a Dallas Star has more twists and turns than most players' entire careers.

Playing forward at rookie camp isn't Marty's first choice. It's been four years since the Stars took him in the fifth round of the NHL Draft (to play goalie, in case you're already confused). He's just finished a spectacular four years with the Michigan Wolverines, winning a (likely unbreakable) record 127 games, and is now anxious to take the next step. But he still hasn't signed a pro contract. His agent doesn't want him to go to rookie camp without one.

"My agent says, 'You can't go. What if you get hurt?' And I say, 'I'm not getting hurt.' And he says, 'What if you suck?' And I say, 'I'm not gonna suck. I just won a national championship.' Finally, I say, 'Can I just go hang out with my future teammates?' He says, 'Fine, but you can't take your equipment.' So I get there, and J.J. McQueen, the Stars' strength coach, says, 'You're a hockey player, right? I'm getting you gear.' And sure as shit, I play forward the entire camp. Brenden Morrow, who would become one of my best friends, has just been drafted. We're in line for a drill, and I'm wearing someone else's bucket, skates and jock. Brenden says, 'Man, I swear I thought you were a goalie.' So I take off, slap the puck off the glass, high-step it back to the line, snow-plow him and say, 'I am!'"

Marty finally signs that first contract later that summer. He didn't attend his draft, so he has never even put on a Stars jersey until his first pre-season game against the Nashville Predators in Little Rock, Arkansas, in September.

"We're playing in some tiny cow palace where the ice is three millimetres thick," Marty says. "Hitch [Stars coach Ken Hitchcock] says, 'Roman Turek is playing the first two periods. You get the third.' The benches are so small, I have to sit in the crowd. I end up with beer, tobacco chew, cotton candy spilled all over me. People around me keep asking if I want a beer. I'm like, 'No, I'm playing next period.' And they're like, 'Sure you are, kid.' Then after two, Hitch says, 'Turek is playing great, so we're going to leave him in.' I have to go back in the stands, and the fans are laughing, saying, 'We thought you were playing, kid? You want that beer now?' I'm like, 'Yeah, actually, I really want that beer.'"

After a bad call in the third, the fans start throwing things onto the ice (not Marty, just to be clear). Stars general manager Bob Gainey grabs the mic in the scorer's box and politely asks them to stop, saying the Stars will leave if they don't. This, of course, makes them throw more.

"So we leave," Marty says. "First time I ever put a Stars uniform on and I sit in the stands getting covered in crap, we never finish the game, bus it straight to the airport. See ya, Little Rock. I'm like, 'Welcome to the NHL!'"

Dallas has future Hall of Famer Eddie Belfour as its starting goalie and Turek as the backup. So Marty is sent to their minor-league team in Kalamazoo, Michigan. Emphasis on *zoo*.

"One night we have four hundred and one penalty minutes," Marty says. "IHL record! At the end of the game there are two of our guys and three of their guys left on the bench. I beat up Pokey Reddick at the end of the first period. I feel bad about it, but he ripped my helmet off, so what are you gonna do? We have the Mangler, Mel Angelstad. Best tough guy ever. He's basically a bar fighter who can kinda skate. Our coach, Bill McDonald, had him in senior hockey in Thunder Bay. Bill keeps getting new jobs and keeps bringing the Mangler with him. Hilarious guy—everyone loves him. Runs a real tight poker game. No one fucks with him. He's the first guy to ever wear sixty-nine in the NHL. He thinks it's funny. Played two games for Washington, about twelve seconds total. Absolute legend."

While Marty and the Mangler are chucking knuckles in the

'Zoo, the Dallas Stars and their two goalies are having a great season. So Marty figures he won't get a sniff of the big league. He's in Kalamazoo, on the ice for a morning pre-game skate near the end of the season, when someone yells that there is a call for him.

"I'm dripping wet, holding some phone attached to a ten-foot wire, and this voice says, 'Marty, Roman Turek hurt his knee. We need you to back up tonight. You have an hour and ten minutes to get to the airport.'"

He makes it, barely. Flies to Chicago, gets a connector to Dallas and gets to the game just before puck drop. He's made it to the NHL. And he still doesn't get to sit on the bench.

"It's the old Reunion Arena and I can't fit on the bench, so I sit on this little wooden stool between the two benches in front of the tunnel," Marty says. "The camera guy comes in just before the game and says, 'Move.' I go, 'I have to watch the game.' And he says, 'No, your job is to tell me where the hot girls are so I can put them on the Jumbotron. Besides that, my camera is way more important than you. So I'm not moving.' I say, 'Cool. Can't argue with that.'"

As Marty strains his neck to see the game past the camera guy, he watches the Coyotes' Keith Tkachuk mix it up with the Stars' Darryl Sydor. Sydor gets cut and is bleeding badly. Stars trainer Dave Surprenant helps him off the ice. Sydor is screaming at Tkachuk. Tkachuk is screaming back from the Coyotes' bench. Marty is right in the middle of it, opening the door for his injured teammate.

"All of a sudden, Tkachuk stands up on the bench and tries to one-hand Sydor over the head with his stick," Marty says. "It hits the glass, so he tries again, but Sydor has gone down the tunnel and it hits Dave Surprenant square on top of the head. He drops like a sack of potatoes. I'm like, 'Oh God, my trainer is dead!' I think I can see the little birdies flying around his head. So I peel my trainer off the ground and help him to his feet. I'm staring at Tkachuk because I can't believe what he did, and he's staring back. Finally he says, 'What the fuck are you looking at, kid?' And I say, 'You're a fucking idiot! You just killed my trainer.' We go back and forth, swearing at each other. Finally, he says, 'Meet me after the game. I'll show you what's up.' And I say, 'Bring your Russian goalie buddy [Nikolai Khabibulin] with you to make it interesting.'"

(At this point we pause to remind you that Marty is a rookie who has never been in an NHL game, jawing with one of the toughest vets in the league.)

What Marty doesn't know is that the tension and animosity between the two teams has been building since Jeremy Roenick knocked out Dallas superstar Mike Modano in a game in Phoenix three weeks earlier. Now Marty has landed right in the middle of it. Five minutes into the game, Stars captain Derian Hatcher catches Roenick coming around the net and breaks his jaw with a flying elbow.

"I'm thinking, 'I woke up in Kalamazoo this morning. I thought I left the minors. This is nuts!' So yeah, that's my first NHL game in uniform. Pretty uneventful."

After the game, Marty is waiting outside the dressing room for a ride to the hotel, unsure if he's staying in Dallas or going back to Michigan. He sees Tkachuk walking his way.

"I'm not sure whether to say something," Marty says. "His head is down—he's not even looking at me. So I just say, 'Fuck it.' And I go, 'Hey, Keith, where you been? I've been waiting for you.' He looks up and his face goes beet red. And I just say, 'Just kidding.' And he puts his head back down and walks to the bus. Brad Lukowich is standing next to me and says, 'What was that?!' I tell him I was just going to kick him in the nuts and run, anyway."

The Stars win the Presidents' Trophy. Marty gets called up to be the third goalie for the playoffs. Eddie Belfour rarely practises, so Marty takes his place. Hitchcock asks him to mimic the opposing goalies. The Stars beat Edmonton, St. Louis and Colorado before facing Buffalo in the Stanley Cup Final. "So I get to pretend to be Tommy Salo, then Grant Fuhr, who I grew up watching, then Patrick Roy, and for the final, Dominik Hasek," Marty says.

During the final, Hitchcock skates up to Marty during a practice and says, "Hasek goes down all the time, and I need the guys to get the mentality of shooting high, so I want you to lie down on the ice."

Marty, super keen rookie, says, "For sure, Hitch."

"I take three strides, turn around and go back, and say, 'When you say lie down, what exactly do you mean?' And he goes, 'Just lie down. Don't move.' So I lie down, stack my pads and don't move. And they are all coming in, firing wrist shots into the open net above me. But soon they get bored. Now they are taking slapshots and one-timers and hitting me in the cans, and up by my throat. I'm getting mad. But hey, this is my job, so I don't move. Finally, Joe Nieuwendyk comes over and says, 'Get up, this is embarrassing.' And I say, 'Thank you, Joe,' and I get out of that net, fast."

You probably remember the next part. Brett Hull scores the controversial triple-overtime goal to win the Stanley Cup. Marty, watching with the other black aces in the dressing room, races on the ice in gear to celebrate. He hoists the Cup, before he has played a single second of an NHL game.

"And we almost do it again the next year, losing to the Devils in the final," he says.

Quarterback Brian Griese is one of Marty's best friends from their days at the University of Michigan. "I win two national championships at Michigan and Brian wins one. Then I go to Dallas and we win the Stanley Cup before I've played a game, and almost another the next year. Brian goes to the Broncos and they win the Super Bowl his first two years. After that second year, we're hanging out smoking cigars and drinking whisky, thinking, 'This shit's easy!'"

This shit, of course, is not easy. Marty would never get a chance to hoist the Cup again (and Griese wouldn't win another Super Bowl). But he has a terrific 11-year NHL career, setting a modern league record with a 1.72 goals-against average in his first season as a starter (later broken by Miikka Kiprusoff). He still holds the Stars' franchise records for most games played (509), wins (262) and shutouts (40). Marty also pioneers the Turco grip, where a goalie's left hand is turned over like a claw, making it easier to handle the puck. Almost every goalie in the world uses it today.

And he most definitely holds the record for "most wild-ass stuff to happen to a goalie before he plays a single game in the NHL."

"Wait, one more I forgot to tell you," Marty says, as we're about to say goodbye.

This one might be another goalie record. During his second year in Kalamazoo, Marty plays four games in four nights in four different cities. A road game in Chicago on a Thursday, another one in Milwaukee Friday, a home game in Kalamazoo Saturday and the IHL All-Star Game in Cincinnati Sunday.

"Thank God I'm still young and in shape, because that would kill most mere mortals," he says.

After the last game, he sits at the Cincinnati airport, exhausted, waiting for his flight home with his wife, Kelly, and fellow All-Star teammate Jon Sim. "We don't play 'til Thursday, so I look up at that big digital board with all the flights and think, 'Where's the warmest spot?' I see Orlando. Our equipment and luggage are already on the flight back to Michigan, but I say, 'Screw it, we're going to Orlando.' I buy three tickets. We're cheap so we get one room with two beds at Treasure Island for a couple of nights, and Jon stays with us."

The last night, Marty and Kelly go to bed. Jon is still down at the bar. "We're in our skivvies, ready to pass out, and I hear the door open. I open one eye and see two people, and I'm like 'Did Simmer bring a friend back? This guy has balls!'"

It isn't Simmer. It's two teenagers with guns.

"They are going through our stuff and I'm thinking, 'If Jon comes in now drunk, it won't be good.' These guys have a Glock and a revolver. Kelly is the real All-Star because she slides off her watch and hides it under the pillow, and when the guy asks where my wallet is, she says, 'He doesn't carry a wallet.' I'm thinking, 'Yes, I do . . . oh wait. Smart, honey.' Somehow, he takes her word for it. They take Jon's winter coat, which has his passport in it, and as they leave, they say, 'You two are the nicest people we've robbed all night.' They leave, and I say to Kelly, 'Well, that was nice of them to say! Should we high-five?' Jon eventually comes back, and we call the cops. Jon is saying, 'I almost died tonight!' I'm like, 'Dude, you weren't even here.' Anyway, four games in four cities in four nights, armed robbery, back to the minors. Pretty solid week."

FREE MEGAN

Megan Keller's Best and Worst Career Moments Happen in Isolation

---

"This can't be happening. Please, please, don't let it end this way. Not with me in here."

Megan Keller has never felt so alone. So isolated. So helpless. The biggest moment of her life, suddenly a nightmare.

When she can finally breathe a couple of minutes later, she tries to get out. But they won't let her. She's trapped.

Wait. Let's pause here for a second. And do what every Netflix documentary does these days—jump forward four years. To the only other time Megan has felt this helpless and trapped.

After all, most of her life has been an endless run of happiness and success. She falls in love with hockey at three years old, following in the skates of her older brother, Ryan. She becomes a star defenceman at Boston College and a stalwart on Team USA.

Now she's getting ready for her second Olympic Games, after a year training with the American team in Saint Paul, Minnesota. It's the middle of the pandemic. The World Championship has been cancelled, and Megan is starving to play for a gold medal again.

"We're pretty fed up at this point," she says. "We are willing to do anything and everything to get to Beijing for the Olympics."

They play a series with their archrivals from Canada just

before Christmas. COVID catches up with a few of the Canadian players, so the last game is cancelled. "We come home, and the final Olympic roster is named," Megan says. "We think we are in the clear. Then we get word that one of our players has tested positive."

Three weeks before leaving for Beijing, Team USA shuts everything down. Training halted. Practices cancelled. Players isolated. "We just couldn't take any chances," Megan says. "But after a few days, the fear started to ease. And then my roommate, Amanda Kessel, tests positive."

They immediately separate, but Megan is in panic mode. "I feel for Amanda, and I'm terrified I'm going to be positive too. It's mid-January. We leave January 24. This is all you are living for, and now it might get taken away for something out of your control."

Then the phone rings, and she hears the two words she's dreading: "You're positive."

Megan, Amanda and two other players—Alex Carpenter and Hayley Scamurra—are completely isolated from the team. But they still need to train. So Megan and Amanda find an outdoor rink in a park near their apartment. "It's crazy, two Olympic hockey players, in their equipment, skating outside in this public park," she says.

And when they aren't training, they are trying everything to get a negative. "We are testing five times a day," Megan says. 'We're going to CVS buying our own tests. We're trying neti pots. We stick hand sanitizer up our noses. You name it. Amanda even rubs the swab on the outside of her nose just to see. And she still tests positive!"

They are eventually allowed to rejoin the team once there is no longer any chance of transmission. But the tests are still positive. The Chinese government has implemented extremely tough rules to get into the country for the Games. They need to be sent negative tests before the athletes leave for Beijing. Megan and her teammates are running out of time.

"We get on a Zoom call with the head doctor from the US Olympic Committee, and he tells us they are preparing to bring alternates," Megan says. "We say we'll do anything. We'll buy our own commercial flight tickets and come over later. But they aren't having any of it. That's when I realize we probably aren't going to the Olympics. And I break down. Amanda realizes we are in trouble when I break down because she had been crying the whole time, and I was keeping it together."

Megan is crushed. They have been isolated for weeks. Overwhelmed with anxiety, helplessness, dread. Imagine working for something your entire life, feeling totally healthy and ready, and being kept home because a swab won't cooperate.

On January 24, all of the American athletes are meeting in Los Angeles to head over on charter flights. Megan and Amanda fly to LA with the team and take their final test. Their last chance. They have to wait 12 hours in their hotel room for the result. Finally, the phone rings, again.

"Negative."

"It's the biggest relief of my life," she says. "I've never been happier to get on a plane for fifteen hours."

This is the part where Megan is supposed to win gold and live happily ever after. Oops. Canada spoils that, beating the Americans 3–2 in the gold medal game. Sorry, no happy ending.

Or... wait. Let's Netflix that timeline back four years to where we started this story. With Megan feeling trapped, alone and terrified. Again.

Except this time it's not an apartment in Minnesota with a pile of positive COVID tests on the floor. This time, it's a penalty box in South Korea. There is 1:35 left in overtime in the 2018 Olympic gold medal game, Megan's first. And she has just taken an illegal hit penalty on Canadian star Marie-Philip Poulin.

"I am shitting my pants," Megan says. "I'm remembering the 2014 gold medal game when the US lost to Canada in OT on a four-on-three. That's all I can think of. I'm going to cost us the gold. I'm praying they don't score."

She finally exhales when time expires without Canada scoring. Shootout. Megan can't wait to escape her panic room and get back to the bench. But the referees and linesmen quickly skate over to block her exit.

"I had no idea of this rule, but I can't leave the box," she says. "They tell me I have to stay in there for the entire shootout."

By this point, we really need "Free Megan" T-shirts.

It's 10 more excruciating minutes. After five rounds of the shootout, it's still tied. Then Jocelyne Lamoureux scores for the US, and Canada's Meghan Agosta is stopped by Maddie Rooney. The US has won the gold medal. Megan is finally free.

"You have never seen someone jump out of a penalty box as fast as I did to leap on the pile of my teammates," she says. "I'd watched Olympic hockey since I was a kid. It's the pinnacle of our sport, and we've just won gold."

And at that magical moment in time, *COVID* is a word Megan Keller has never heard of.

JUMPMAN

Future Captain Nick Foligno
Learns the Ropes as a Rookie

We'll get to the jump. Of course we will. But we begin with Nick Foligno having both skates firmly on the ice. It's the end of a morning skate in the fall of 2007. He's chatting with Ottawa Senators goalie coach Ron Low. Nick is a keen rookie, eager to sponge knowledge from everyone on a veteran team that just went to the Stanley Cup Final. The retired NHL goalie they call "Low Tide" is no exception.

Scattered around the ice are players engaged in one-on-one battles, something captain Daniel Alfredsson started at the end of practices. A way to get their hands going and raise the compete level. Dean McAmmond and Shean Donovan are two of the guys going at it. They are battling while skating backward. At full speed.

SMACK! BOOM! WHAM! Choose your favourite *Batman* caption.

Nick gets smoked from behind by McAmmond or Donovan (neither would admit to it). Nick's head, playing the role of a sledgehammer, drills Ron Low's face.

"Low Tide goes straight backward on his head, and he's out cold on the ice," Nick says. "He has these false teeth or dentures, and they pop out and go flying. It's wild. Trainers are running out on the ice, and I'm like, 'I just killed our goalie coach.' He's carried off the ice, goes straight to hospital. They had to check for internal bleeding. It's scary."

The rookie feels terrible, even though it's not his fault. But when he gets back to the rink for the game, guess who strolls into the room.

"Low Tide walks in with this full Civil War tourniquet wrapped around his head," Nick says. "That guy is so tough, there is no way he is missing a game. But he doesn't remember anything. So the guys tell him I hit him, that it was all my fault. The entire pre-game and warm-up, he's swearing at me. 'Where's that Nick?! That fucking kid! We're sending him down!' I'm just shitting my pants. Dean and Shean are laughing their heads off." Welcome to the NHL, kid.

His teammates are much more encouraging when giving advice on how Nick should celebrate his first goal. His dad, Mike Foligno, would famously leap in the air after he scored. As soon as Nick makes the team, the Senators veterans tell him he has to become Jumpman Jr. At least for his first goal.

"I had been thinking about it," Nick says. "But the fact they are all pushing me to jump is pretty cool."

On October 18, 2007, the Senators are hosting the Montreal Canadiens. Nick picks up a loose puck and tucks a wraparound past Carey Price. He leaps about three feet in the air.

"I call my dad right after the game," Nick says. "He's still coaching Sudbury at the time, and he tells me he was watching on the team bus and started crying after the goal and the celebration. So I'm really glad the guys pushed me to do it."

Later that season, Nick lines up for a faceoff opposite Brendan Shanahan, then a New York Ranger. "Here's this legend I grew up watching, and he leans over and says, 'Hey, I thought that was pretty cool the way you paid tribute to your dad with the jump. I hope my boys would do something like that for me one day if they had the chance.' It's such a classy thing for Shanny to say. I'll never forget it."

Moments like this help shape a rookie. Nick has a bunch of class acts in Ottawa to learn from. And one class clown.

"Shean Donovan is the funniest guy I've ever played with," Nick says. "We go on a short road trip, and he tucks a toothbrush into the pocket of his suit jacket, and that's all he brings! No bag. No extra underwear. No charger for his phone. Nothing. Just a toothbrush. He says, 'We're gonna be home in a couple of days. What else do I need?'"

Nick's captain, Alfredsson, travels a little heavier. On a road trip in Tampa, he takes the rookie shopping. "We're walking around all these designer stores that I've never been in in my life," Nick says. "We're in Burberry and I'm looking at the price tags, and these shirts are like six hundred dollars! I'm thinking, 'Who would ever buy these?' Then Alfie walks by with three of them in his arms. I go, 'Alfie, do you know how much these are?' He just smiles and says, 'I don't look at price tags.' He's the least arrogant guy you'll meet, but he has this swagger, always mixed with a sense of humour. These guys teach me it's okay to have a personality, to have some fun."

But it isn't always fun those first couple of years in Ottawa. The Sens go 13-1 to start Nick's rookie season ("I'm thinking, 'The NHL is awesome, we never lose!'"), but they stumble after and get swept in the first round by Pittsburgh.

His sophomore season is worse. Craig Hartsburg becomes Nick's third coach in a year. And by early January 2009, there is heavy speculation he's about to get a fourth. The Senators lose for the 10th time in 13 games in New Jersey. They fly to Buffalo right after.

"We land at about eleven, and Hartsy pulls the bus over at this shitty strip mall," Nick says. "He says, 'Everyone off the bus!' The entire team goes into this rundown bar, and we just drink all night with the coaches. I think Hartsy was pretty sure he was getting fired the next morning. But we show up at practice the next day, and he's still there. He says to us, 'Well, this is awkward.' Then he blows the whistle and we start the practice. I've never seen that, before or after, where a coach says, 'Screw it. I'm probably done so I'm getting hammered with my players.'" (Turns out Hartsburg was just a little early. He gets fired three weeks later.)

Despite the team's struggles, Nick treasures those first years in Ottawa. He learns to be a pro—and a leader, from the likes of Alfredsson, Mike Fisher and Wade Redden, whom he lives with for a while as a rookie.

"Wade married my cousin Danica, so he takes me in, and I'm basically his annoying little brother," Nick says. "I read the paper over his shoulder, eat cereal in his ear. We drive to the rink every day and I'm so excited, talking the whole time, asking all sorts of dumb questions. At one point, he finally says, 'Nick, just stop talking.' But he is just amazing to me."

There's a *Lion King*–like circle of life to hockey. The rookies watch. Learn. And someday, some become leaders themselves. Nick Foligno is 38 now. He can't jump quite as high. But the kids still look up to him. He's captaining his second NHL team, the Chicago Blackhawks. He remembers how Alfredsson would have him over for dinner when he was a rookie. Let him play with his kids. Make him feel like family. Almost two decades later, Nick now does the same for Connor Bedard.

"The first time Bedsy comes over, my boys, Landon and Hudson, are so excited," Nick says. "They are waiting for him at the door with mini-sticks. They hand one to him the second he walks in. He laughs, and off they go to play for hours. But this stuff is important. Because Bedsy, his whole life is hockey. I want him to see that I'm a hockey player, but this is my family. This is what matters to me. And I want him to know he has a friend here who cares about him no matter what happens on the ice. Because that's how Alfie made me feel."

The rookie is now the vet. The pupil now the teacher. And there's a lot to teach. During a TV time out in Bedard's rookie season, the big screen in the rink plays Freddie Mercury's "Day-O" performance from the late '80s. Nick elbows Bedard and says, "Do you know who that is?"

"The Beatles?" Bedard replies, with little confidence.

"Oh man," Nick says, shaking his head.

"Eddie Vedder?" Bedard tries on the rebound.

Nick sighs. "I have so much to teach you."

VINNIE'S PRIVATE PLANE

Vincent Damphousse Gets
Traded in the Sky

If you could time-travel back and ask 16-year-old Vinnie Damphousse who would be most likely to have a 747 all to himself someday, he would pick his junior teammate in Laval. Some kid by the name of Mario Lemieux.

"My rookie year in junior is Mario's last, and he gets four points a game . . . for the whole season!" Vinnie says. "The last game of the year he's at 130 goals. The record is Guy Lafleur's 133. So Mario needs three to tie it, four to break it. He gets six goals and five assists. Unreal. It's so obvious he's going to be a superstar in the NHL from the moment he gets there."

And of course, he is. But on March 23, 1999, it's not Mario alone with an entire flight crew, 35,000 feet above Canada. It's Vinnie, at the end of one of the craziest and most emotional days of his life. He's not popping bottles and eating caviar. He's quiet, wiping away tears, reflecting on the long journey that led him here.

Though he's not Mario, Vinnie tuns into a junior sensation himself, racking up 318 points in his three years in Laval. He goes sixth overall to the Toronto Maple Leafs in the 1986 NHL Draft and becomes a terrific NHL player in his five seasons there. In 1991, he's part of a blockbuster deal with Edmonton that brings Grant Fuhr and Glenn Anderson to the Leafs.

The following summer, Vinnie's on the move again. This time, it's a childhood dream come true.

"I love Edmonton. I learned how to win there. But I'm going into a contract year and know I'm not going to re-sign. I want to go home. So I ask my agent, Pierre Lacroix, to try to get me to Montreal."

He's in his brother's office that summer when the phone rings. It's Lacroix. "You're a Montreal Canadien," he tells Vinnie.

"My brother and I have the biggest high-five in history," he says. "I grew up twenty minutes from the Forum. I never thought it was possible that I would get to play for les Canadiens."

The dream turns surreal, quickly. In Vinnie's first year with the Habs, they win 10 overtime games in the playoffs behind Patrick Roy. And win the Stanley Cup. "Being in that parade, seeing my entire city line the streets, it's hard to even comprehend how much it means," he says.

Vinnie has six more solid years in Montreal, surpassing 90 points three times. But as the trade deadline approaches in 1999, he knows the dream might be coming to an end. He's 31 and about to become a free agent.

"We try to work out a new contract, but it becomes pretty clear it's not going to happen," he says. "It's just before George Gillett Jr. buys the team, and they just aren't putting much money into it. So I know I might get traded."

On trade deadline day, the Canadiens are scheduled to fly to Edmonton at noon to start a road trip. The day before, Vinnie gets a call from general manager Réjean Houle. "He says, 'Thank you for your time with the Canadiens. I'm going to try to trade you today or tomorrow.' I appreciate the call. But . . . what do I do about the flight to Edmonton tomorrow? After some thought, Réjean says, 'Get on it.'"

Houle makes the same call to Stephane Quintal. So both Vinnie and Stephane pack their bags for a road trip to... who knows where.

Montreal to Edmonton is already a long flight. But this one feels eternal. It's 1999. There are no cellphones, no free wi-fi on the plane.

"I'm playing cribbage with Brian Savage and Martin Rucinsky, and I keep looking up toward the front of the plane where the media are sitting because they are the only ones with communication," Vinnie says. "Every fifteen minutes I ask, 'Did you hear anything yet?' But there's nothing."

The deadline is 3 p.m. Eastern. The hours go by. Crickets. Vinnie starts to wonder if a deal fell through. Maybe he'll remain a Hab after all. Then at 2:55, he sees Habs medical trainer Gaétan Lefebvre stand up and walk toward the back of the plane. Lefebvre taps Vinnie on the shoulder.

"Alain wants to see you up front." He knows right away what it means, and walks up the aisle to coach Alain Vigneault's seat.

"You've been traded," Vigneault says.

"Where am I going?" Vinnie asks.

"San Jose."

"Is anyone else involved?"

"No, just you."

Vinnie takes a moment for it to sink in.

"Okay, so... what do I do now?"

"Well, your team is playing in Toronto tomorrow, so stay on the plane once we land in Edmonton. They'll refuel and you'll fly back to Montreal with the crew."

Vinnie returns to his seat and is overcome. "We're in the sky over Saskatoon or Winnipeg or something, and I just sit down and start crying in my seat. My buddies Brian and Martin are with me, plus the other guys, and they really don't know what to do. Finally, I gather myself and say, 'Guys, I just got traded.' There's still an hour or two left in the flight, so they say, 'What do you want to do?' I just shrug and say, 'Deal 'em up!' It's so weird. I'm flying to Edmonton with my team, but it's not my team anymore. One of the media guys does an interview with me, and then we land. I call my parents and ask them to pack my stuff because I have to meet the Sharks in Toronto. Then all my teammates say goodbye and get off the plane. I'm all alone, on this huge Air Canada charter."

And so begins the most surreal five hours of Vinnie's life. They sit on the tarmac for an hour refuelling. And then he soars back across Canada. By himself. "It's so strange being alone on this massive plane," he says. "I just stay in my same seat at the back, thinking about my whole career, wondering what it will be like in San Jose. It's not like I'm royalty and the entire crew is waiting on me. But I think I get an extra bag of chips and a chocolate bar or two."

He's been on the plane for more than 10 hours when he lands in Montreal. He rushes home, packs and grabs a commercial flight to Toronto. The private plane life is short-lived. He's back with the rest of us in 17C, with a tiny bag of pretzels and no room in the overhead.

The next night, he makes his debut with the Sharks.

On a five-on-three early in the first period, Vinnie plays the point on the power play. He fires a shot from the blue line and scores. He adds another later as the Sharks win 8–5. The sadness fades quickly. He likes San Jose right away, and signs a five-year deal with the Sharks in the off-season.

The trade ends up being a disaster for Montreal. They get three draft picks that turn into Marcel Hossa, Kiel McLeod and Marc-André Thinel. Only Hossa makes the NHL, playing just 59 games for the Habs over three seasons.

Vinnie, meanwhile, retires in 2004, just before the lockout. His final stat line: 1,378 games, 432 goals, 773 assists and the biggest private jet in NHL history.

STRUDDY'S (ACCIDENTAL AND INTENTIONAL) SCRAPS

Jason Strudwick Fights Everyone Except a Hungarian Riot Squad

---

The Hungarian riot police are trying to pull Jason Strudwick's coach over the boards. His teammate is slashing one of the officers with his stick. All hell is breaking loose inside the rink in Budapest.

Struddy looks at his cousin, Rob Niedermayer, and says. "Let's get out of here!"

It's not the first time Struddy has run from a fight. It's just . . . been a while. The website HockeyFights.com lists 112 scraps in his NHL career, counting the pre-season (which we'll get to later). But despite that stacked resumé, Struddy starts out as a reluctant combatant.

"I don't fight a ton in junior," he says. "I think my last year I have eight fights and the stick boy has eleven. But when I get to the minors in Worcester in 1995, I have this old-school coach, Jimmy Roberts. He tells me if I want to make the NHL, I need to learn how to fight properly. So I get in a few scraps and . . . it's not going very well. I go out of my way to avoid the heavyweights so I don't get killed. But it becomes an ongoing joke that I keep ending up in fights I don't want to have."

Struddy always likes to be the last man off the ice in warm-ups. But one night during his rookie pro season in Worcester in the American Hockey League, two of the opposing Binghamton Rangers players are lingering. As they leave, one fires a puck at the IceCats' net.

"I just snap," Struddy says. "I skate over, pull the puck out of the net, and as he's walking down the tunnel I take a slapshot as hard as I can and hit him in the back of the leg."

Couple of thoughts here. First, great shot, Struddy. You should have done shooting accuracy at the All-Star Game. Second, perhaps consider having a good look at your target before you fire. Because he is hard to miss. It's 6-foot-5, 250-pound mountain Eric Cairns. Also known as one of the toughest guys in hockey.

"Oh my God, what did you just do?" says Struddy's defence partner, Jason Widmer, the only teammate still on the ice with him.

The second Cairns gets hit, he freaks. "I'm going to kill you tonight, Struddy!" he screams.

The other Rangers player still out there, Ryan VandenBussche, holds Cairns back and pushes him toward the dressing room, just to avoid an unfortunate pre-game murder.

"Now I'm like, 'What am I going to do—I'm dead!'" Struddy says. "I stay out as long as I can for warm-up until the rink guy finally kicks me off. I have to walk right by their dressing room. The door is open and Cairns is still yelling, 'You are going to die tonight!'"

When Struddy gets back to his own dressing room, Widmer is apoplectic. "Why would you do that?!"

"I don't know, I couldn't help myself," Struddy says. "What am I gonna do now?" There is silence for a moment, before Widmer decides to reassure his panicked partner.

"Maybe you'll be okay. Two defencemen never hook up to fight."

This settles Struddy a little. Widmer's right. Odds are, he won't be on the ice much with Cairns. Even if they are, the giant likely won't get close enough to start something. And at that exact moment, coach Roberts walks into the room. "Struddy, one of our wingers can't go tonight. You're playing left wing."

If I could type the wide-eyed scared emoji, I would place it here.

"I'm so dead," Struddy says to himself.

He starts at left wing on the IceCats' top line, keeping one eye on the puck and the other on the Rangers' bench, to see when Cairns is coming on.

"Every time I see him stand up, I change right away," Struddy says. "It works for a while, but finally I can't get off and he grabs me. He proceeds to beat the wheels off me. I'm bobbing and weaving, just trying to survive, but he's annihilating me. And as we go to the box, he says, 'We're going to fight three times tonight! I am going to beat the crap out of you three times!'"

Struddy sits in the penalty box, dazed and terrified. He's staring at the clock, wishing he could time-travel to the final buzzer. A couple of minutes into their majors, he hears Cairns yelling at him again. "Hey, Struddy, bad news. My hand is sore and I can't fight you anymore tonight."

It's the single greatest sentence he's ever heard. "I'm so happy," Struddy says. "It's my stay of execution."

Of course, he can't show Cairns that. So he responds with some all-time false bravado.

"You got lucky this time, big guy!" Struddy screams back from his box, knowing full well who the lucky one really is. That's confirmed when he gets back to the dressing room at the end of the period and finds a crack in his helmet, courtesy of a Cairns punch.

Struddy's entire rookie season is baptism by fire . . . er . . . fists.

"I have a black eye the entire year," he says. "I just don't know how to fight, but I keep ending up fighting thirty-year-old men who know what they are doing. I have twenty-two fights that season and end up 0-21, with one tie against this little hobbit."

By his second AHL season, now with the Kentucky Thoroughblades, Struddy is starting to learn the ropes. But he still desperately tries to avoid scraps with other teams' enforcers. One of them is Craig Martin, who has been chasing him for a year.

"For some reason, he doesn't like me," Struddy says. "He keeps asking me to fight and I keep saying, 'No, I'm not fighting you. I want to live.' I do fight one of his teammates one night and actually do pretty well. So Martin comes back and says, 'Okay, now we're definitely fighting.' But I keep saying, 'No!'"

Later in that game, they line up against each other on a faceoff in Kentucky's end. And it quickly turns into a *Seinfeld* episode. The puck slides to the corner and Martin chases it, with Struddy right behind him. "And as I'm skating, somehow one of my gloves falls off and slides right by him," Struddy says. "He sees it and thinks I'm jumping him. So he says, 'You're dead!' I'm yelling, 'No, it was an accident!' I'm trying to pick my glove up, but he jumps me and just tosses me all over the place, saying, 'I can't believe you jumped me!' As I'm getting pummelled I keep yelling, 'IT WAS AN ACCIDENT!'"

By the time he makes the NHL a year later with the New York Islanders, Struddy is no longer the Accidental Scrapper. It's part of his game. He no longer avoids the heavyweight legends. In fact, he challenges one, under the strangest of circumstances.

"I'm in my rookie year and I think I'm going to be an Islander forever," Struddy says. "Then we arrive in Vancouver for a game, and the second I check into my hotel, the phone rings. It's Islanders coach Mike Milbury. He says, 'Hey, Struddy, I just wanted you to know we traded you. Good luck.' My roommate, Claude Lapointe, tells me someone is probably pranking me, but then the phone rings again and it's Canucks coach Mike Keenan. He says,

'We just traded for you. Go downstairs—someone is going to take you to a press conference.' So I grab my bag and I'm gone."

When he arrives at the press conference, Struddy finds out the player he's been traded for is Canucks fan favourite Gino Odjick. Gino happens to be having his own goodbye press conference in the same room, right before Struddy's.

"Gino finishes and walks by me and gives me a bit of a dirty look," Struddy says. "Then I walk in and the first reporter says, 'Gino said he didn't mind getting traded, but he hates getting traded for a nobody.' I'm like, 'What did he say?' Now I'm mad. And we're playing the Islanders the next night. So I decide I'm fighting this guy. He's way out of my league, and everyone loves Gino. All the fans love him. All the players on the Canucks, the team I've just been traded to, love him. But I don't care."

Struddy chases Odjick all over the ice. Finally, Gino gives in to the hotheaded kid. "Fine, let's go."

Struddy starts firing punches like a wild man. He can't understand why Odjick is just taking them, holding on to him, not punching back. This goes on for 30 seconds or so, before Struddy finally figures it out. Too late. Odjick has let the rookie tire himself out. Struddy is exhausted by the time Odjick finally lets loose, hitting him with a flurry of fists and taking him down.

"I'm like, 'Oh no. What a way to start my career with the Canucks.' I've just gotten beaten up by the guy everyone loves. So I sit in the box feeling shame for five minutes. But then I skate back to the bench and my team is going crazy. Mike Keenan, Mark Messier, Brad May, they are all saying, 'That's how you compete!' So unknowingly, it was the best thing I could have ever done. Standing up for myself and getting destroyed by Gino."

After the game, the media gathers around Struddy for the second time in two days, wanting to know what happened with Odjick. And he fires one last shot. "He said he didn't know who I was, so I thought I'd introduce myself."

A year later, they run into each other at a rink, and Odjick apologizes for what he said in the press conference. Struddy has nothing but respect for the legend, and still can't believe he went after him. "My ego was writing cheques my body couldn't cash," he says with a chuckle.

At the end of that first season, Keenan tells Struddy he needs him to show up to camp the next fall ready to make a statement. Struddy figures that means he needs to fight . . . everyone.

"We get to the exhibition games and I end up fighting seven times in six games—it's crazy," Struddy says. "In the sixth game, I fight in the second period, and I'm just done. The trainer takes me to the trainer's room in Vancouver and I'm icing my hand. Todd Bertuzzi walks in and says, 'Struddy, enough. No more fights. You've proven yourself.' Then the trainer says, 'He's right, you're done. I'll tell Keenan we're taking you out for precautionary reasons.' I'm so thankful, because I'm totally spent. Then Keenan walks in the training room and says, 'Struddy, you got a third period in you?!' And I jump off the table and say, 'Sure do, coach!' I just had to make that team and was willing to do anything. And fight anyone."

He makes the team. And goes on to play 14 seasons and 674 games in the NHL. Never backing down from a fight again.

Wait. Except for one.

Which brings us back to that rink in Budapest, during the 2004–05 NHL lockout. Struddy and his cousin and close friend Niedermayer decide to go over and play together with a club called Ferencváros.

The Hungarian League isn't exactly Europe's finest. Quick case-in-point side story: Struddy becomes addicted to the Gatorade-like electrolyte drink they have in a big jug in the dressing room.

"It tastes unreal," he says. "I'm just downing this stuff by the gallon. But I notice that no one else is drinking it. I can't figure out why. Our trainer is this seventy-five-year-old Hungarian guy. He brings in the drink every day. One day I get to the rink early. I'm sitting in the room and he comes in with the jug and pours the crystals in. Then he pours the water in. And instead of grabbing a big spoon, he just puts his big hairy arm in and starts stirring it with his arm! I almost had to go get steel wool to scrub my tongue. I go to all the guys later and they say, 'You didn't know that? That's why none of us drink it.' I have been pounding this stuff for a month!"

Apologies if you are eating. Or drinking any hydrating substance. You get the picture. Hungary is a long, long way from the NHL. Money is always an issue. The teams practise at night, because most of the players have day jobs. One night, they show up for practice at the main rink in Budapest, and the buzz in the dressing room is that there might be an issue with the ice time. Struddy and Rob don't understand much of what is being said. It's mostly in Hungarian or Russian. So they shrug it off and hit the ice.

A few minutes into the skate, two beer-league teams show up. They are scheduled to have a game at the same time. Turns out Struddy's team hadn't paid for the ice, so the arena rented it out. No one is sure what to do. But Struddy's Russian coach tells the team, "We're not leaving."

The beer-league teams don't leave either. They start their game. "It's just complete chaos," Struddy says. "They are playing an actual game with referees while we are doing full-ice horseshoe drills!"

After 10 or 15 minutes of this madness, the two captains of the beer-league teams say "enough" and agree to leave. But apparently someone had already called the cops. The Hungarian police show up on the bench in full riot gear. "And I mean Eastern European riot gear, ready for battle," Struddy says.

The team's assistant coach goes over to talk to them, and it gets animated, quickly. "All of a sudden, one of the cops grabs our assistant coach and tries to pull him off of the bench. So the entire team, besides Rob and me, skate over and start getting into it with the cops. Now they are battling. One of our guys slashes the arm of the cop who is holding the coach. It's mayhem."

That's when Struddy does something he hasn't done since that first season in the minors. He runs from the fight. As fast as he can. "Rob and I just look at each other and say, 'Let's get out of here!' I've never skated off the ice faster in my life!"

A few minutes later, the rest of the team are back in the dressing room with them when the police barge into the room, looking for the slasher. They demand all the players' passports and make them stay in the room for three hours.

"I think I'm going to a Hungarian jail," Struddy says. "I'm ready to sing and give up the guy who slashed the cop in a heartbeat."

Finally, the team agrees to apologize, and the riot squad lets them leave. And as a peace offering, Struddy offers the cops a complimentary jug of the team's tasty electrolyte beverage.

HOCKEY NIGHT IN KENYA

This African Nation Wants to Take On the World

This story, like most these days, begins with a Tweet. (Or an X, or whatever we are supposed to call it now.)

It's September 2024. A video post pops up on my feed. It shows a man sitting at a desk watching a computer screen. The International Ice Hockey Federation logo is in the top left corner. Suddenly, the screen changes and dozens of green squares populate it. The man yells and throws his arms in the air. A female voice doing the filming says, "We're in, people!"

The caption reads "Kenya Ice Hockey finds out they've been added to the IIHF, and their reaction says it all." I do a doubletake. Kenya? In the IIHF?

Wait. Kenyans . . . hockey . . . it does ring a bell. Wasn't there a great Tim Hortons ad a few years ago with Crosby and MacKinnon playing hockey with a Kenyan team? Commercials tend to run for a couple of months, then vanish. (Except that 1-877-Kars-4-Kids ad. Those little actors pretending to play instruments are probably 47 now. And their catchy damn jingle still haunts me.) Point is, the Timmy's ad is a bit of a blur. I google it to make sure it was real. It was . . . it is. And it's pretty great. But I haven't heard anything about hockey in Kenya since. Joining the IIHF seems like a major leap for a country you don't exactly associate with skates and frozen rubber.

So I send a message to the account out of curiosity.

When Ali Kilanga starts working at the rink, he doesn't pay much attention to the hockey players.

They come in every Wednesday night—expat diplomats from Canada, the USA, Finland, Sweden—to play a pickup game. A group of scientists on exchange from the University of Manitoba become regulars soon after.

It's their only hockey option in Nairobi. In fact, the small rink attached to the Panari Hotel is the only ice in East Africa. It's right next to the Nairobi National Park. Lions, giraffes and gazelles roam just across the highway.

Ali, 29, works as an ice marshal for public skating. He makes sure no one is going too fast, helps the newcomers who have fallen get back up. He wears figure skates because they are more comfortable than the plastic ones they rent at the rink. Ali has seen hockey on TV before, but never really cared for it. But one afternoon, the expats are short a player and ask him if he wants to join.

"Sure, why not,'" Ali says. He has no equipment—no shoulder pads, no shin pads, no helmet . . . no jock. They just hand him a stick and off he goes, figure skates and all.

"I like it right away," he says. "The other players are much better than me, but I'm up for the challenge."

Ali scores that first night. Full disclosure: The goalies don't move very well. There is no one to play net, so they stick two three-foot-high plastic penguins between the pipes—the ones kids use to balance while learning to skate. But hey, a snipe's a snipe. "I score many goals," Ali laughs. "More than Gretzky." He's hooked.

It's 2007. As the months and years pass, other Kenyans join in. But it's hardly a wave of hockey popularity in Nairobi. Just a slow, steady drip.

Robert Opiyo first gets on the ice at 18, while he's away at school in Malaysia. He buys a pair of skates and brings them home to Kenya after he graduates. His brother tells him about the rink in Nairobi. He goes there to skate and soon gets the hockey bug too.

"When I step on the ice, I forget about everything," Robert says. "There may be voices everywhere, but the moment I get out there, it's just peace and quiet. That's what I love about hockey. I lose myself."

For years, the small group of Kenyans join the expats in the Wednesday night games, tossing their sticks in a pile to choose sides, like we've done forever on the outdoor rinks in North America. They call themselves the Panari Penguins (those plastic goalies can now double as mascots).

By 2016, the Kenyans have enough players to take on the expats in a game. The Madaraka Cup is born, named after a national independence holiday. The Expats beat Team Kenya 14–12 in the first one. The trophy gets lost in a bar after the game (as every good hockey trophy has at some point). Never found it. They'd get a new one eventually. Soon, the Kenyans decide it's time to have their own permanent team. The Ice Lions are born.

There are no tryouts—not enough players for that. Anyone who shows up is in. Kind of like the '90s Leafs. One of the Canadian expats, Tim Colby, who used to coach minor hockey in Ottawa, volunteers to help out. "One day, they tell me a doughnut store in Toronto called, asking about sponsoring the team," Colby says. "I'm confused, thinking what mom-and-pop doughnut store wants to help Kenyans play hockey? So I keep asking them the name, and finally someone says, 'Tim something.' And I go, 'Tim . . . Hortons?! Holy shit." Yeah, *that* little mom-and-pop donut store. Tim's wants to bring the Ice Lions to Canada. They make an 18-minute documentary about the journey, along with the commercial I remembered. The players are all given new equipment and team jerseys (which are spectacular). Then Crosby and MacKinnon surprise them in the dressing room in those same jerseys, and join the team for a game.

"It's incredible," Ali says. "It's the first time I've had full equipment on. Including a jock! It's the first time we feel like a real team. And playing with Sidney and Nathan is surreal."

Tim Hortons also gives the Kenyans $30,000. The commercial and doc get the Ice Lions a lot of attention. An illustrated children's book is published called *Hockey Night in Kenya*. But like everything that goes viral, the spotlight soon fades. And not much changes. Except for the addition of a few lionesses to the Lions.

In 2018, Faith Sihoho is walking through Nairobi's Central Business District when she spots a group of men playing in-line hockey in a parking lot. One of them tells her they also play the sport on ice. "I don't believe him at first," Faith says. "There can't be ice in Kenya. But when I see it, it intrigues me." She soon joins in.

"I love body-checking," she says. "I love that the sport is fast. After playing, I feel like a new human being. I feel like I've left all the bad energy at the rink."

Faith is afraid to tell her parents. She sneaks off to the rink after church. When they finally find out, they tell her they are proud of her. But they still aren't sure she should be mixing with men on the ice.

"Kenya is behind much of the world in terms of equality for women," says Colby, the Canadian expat. "They are where we were generations ago. The women are expected to marry young and stay home. The gender stereotypes are much heavier here."

"Women playing sports is not as accepted here," Faith says. "But all the men on the Ice Lions are very welcoming to us. There are a dozen women now. Someday, we will have our own team."

I ask Faith her favourite hockey player. "Auston Matthews," she says. "But the others here don't like him. They like MacKinnon."

Getting enough gear for all the players remains a challenge. At one point, they hear the International Ice Hockey Federation is giving out green pucks as part of an anti-doping campaign. They write, asking if they could have some. The IIHF responds that it can only give pucks to member nations.

A light bulb goes on. Could Kenya get into the IIHF? Worth a shot.

Kellen Maina, who runs the rink and is a hockey mom to son Liam, does much of the groundwork. There's a detailed application where you need to confirm you are the sole federation overseeing hockey in the country. With just one tiny rink and 30 players, Kenya doesn't meet the requirements for full membership, so they apply to be an associate member, hoping the IIHF will want to help them grow the game in Africa.

It's a long process, interrupted by a pandemic. But in September 2024, the Kenyans are invited to the IIHF Congress in Greece for the vote. They don't have the budget to travel there. So on voting day, Kellen and Robert—one of the players you met earlier and now the chairperson of the Kenya Federation of Ice Sports—find a quiet room and join online.

It's the first time the IIHF has done digital voting. Every member nation votes. When someone votes YES, their box turns green. NO, and the box turns red. Once all votes are in, the coloured boxes appear instantly on the screen. You need 85 percent of the votes to get in. "We are so nervous," Robert says. "We had never gotten this far, and we've worked so hard. Now it's down to a vote."

Kellen starts recording on her phone. Robert stares at the computer anxiously. Suddenly the screen changes, and all the boxes are green. Robert reacts like he just scored an OT winner.

"It's just pure joy," Robert says. "To be able to say Kenya is now a hockey nation."

So what exactly does an associate member of the IIHF get? "The short-term thing is the buzz," Colby says. "The players are really proud of it. They feel accepted into the international hockey community."

Colby is now the Lions' full-time coach. He's retired, and Nairobi is home for his family. Teaching Kenyans to play the game he loves is his passion.

"We have a long, long way to go," he says. "But what matters now is the players really love it. They are so aspirational, it's phenomenal. Many of them take two or three buses to get to the rink. It eats up their whole daily wage."

The team has a GoFundMe page, and the expats, who still play every Wednesday, chip in cash and gear. They sponsor players from the Nairobi slums and keep them in school. "These are young people who have little to no hope," Colby says. "Through hockey, we give them hope and something to accomplish. They come here never having skated, then one day they're doing backward crossovers and scoring goals. They are so proud of themselves."

The junior program, which includes kids from local orphanages, is booming. They can't keep up with demand. The primary goal now is to get an Olympic-size rink in Nairobi. "It's going to happen," Colby says.

But this will not be another Jamaican bobsled story, where Kenya makes the Olympics out of nowhere. The lowest competitive group in the IIHF is Division Four, with countries like Malaysia, Kuwait and Indonesia. Kenya is years, maybe decades, from even getting to that level.

"Kenya is not going to be in the World Juniors or the Olympics anytime soon," says Ali Kilanga, the former public skating marshal turned hockey trailblazer. "But we will keep that dream alive. If we keep focusing on development maybe ... someday ... Kenya will be there."

Back at the rink, the juniors are getting ready to take the ice. A little girl named Blessing, one of the sponsored players, is having trouble finding a helmet. Colby digs one up and off she goes, smiling ear to ear.

"They love it so much," Colby says. "And even when they struggle at first, they just never quit. It's inspiring."

Blessing. Truly.

"THE BIGGEST BUNCH OF BEAUTIES EVER ASSEMBLED"

Matthew Tkachuk and His Florida Panthers

This book began with a Tkachuk brother messing up a prank. By law, it requires one more before it ends.

The 2022–23 Florida Panthers are, in the words of Matthew Tkachuk, "the biggest bunch of beauties ever assembled." Tkachuk figures this out on day one of training camp. Paul Maurice is the Panthers' new head coach and wants to send an early message.

"We have a ridiculously hard camp," Tkachuk says. "Paul has this crazy-tough skate, where we do one-on-one battles for fifteen seconds, laps for thirty seconds, for ten reps on day one. It's gruelling. Guys are puking. So the last rep, my group of six—myself, Colin White, Eric Staal, Patric Hornqvist, Sam Bennett and Ryan Lomberg—say, 'Fuck it,' let's have some fun. We throw one puck in the corner and have this wild melee fighting for it. This is at the end of the toughest skate imaginable! When that happens, I know this is going to be a fun group."

Every NHL team has one or two guys who stir things up off the ice. They aren't all Todd Simpson–level pranksters, George Parros–quality game inventors or Darcy Hordichuk–crazy alligator wrestlers. But you need a couple of personalities to keep a room light. Except the Panthers don't have a couple. They have half the team. Roll call:

"Nick Cousins and Brandon Montour lead the way," Tkachuk says. "They pull crazy stuff every day. Josh Mahura and Colin White aren't far behind. I'm in the middle tier of shit disturbers. Guys like Carter Verhaeghe and Aaron Ekblad pull shady stuff on the side. No one stirs the pot more than Marc Staal. He's constantly telling me to prank Montour, and then going to Montour, saying, 'I think Chucky is after you—be careful.' Eric Staal doesn't pull anything, but encourages everyone else to, just so he can laugh. The list goes on and on."

"He's right, and it lasts all season," Cousins says. "My wife gets me this new Louis Vuitton tie, and I mistakenly leave it in the room where we autograph jerseys. I come in the next day and about six of them have signed my tie. Another time, Montour buys this two-hundred-dollar pair of dress socks. Who buys two-hundred-dollar socks? So I cut the toes out of them. He's genuinely pissed."

Tkachuk volunteers to help Montour get even with the sock slasher by pulling what Kevin Hayes would call "the Yandle."

"Cousy comes to the practice rink in his car. I come in my golf cart," Tkachuk says. "I go into his stall, grab his keys, shorts, shirt and shoes. I leave only his underwear. There is this massive empty field down from the rink where I'm going to put his car. But as I'm taking his car, I realize I don't want to have to walk back. Verhaeghe comes by in his golf cart. So I go, "Swaggy, don't ask questions, just follow me." He knows exactly what's going on. I park at the farthest point away, Swaggy drives me back, and I put Cousy's keys back in his stall. When he gets there, he just says, 'Oh no.'"

"I get to my locker in my gitch, and all that's there are my keys, my phone and my wedding ring," Cousins says. "I question all the boys—no one is saying a word. Then I go outside and my car is gone. I ask Frank, the parking lot attendant, where my car is, but he's in on it so he gives me nothing. So I have to do this walk of shame in my underwear down the street until I see it across this field. At least he left my clothes in the car."

"I plan my exit so that I drive my cart by just as he's getting dressed at the car," Tkachuk says. "I'm pissing myself laughing."

You would think these kinds of hijinks would cease come playoff time. But with this team, it just gets worse.

"Game 6 against Boston, we're down 3–2, facing elimination, and just before the pre-game skate, Mahura, Montour and Cousins are all missing their sticks," Tkachuk says. "They all hid each other's without the other guys knowing. It just shows how loose our group is. No one is even remotely worried that this could be our last day. Of course we win the game and the series."

On the plane to Las Vegas to start the Stanley Cup Final, Tkachuk hears Colin White say he only brought one pair of pants. (The Panthers all wear ABC pants, a Lululemon style, on practice days and to morning skates.) "Some guys bring two pairs, some one, but when I hear Colin say he only has one, I say to myself right away, 'I'm going to ruin those pants, and he will look like an idiot the entire trip.'"

Tkachuk sneaks into the dressing room the next day with a pair of scissors. He cuts out the zipper from White's pants and the buckle from his belt. He giggles with excitement at the thought of White showing up to Stanley Cup Final Media Day zipperless.

But like his brother Brady did with Claude Giroux and the cut sticks, Matthew makes a costly mistake. "It's confusing with all the stalls so close, and it turns out I cut the wrong guy's pants," Tkachuk says. "And when I say wrong guy, I mean *really* wrong guy. I ruin the pants of Radko Gudas."

When he first says this, my mind automatically wanders to the long list of punishing and occasionally suspension-worthy hits by the tough Czech defenceman. I figure Tkachuk is terrified he will be pummelled. But this is not the reason for his regret.

"Guds is the best guy in the world, and one of the few guys who hasn't been involved in any of this idiocy all year," Tkachuk says. "He only has one pair of pants too, so now he has no fly for the first road trip of the Cup Final! I walk up to him, tail between my legs, and say, 'Guds, you likely won't believe this story, but this is what happened...' And incredibly, he just laughs it off."

Maybe Radko enjoys a cool breeze through his groin on those smouldering June Vegas days. Tkachuk still isn't sure how he pulled off Media Day zipperless. "I think he just wore an XXL-size hoodie to cover his fly," he laughs.

Gudas isn't the only Panther to have unwanted wardrobe alterations. Cousins buys brand new white Givenchy shoes, which he debuts on Media Day. You can find the interview on YouTube where reporter Jonny Lazarus says, "I'm looking at your shoes... it looks like you just took the laces out of your skates." Cousins looks down and starts laughing. Montour has replaced his designer shoelaces with his chunky skate laces. And Cousins realizes the real laces are hanging out of his hoodie pouch. All live on TV.

"I've never seen anything like this group in my career," Tkachuk says. "We're just a bunch of goofball animals who need this stupid stuff to get fired up to play. I truly believe it's why we made the Cup Final. And this group set the tone for our teams that would win it all the next two years."

When I chat with players for these *Beauties* books, there are no rules about what kind of story they can share. My ask is simple: Just tell me your favourite hockey story—craziest game, most memorable moment, funniest teammate—whatever you want. As you've read, more than a few end up being pranks and off-ice idiocy.

I ask Tkachuk why hockey, more than any sport, seems to

need—and breed—the "goofball animals" he so adores from that Florida team. "It's such a long season, longer than any sport if you go deep in the playoffs," he says. "I get to Florida in late August and my goal is always to win and not go home until early July. So you need little things to brighten your day. You can't possibly focus on hockey 24/7. You'll be mentally drained. We need laughter and joy, and different reasons to be excited to come to the rink for practice.

"Some teams don't value off-ice camaraderie enough. Hockey today is very numbers- and analytics-based. But I would argue a certain guy is way more valuable than another because of what he brings off the ice. Obviously, you can't have too much of it without on-ice abilities because you won't win. But it's so crucial to have that mix. To have guys that can bring a team together. We need characters . . . beauties. It's what drives a culture, what drives a team."

And sometimes . . . a book.

(This was going to be the final chapter. Until Ray Whitney called . . .)

REVENGE OF THE CABBAGE ROLLS

**Ray Whitney Takes the F
Out of Opening Shift**

Ray Whitney needs to get off the ice. RIGHT. NOW. But he can't. If he leaves, it's a penalty. No chance Ray is doing that to his team. So he's stuck. It's not an injury. Though he'd trade this feeling for a pulled groin or separated shoulder in a heartbeat.

No, this is worse. This is rock bottom. The lowest moment of an otherwise terrific 21-year NHL career.

"Shitty feeling," Ray says. "Really, really shitty."

You know that old expression about going from the penthouse to the outhouse? Few have ever lived it as quickly (and literally) as Ray.

In the spring of 2006, his Carolina Hurricanes make an unlikely run to the Stanley Cup Final. They go up 3-1 on Edmonton in the series. After 12 long seasons, and a lifetime in the game, Ray is one W from his dream.

"We're on the power play in overtime in Game 5, with the Cup in the building," Ray says. "And Fernando Pisani scores shorthanded. We lose. Then we go back to Edmonton and get blown out in Game 6. Our families had flown in for that game, and my wife,

Brijet, has tears in her eyes after. I say, 'Why are you crying? We're fine. There is no way we're losing three in a row.' She says she's never seen me more calm in a worse situation. But I just know. The day of Game 7, Mark Recchi and I are sitting in the lounge thirty minutes before warm-up watching *Seinfeld*. Giggling like two little school kids. I just have zero doubts we are going to win."

Three hours later, Brijet is crying again. The joy tears. Ray was right. The Hurricanes are Stanley Cup champions. It's Bret Hedican who hands him the Cup. Ray lets out a primal yell and the happiest "Fucking right!" of his life as he hoists it above his head.

"I think *The Hockey News* had us ranked twenty-ninth of thirty teams before the season," he says. "So to win it all with this group of guys is just the greatest feeling ever."

This moment, right here, is the penthouse. Top of the world. But it takes less than seven months to get to the outhouse. Well, technically, Ray doesn't get there. And therein lies the problem.

It's Christmas 2007. The Hurricanes have two days off for the holiday, then a game Boxing Day at home against Florida. One of the Whitney family traditions is Great-Gramma Leona's cabbage rolls. A delicious combo of rice, bacon and onions wrapped in cabbage and drenched in vinegar. "I absolutely love them," Ray says. "My favourite thing every Christmas."

Brijet makes this year's batch. Ray wolfs down about a dozen of them at Christmas dinner. On Boxing Day, he comes home from the morning skate and inhales a half dozen more. "Questionable game-day decision in retrospect," he says.

By the time he takes the ice for warm-up, there is a full bench-clearing brawl going on in Ray's stomach. And he feels every punch. "Cabbage does some nasty stuff to you," Ray says, with the tone of a man who has seen some things.

Carolina coach Peter Laviolette puts Ray in the starting lineup, which means he is standing on his blue line for the national anthem. There is a young boy next to him. Part of the Hurricanes' routine is to have minor-hockey players stand shoulder to shoulder with the players during the anthem.

"The remnants of the cabbage rolls have been trying to escape for a while now, and I can't hold them in any longer," Ray says. "So I try to squeak a tiny little fart out. But instead, it's an explosion. Just a full pile of poop. I'm not talking about some wet fart where a tiny bit sneaks out with it. This is my entire stomach emptying at the same time. Full load. And I wear these tight compression shorts under my gear. So . . . yeah . . . apocalypse."

Ray is horrified. He looks down at the kid next to him, wondering if he can smell the toxic environmental disaster Gramma's delicious cabbage rolls have morphed into inside those compression shorts.

The anthem is eternal. Ray quietly begs the singer to stop lingering on every note.

"*. . . And the hoooommme . . . offfff thhhhhe . . .*"

"Oh, God. I think it's flowing into my skates."

. . . bray-ayyyyyyyyvvvvve."

Usually, when the last note hits, Ray's routine is to take a quick lap, stop by the bench for a swig of water, then line up for the opening faceoff. But he's terrified to move. He can't go off the ice. It's a penalty if a player listed in your starting lineup doesn't actually start the game. So Ray puts his helmet on, leans forward on his skates and glides gingerly to his spot on the left side of the circle.

"I don't know what to do," he says. "Roddy Brind'Amour wins the draw, of course. We go D to D and dump it in." (Second dump-in of the night.) "I go chase the puck, but my legs have to be four feet apart. I don't want to bring them together and squish the mess further around my shorts. So I just skate bow-legged into their end. I take a swipe at the puck and head straight to the bench. I pass the forward bench door, go right in the D door, and right down the hall into the handicapped stall."

The Hurricanes' trainers follow close behind, thinking Ray has pulled his groin again—he'd had issues the season before. "I'm not hurt," comes the voice from inside the stall. "I need a plastic bag. I need you to turn the shower on and get me all new hockey underwear—compression shorts, long pants, socks. Everything!"

He gets completely undressed and tries to gather all the poop he can in the plastic bag.

"Mr. Whitney, when the doctor asked for a stool sample, he didn't mean..."

An unlucky member of the training staff has to transfer the bag to the dumpster outside.

"I jump in the shower, get dressed in the clean gear and hustle back to the bench," Ray says. "So I have a nine-second shift to start the game, and I don't show up again until there are eight or nine minutes left in the period. I'm walking behind the players in front of the coaches to take my spot, and Lavy looks at me and says, 'What, did you shit yourself or something?' I stop, look at him dead serious and say, 'Full shit.' He just starts laughing in the middle of the game.

"So yeah, I go from carrying the Cup around that ice to shitting myself in front of fifteen thousand people."

Ray plays seven more clean-underwear years in the NHL, before retiring in 2014. He still enjoys Gramma Leona's cabbage rolls every Thanksgiving and Christmas. He was kind enough to share her secret recipe.

Gramma Leona's Sour Cabbage Rolls

1 head cabbage
½ cup chopped sautéed onion
2 cups cooked white rice
1 cup chopped fried bacon
1 tbsp butter
1 cup vinegar

Boil head of cabbage until soft enough for leaves to peel off easily.

Mix onions, rice, bacon.

Tear cabbage leaves off and fill with rice mixture. Fold sides of leaf over filling. Roll up from base to tip of leaf. Place cabbage rolls in a buttered casserole dish, adding 1 tbsp butter between layers. Pour vinegar over cabbage rolls and bake at 325 degrees for two hours or until tender, adding butter and vinegar to taste. Do not eat 18 right before playing in an NHL game. There will be consequences.

—Gramma Leona

ACKNOWLEDGEMENTS

I wrote this book during a home renovation.

I would sit on a lawn chair in our laundry room, which doubled as our kitchen, which tripled as our dining room, and interview players on the phone, while real men tore up drywall all around me, and my wife, Cheryl, held up seven different beige paint samples which looked exactly the same.

"Do you like Baby Fawn, September Fog, or Dumpling?"

"Umm, could you hold on a minute, Brady? I just have to stick a fork in my eye."

If you are reading a purchased copy of *Certified Beauties*, and not one you borrowed from Larry, the goalie on your beer league team, thank you for funding the Restoration Hardware sconces we absolutely did not need.

Sorry, honey. That's my awkward way of apologizing for leaving you completely alone to make every single decision in the reshaping of our home, while I wrote Pulitzer-worthy content like Ray Whitney pooping his pants during the national anthem of an NHL game.

I am not the best husband/father when I write; I tend to get lost in the stories and not hear questions from my loved ones until roughly the seventh asking.

"Dad? Dad? Hey Dad? Yo Dad!?! Father? Daddyo? James Duthie?!?" is a common refrain in our house.

I promise the loves of my life—Cheryl, Jared, Darian, Gracie,

ACKNOWLEDGEMENTS

and our Frenchie Hugo—that you have my undivided attention from here forward.*

Cheryl likes to joke that I have written more books than I have read. Which is harsh, but close. Fortunately this is not the case for my invaluable team of editors:

- My wonderful Mom, 92, and sharp as a tack. Mom, I'm sorry for the f-bombs in the book. I never said them out loud. Promise.
- My brilliant sisters Merydee and Kristy, who aren't the biggest hockey fans, but read every word and made countless good suggestions. My favourite text from Kristy outlined five egregious errors over the span of four pages, followed by "Rough chapter. What were you drinking that day?"
- The TSN Quizmaster, Steve Dryden, who I'm quite certain sobs over the sheer volume of grammatical and punctuation mistakes in the first draft I sent him. I'm pretty sure he believes that, though we both have a journalism degree from Carleton, mine must be honorary.
- Terrific copy editor Patricia MacDonald, who somehow found more mistakes my crack editors missed, and production editor Canaan Chu, who made *Certified Beauties* look great.

I cannot thank Brad Wilson and his entire team at Harper-Collins enough. Brad, the dedicated hockey dad of a terrific goalie, is the most supportive friend a writer could ask for. We're already working on another book together because he can't get rid of me. I'm clingy like that.

---

* (unless the playoffs or golf are on.)

ACKNOWLEDGEMENTS

Thank you also to Brian Wood, who helped give me my start in the book business and taught me a great deal. And to the leaders at TSN and Bell Media, who always show unwavering support for this side hustle: Sean Cohan, Shawn Redmond, Ken Volden, Mike Lane—I promise I never wrote a single word of *Certified Beauties* on company time. Except for this part, which I'm writing during a lull on Tradecentre (which is . . . most of Tradecentre.)

I wasn't going to write another *Beauties*. Mostly because TV keeps me busy enough, and a book eats a year of your life. Also, it turns me into a pain in the ass. It's not fun hassling hockey players during their long seasons. Asking them to give me hours of their time to tell their favourite tales. And then following up with endless questions about tiny details.

So before you wrestled the alligator, captured it, and left it on your teammate's porch, did you lure it with chicken or bread?

This was an actual text to Darcy Hordichuk. I owe everything to all the characters who bring *Certified Beauties* to life.

Finally, a special thank-you to the Gaudreau family. Madeline, Meredith, Jane, Guy, Kristen and Katie answered calls and countless texts from me during the most painful year of their lives. Their stories, and their love for John and Matty, are the soul of this book.

—*James*